Passionate Quests

By the same author

Tell Me Honestly
Someone Is Missing

Passionate Quests

FIVE MODERN
WOMEN TRAVELLERS

Sonia Melchett

Faber and Faber

BOSTON ● LONDON

First published in the United States in 1992 by Faber and Faber, Inc.,
50 Cross Street, Winchester, MA 01890. First published in
Great Britain in 1991 by William Heinemann Limited, Michelin House,
81 Fulham Road, London SW3 6RB.

Library of Congress Cataloging-in-Publication Data

Melchett, Sonia.
Passionate quests : five modern women travellers / Sonia Melchett.
p.   cm.
Includes bibliographical references (p. 209).
ISBN 0-571-12946-3 (paper orig.)
1. Women travelers—Biography.   I. Title
G200.M38   1992
910'.82--dc20   91-36588
CIP

Published by arrangement with William Heinemann Limited

Cover photograph: Paradise Bay, Antarctica ·
ASPECT PICTURE LIBRARY

Cover design: John Hamilton

Printed in the United States of America

To Peter, Kerena and Pandora

Contents

Acknowledgements

First I am indebted to Helen Fraser who, when she heard I was intent on writing this book, was brave enough to want to publish it. But without the full co-operation of my chosen travellers, and permission to quote from their books and interviews, this would not have been possible. All busy people, they have been more than generous with their time whenever I managed to catch them in between continents and have pointed me in the right direction when I strayed off course.

I would like to thank all the individuals who have advised and helped me in my quest while writing these pieces. At the Royal Geographical Society my gratitude goes to the ex-President, Lord Shackleton, for his encouragement from beginning to end; to the Director John Hemming for his constructive suggestions; and to Shane Windsor of the Expedition Advisory Centre, who has been so helpful with my enquiries.

To Julie Donnelly I owe special thanks for allowing me to quote from *The Windhorse*, which she wrote with Elaine Brook; to Audrey Salkeld, the well-known writer on mountaineering, for her advice on the technicalities of the climber's world. For the description of the 'advantages of women climbers as mountaineers,' I am grateful to an article by Rosie Andrews, No Spare Rib: 'The Advent of Hard Women Rock Climbers'; to Michael Richey, the former Director of the Royal Institute of Navigation who saw that I didn't get too knotted up in my sailing terminology; and to Neil McIntyre of Earth Observation Sciences Limited, who explained the more technical aspects of Antarctic exploration and gave me his account of the 90° South Expedition. I would like to thank Jock Murray for chatting to me about Dervla Murphy and for supplying photographs of her and her daughter Rachel. Sarah Anderson and her Travel Bookshop have been a mine of information and that great travel writer, Dorothy Middleton, a source of inspiration and generosity.

I am also grateful to Nadia Lawrence, my editor, for her patience, and to Liz Spicer for deciphering my handwriting.

And finally thanks must go to my husband, Andrew, for finding the books needed for the research, but, more importantly, for keeping up my morale in the low moments and seeing that I reached the end of the journeys.

Foreword

by The Rt. Hon. Lord Shackleton, KG, FRS

In this book Sonia Melchett has tackled a very difficult task. As her Preface makes clear, she has described the achievements of five remarkable women who have devoted much of their lives to adventure. All of them are themselves writers of ability and sensitivity. This is an ambitious undertaking but Sonia Melchett is herself a dedicated traveller. Furthermore, she seeks to describe the complex nature of the women and one is left gasping at the rigours and optimism of these travellers. One wonders at times how they survived at all.

None of them except Monica Kristensen took part in scientific expeditions and whereas she did first-class work which brought her one of the Gold Medals of the Royal Geographical Society, there is a deep streak of adventure running through her dangerous journeys, as there is in all the essays.

An important part of this book is Sonia Melchett's own preface which helps to interpret and highlight the unusual qualities and indeed the spirit which underlies the motivation of these five women.

I recommend *Passionate Quests* to anyone interested in courageous travel.

'All thoughts, all passions, all delights,
Whatever stirs this mortal frame'

'Love', Samuel Taylor Coleridge

Preface

What made me want to write about modern women travellers? And why these particular women? Not easy questions to answer, but I will try.

They say all our dreams begin in youth. Mine certainly did. My most vivid early memories are of travelling with my parents in India; by car along dusty roads, pulling a horse-box behind us and being held up for hours by flooded rivers; by train, winding for days and nights round the foothills of the Himalayas; and by pony, accompanying my father when he went on hunting trips. My father was an Army doctor and we were always on the move. Even when we came 'home' we never put down roots for long. Except for a few years at boarding school, travelling was a way of life. But travelling for adventure has also been a compulsion for me. When I was about nine and at a convent in Dover, I persuaded my younger sister to run away with me to Dover Castle – a distance of four miles – taking a few basic provisions and to stay there for three nights. It was much more frightening that I had imagined and, luckily for us, we were discovered by the British Army within twenty-four hours and suitably chastised. This set-back in no way deterred me. I have been a passionate 'escaper' all my life – going anywhere that circumstances and commitments allowed.

The excitement of visiting an unknown country, meeting people of other cultures and religions, experiencing strange vegetation and new smells and foreign food has as strong a hold over me now as it ever had. The thrill of sailing in distant waters, whether it be the Indian Ocean or the Aegean or the Caribbean – leaving the sanctuary of one harbour to set sail for another – not quite knowing what the elements have in store – is to forget time, to lose count of the days, to live completely in the present, and to feel at one with nature. Of course, when I look back I forget the fears and the occasional hardships and sickness and remember only the joys. My travels have seldom been alone – they were nearly always shared with parents, friends, lover, husband, children or a group of strangers. And enjoyable as it is to share the experience of new and strange sights, no doubt it can dissipate the intensity of the experience of the lone traveller. This is why the books about the exploits of solitary wanderers, particularly women, have always fascinated me and left me full of admiration, curiosity and even jealousy. Why did I never have the guts? What is it that makes a woman subject herself to the loneliness of exploring uncharted territories, sailing across stormy oceans or climbing snowbound peaks?

It is no new phenomenon. In the Victorian age, countless women left their comfortable homes to embark on a frenzy of global navigation. We have had biographies of Lady Hester Stanhope, Jane Digby el Mezrab, Mary Kingsley, Gertrude Bell and Isabella Eberhart, to mention but a few. They also bequeathed their own wonderful descriptions of their exploits. In *On a Sledge and Horseback to Outcast Siberian Lepers*, of 1823, Kate Marsden revealed the obsessive religious fervour which drove her to seek in the forests of north-eastern Russia the forsaken lepers of Yakat. In *A Thousand Miles Up the Nile*, of 1877, Amelia B. Edwards left us one of the classics of the history of the river and became a leading authority on Egyptology. Many of these women were anything but strong. Isabella Bird Bishop, one of the earliest and most dramatic of Victorian travellers, was an invalid as a child and suffered from chronic ill-health, yet she still managed to scale Mauna Loa, the world's largest volcano, and she ascended Long's Peak – known as America's Matterhorn – accompanied by Rocky Mountain Jim, a one-eyed trapper.

Since the Victorians, there have been equally famous women, seeking adventure and giving us a wealth of autobiographical descriptions of their journeys. Rosita Forbes, journeying to Kufara in the heart of the eastern Sahara in 1920, would have been killed by the fierce fanatics of the Libyan deserts, had she not disguised herself as a Bedouin and learned tracts from the Koran. The lone pilot, Beryl Markham, in spite of being one of the frivolous 'Happy Valley Set', wrote *West With the Night*, an account of her flight across the Atlantic in 1936 in a small Gipsy Moth – the first woman to make the solo flight. Freya Stark found time to pen millions of words in between her amazing voyages round the coasts of Turkey and her travels in Persia, Arabia and the Near East.

It might appear that the enormous explosion of tourism has left few virgin parts of the globe for today's generation of women travellers to discover, but this is not so. The challenge for present-day women is even greater and stretches their imagination and powers of physical endurance to the limit. The mantle of feminism has been thrown over them and their role in society is constantly being redefined. The need to escape from consumerism with its answerphones, noise pollution and constant bureaucratic demands, and the urge to explore remote regions, is greater than ever. Those who have consciously chosen to live much of their lives without the accepted comforts of the West have found that, by breaking free, their lives have become richer. They have not just been escaping from a humdrum existence, but reaching for a kind of liberty. The word 'travel' comes from 'travail', with its meaning of hurt and work. Maybe by risking hardship, sickness, boredom and even death, and then by surviving, we validate life.

I made a list of the five present-day women travellers whom I most admired. Through a series of encounters and events which seemed almost fatalistic, I was able to meet, interview and write about the five people I had chosen. For instance, I was at a crowded gathering and was introduced to a stranger who asked me what I did. I replied, 'I'm writing a book about contemporary women travellers.' 'Are you doing a mountaineer?' she asked. 'Yes,' I replied, 'Elaine Brook, if I can make contact with her.' 'Oh,' she said, 'she's one of my greatest friends – she's normally in Tibet, but it just happens she's arriving here next week.' Elaine agreed to be interviewed shortly afterwards. Chance supported choice.

Obviously my choices are subjective, and the reader may well ask why her, and not another. The answer is that these are the women I most wanted to meet and discover for myself the motivation behind their extraordinary voyages. Luckily, like most of their predecessors, they have all kept diaries and records and written books in between their exploits to the far corners of the earth. The descriptions of their travels have been even more rewarding than I had hoped. They are all predominantly loners and don't need the support of a husband or a companion to go along with them.

It is true that Dervla Murphy was sometimes accompanied by her daughter Rachel, yet some may think that taking a five-year-old to explore Southern India was a handicap rather than a support. But Dervla was in no way inhibited by the presence of a small child in remote places, and it did not stop her from living among nomads in Baltistan. She holds the view that the only valid and rewarding search is not for the differences between people of all races and cultures, but for the similarities. She believes, too, in the enduring nature of travel, finding nothing ephemeral about the effects of journeying through primitive countries.

Monica Kristensen, when attempting to follow in Amundsen's footsteps to the South Pole, was the leader of a three-man team and twenty-two huskies. But when she had to make her most difficult decisions, she was alone in her icy tent in Antarctica.

Clare Francis raced across the Atlantic in her 32-foot yacht, revelling in her solitude and independence while she battled through the raging seas. And in the Round the World Race, when she was the skipper of a crew of twelve, it was she alone who had to make the final judgements of seamanship.

Christina Dodwell's intrepid lone voyages over unchartered deserts, lakes and rivers have brought her a sense of achievement which has nothing to do with reaching for goals or ambition. After riding her Arab stallion in the mountains of north-east Turkey, she said, 'I never wanted that day to end.'

Climbers can seldom be completely solitary, but Elaine Brook is unique in the fact that she took a different route from other climbers. When she led the blind Julie Donnelly up Mount Everest and had to be her eyes as well as her guide, she had no one with a rope pulling her towards the summit. After attempting the most difficult of the mountain peaks, she has sought challenges of another nature which are proving even more compelling.

All these women's lives defy simple definitions. I have attempted no psychological analysis but have relied on them to reveal themselves through their words and actions. Their singular means of travel express their individualities, travelling fearlessly in their inimitable styles. They have measured themselves against their own natures and nature itself. Without thought of material gain or the wish for fulfilment, they have become fulfilled. It has been a privilege to feel I was journeying with them.

Sonia Melchett 1991

Dervla Murphy

For my part, I travel not to go anywhere but to go.
I travel for travel's sake. The great affair is to move,
to feel the needs and hitches of new life more
nearly, to come down off the featherbed of
civilization and find the globe granite underfoot and
strewn with cutting flints.

Robert Louis Stevenson

Dervla Murphy is both a compulsive traveller and a compulsive
writer. Although she has been compared to Lord Byron and Isabella
Bird Bishop, her unique personality and approach to every aspect of
life defy comparisons. Exploring the remote corners of the globe on
foot or mule and by bicycle, she has journeyed through India,
Baltistan, Karakoram, Poland, Ethiopia, Madagascar, the Peruvian
Andes and Cameroon. Sometimes she has been alone and sometimes
with her daughter Rachel, who was only five years old when she
first accompanied her mother. After each trip she returns home to
write up her journeys from her diaries. Apart from her nine travel
books, she has written about three of the most controversial and
important contemporary subjects. *A Place Apart* is an honest and
sympathetic account of the problems of Northern Ireland; *Race to
the Finish?* deals with nuclear fission and the possible end of
humanity; *Tales from Two Cities* examines race relations in Britain.
She has also written an autobiography of her adolescence, *Wheels
Within Wheels*.

Her home in Lismore, County Waterford, is surrounded by
countryside which has scarcely changed since Thackeray's day. It
was originally the town market, and is a series of separate outbuild-
ings, surrounded by cobbled courtyards. The same lofty hand-hewn
stone walls sheltered travellers of another age when the main yard

was a stop for the Cork-Dublin mail coach. The rooms have been restored in wood and stone with the minimum concession to luxury. Nearby is a convent and Dervla remains on good terms with the nuns, even though she is a lapsed Catholic. She shares her home with an assortment of cats, dogs, goats and bantams. 'Admittedly my home is pretty primitive by the standards of most people nowadays,' she remarks in her deep Irish brogue, '*sans* gadgets, *sans* television, *sans* motor car. Yet I do appreciate some mod cons – a radio and record player, electric light, a wood stove to heat water in winter, a tiny gas cooker, a basic bathroom converted from a pigsty across the courtyard. I'm no permanent back-to-nature type.'

Sipping cider, which she now drinks instead of whiskey, and smoking thin cigars which have replaced cigarettes, she explains that she still wants to be cycling around Ireland when she is eighty. She has a self-deprecating sense of humour and a shy, gentle manner which belie an iron will and strongly held opinions. Both solitary and gregarious, anxious to be off on her travels and anxious to return, her character is wildly contradictory. Stockily built, she dresses in baggy corduroys and open-necked shirts, mostly bought from Oxfam shops. She has a kind, weatherbeaten face, curly grey hair and deep-set thoughtful eyes. Blessed with a completely trusting nature, she finds that people usually respond by being equally trusting and protective. Once, when sleeping on a mountainside in Afghanistan, she awoke to find that some tribesmen had set up a goat-hair tent around her to protect her from the fierce sun. 'I think it's true that most human beings are trustworthy,' she says. 'I like most people.'

From the age of four Dervla had two ambitions. One was to travel in distant lands, and the other was to be a writer. Yet the two weren't linked in her mind, they existed in different compartments. Soon after her tenth birthday she decided to cycle to India for the simple reason that her atlas had revealed how very little water there was between Ireland and India. 'Had anyone told me then that my first published book would be a description of that bicycle journey and not the greatest twentieth-century novel, my disappointment would certainly have been acute.'

In fact it was not until January 1963, when she was around thirty, that Dervla began to plan her cycle ride to India, during the worst winter Europe had known for a century. It would take her through France, Italy, Yugoslavia, Bulgaria, Turkey, Persia, Afghanistan and Pakistan to New Delhi. Infinite care went into the planning. Spare parts and new tyres (she wore out six) were sent ahead to strategic points, and although she had no foreign language except a little German, she prepared for the journey so thoroughly that she carried street maps of several remote towns. She had no sleeping bag or tent, but with a .25 revolver, her maps, traveller's cheques and spare clothes packed in two saddle bags, she set off on her bicycle, Rosinante, named after Don Quixote's horse.

In *Full Tilt*, she describes her feelings. 'I shall never forget that dark ice-bound morning when I began to cycle east from Dunkirk; to have the fulfilment of a twenty-one-year-old ambition apparently within one's grasp can be quite disconcerting ... I felt as though some favourite scene from a novel had come, incredibly, to life. However, within a few weeks my journey had degenerated from a happy-go-lucky trek to a grim struggle for progress by any means along roads lost beneath snow and ice.'

She arrived in Belgrade in cold so biting that starving wolves were entering the city. Hearing that the thaw had started further south she hitched a lift from a lorry, but within a few hours they had skidded into a ditch in mountainous, wooded country. The driver was hurt and Dervla left him to seek help from a nearby village. Suddenly she came face to face with three wolves. The two smaller animals attacked her, one clinging to her ankle, the other to her shoulder, while the third looked on. She was able to reach her revolver and, putting the muzzle against the head of the wolf at her shoulder, she pulled the trigger – the first time she had shot a living target. The wolf dropped dead and a second shot drove off the other two. 'They must have been crazy with hunger or they would not have attacked in such small numbers. I was pretty frightened myself, but I managed to reach the village and persuaded the people there to send a pony sleigh for the lorry driver.'

Keeping her spirit up with the odd nip of rum and brandy, Dervla had to use her revolver twice more before reaching Afghanistan – once when she was attacked by three shovel-carrying men near Tabriz who took a fancy both to her bicycle and herself, and again when she woke in a local doss-house in Turkey to find a scantily clad Kurd bending over her in the moonlight. In both cases shots over their heads put a stop to their approaches. She was advised that hotel bedrooms without locks called for empty bottles balanced on tops of doors to deter wandering lechers. 'As creating empty bottles is one of the things I'm good at, this seemed an appropriate suggestion.'

Having finally escaped from snow and ice, Dervla had one of the more unforgettable days of her entire journey, a fifteen-mile cycle run around the base of Mount Ararat, the mountain which seems to inspire strong emotions in every traveller. She felt so deeply that she thought of it as a personality encountered rather than a landscape observed.

Dervla attracted curious, friendly crowds wherever she appeared. The idea of a woman travelling alone was so incredible that most people thought her a man with her short haircut and baggy trousers. But on her way through Azerbaijan, a young police officer was under no such delusion and asked her to accompany him to the police barracks to fill in some forms. In fact, he took her to a deserted private house, where he locked her in and became a little too friendly. This time she refrained from going for her gun and instead used other tactics which reduced him to a state of temporary agony. Freed for a moment, she escaped by grabbing his trousers, which were on the ground, and she raced back to the town. Perhaps this incident influenced her feelings towards the Persian people, whom she found impossible to like as she had the Turks – but more to be pitied than censured. While cycling through the beautiful countryside between Tehran and Deh-Namak, she was moved by the pride of the farmers, whom the Shah had at last allowed to own their own land; their love of him and his Empress was obviously genuine. 'When I think of those wretched Mullahs,' Dervla wrote, 'who try to persuade the villagers that it is immoral and against the Koran for the masses to own land – just because they themselves own so much of it . . . it's disconcerting how men in the religious saddle repeatedly abuse their spiritual authority for personal gain.' Seeing one of the oldest and richest civilisations in the world long past its zenith had its fascinations, but Dervla was soon to find a greater affection and affinity with the people of Afghanistan.

By the middle of April she was pushing the bicycle over the Shibar

Pass at 10,380 feet above sea level. She reached the cold splendour of the snow line where the highest peaks of the Hindu Kush crowded the horizon in every direction, and Dervla felt she understood why some people believed that gods live on mountain tops. At Bamian she spent the night in a hotel built on a cliff and, as she looked across the valley, she saw a 120-foot high statue of the Lord Buddha standing, as it had for over two thousand years, in a gigantic alcove in the golden sandstone mountain. Guarding the god were many caves where Buddhist monks lived near a second eighty-foot high statue. 'Even though I was mentally prepared for those Buddhas, the impact was tremendous when I actually saw them presiding impassively over the valley.' Dervla not only fell in love with the country, but with the Afghan people. At moments she even considered settling in the Hindu Kush. 'Nothing is false there, for humans and animals and earth, intimately interdependent, partake together in the rhythmic cycle of nature. To lose one's petty, sophisticated complexities in that world would be Heaven – but impossible, because of the fundamental falsity involved in attempting to abandon our own unhappy heritage. Yet the awareness that one cannot go back is a bitter pill to swallow.'

Dervla had cycled 4,445 miles when she reached Peshawar in Pakistan, four months after leaving Dunkirk. She had suffered three broken ribs when an Afghan rifleman had accidentally jabbed her with the butt of his rifle in a crowded bus, but even this painful incident had failed to quell her passion for Afghanistan. The Kybher Pass itself had no charm for her compared with the Hindu Kush, but her natural curiosity for a new country soon overcame her nostalgia. In Tehran she had made friends with some Pakistani officers, and one, Colonel Johan Zeb, gave her an introduction to his brother, Aurang Zeb, who lived in Saidu Shariff. Much to her amazement, she found he was a prince and lived with his father, the President Wali of Swat, in a palace guarded by sentries. She felt singularly ill-equipped to deal with this grand Pathan household, but the informality with which she was greeted soon put her at her ease. 'Being entertained by oriental potentates is fine – among other things I have a complete set of Beethoven symphonies at my disposal, presented to the President by Dr Adenauer. But the position also has its snags, one of them being that it's considered very bad form for a house-guest of the ruler of the state to transport herself on a lowly cycle.'

In June she flew to Gilgit in north Pakistan, close to the Russian and Chinese frontiers, intending to cycle across the Babusar Pass. But before reaching this ambitious stage of her journey, she was to experience a bizarre and somewhat romantic encounter. Temporarily exchanging her bicycle Rosinante (or Roz, as she called it) for a horse, to explore the Karakoram Mountains, she was surprised one day when a horseman, who came galloping towards her in a cloud of dust, pulled up suddenly and handed her a visiting card which read, *Where Heaven and Earth Meet – Raja Jan Alam Punial, West Pakistan*. He signalled that she should follow him to the Raja's residence. In her book, Dervla gives a hilarious account of her three-day stay with the Raja. He lived in a modern bungalow built to replace the old stone fortress of his ancestors, virtually unfurnished 'except for about half a ton of silver polo trophies'. The Raja governed his tiny state like a benevolent father. As Minister of Finance, Social Welfare and Justice, he settled disputes, decided on grain sales and personally supported any family who had suffered disasters. He took her riding in the mountains and to watch an eccentric game of polo. 'Never have I seen such a thrilling spectacle . . . there are no rules and every sort of attack is allowed. Blood was soon streaming from over half the twelve players' heads, hands and backs, but they carried on regardless . . . the band played non-stop in time to the thudding hooves and clashing sticks – the faster the game, the faster the music.' In spite of being married, the Raja urged her to stay, and offered her a present of a little farm under the mountains. Refusing as tactfully as possible, she explained that she could never be happy permanently exiled from Ireland, but he remained unconvinced until she bade him farewell, leaving him 'disproportionately devastated'.

Reunited with her bicycle, she cycled through the desolate and magnificent Indus Gorge in a temperature sometimes reaching F 114 degrees, with Mount Nanga Parbat thrusting up from the surrounding peaks, the most impressive mountain she had seen after Ararat. 'I don't wonder at people risking their lives to climb mountains; even getting up to 12,000 feet and standing looking down on what one has conquered is wonderfully satisfying.' She would start off at

4 a.m., sometimes pulling Roz up vertical hills. These were the toughest conditions she had yet encountered, and she suffered from the stench of burning sand and acute thirst. The River Indus, out of reach but always visible a thousand feet below, was the 'quintessence of torture. I have often thought that death by thirst must be grimmer than most deaths and now my surmise has been confirmed ... but the sheer magnitude is overwhelming, the perfect stillness and the brutal sun; despite being half-dead it was an experience worth the exhaustion.' Dervla had, in fact, developed a severe attack of sun-stroke, or what the locals called 'sun devil', and when she reached Chilas village and water she was stumbling and talking to herself. But the hospitable villagers, overcoming their amazement, as they had not seen a bicycle before, fed and cared for her until she was well enough to set out for the 16,000-feet Babusar Pass.

Following in the wake of a pony caravan, she struggled for nearly twenty miles up the barren moors leading to the pass. Sometimes pushing and sometimes carrying Roz, she almost reached the top, only to find her way blocked by a vast glacier. Trying to skirt it, she found herself struggling through deep snow and ice. 'I was at that peculiar stage when one doesn't really believe that one's objective will ever be reached and when one's mental awareness concerns the joy of driving one's body far beyond the limits of its natural endurance.' Then, suddenly, they were on a level plateau about a quarter of a mile square. She had reached her destination and realised that on Babusar Top she was higher than she had ever been before. Free-wheeling down a track to the River Nullah below, she found the bridge had been washed away. A small black cow provided the solution. Hoisting her bike over one arm, she threw the other arm round the neck of the surprised cow and, clinging to her, made the crossing safely through the thundering icy water. Before she caught up with the pony caravan, she had to cross many more glaciers and climb yet another mountain. 'Being in a weakened condition the ludicrous aspect of the situation struck me with special force and whenever I stopped to rest I wasted precious breath giggling at my own dottiness.'

But Dervla's sense of wonder soon reasserted itself when she reached the Kagan Valley. 'What a wonderful place the world is! Here was a valley of glorious beauty, yet quite unique – different from the Ghorband or Gilgit or Indus valleys – with its snow-peaks and regal fir trees, green meadows right up to the snow line, glistening glaciers, waterfalls, jewel-like wild flowers and the clean aroma of some unfamiliar herb.'

Now that she was nearing her final goal and the fulfilment of the ambition conceived on a hillside in Ireland as a ten-year-old, she surprisingly felt no sense of elation. On reaching New Delhi in July, she once again went down with heat-stroke. She and Roz had covered about seventy to eighty miles a day on average, and her longest run had been 118 miles. She had religiously kept a daily account in her diary with a view to publication, but when Mrs John Betjeman – met cycling in Delhi – suggested she send her manuscript to the distinguished publishing house of John Murray, she was full of trepidation. 'I had always heard my father talk so highly of them. I didn't imagine they would want a book by me.' And when a telegram came back saying they would like to publish her, it was the beginning of a working relationship and friendship that was to last. Jock Murray, recalling their first meeting, said, 'I felt I'd known her for years. She has a natural talent for narrative description and for communicating with people. Although one journalist who interviewed her years later said it was like trying to open an oyster with a bus ticket, I've always found she has an enormous sense of fun. She possesses very decided views on many subjects but is not at all bigoted. And she has that over-riding determination to put words on paper and the stamina to do it.'

Full Tilt was universally praised and Dervla Murphy joined the ranks of the unique breed of courageous lone lady travellers. She is quick to refute this reputation. 'The popular view that a solitary woman who undertakes this sort of journey must be very courageous is a fallacy.' She quotes Epictetus, 'For it is not death or hardship that is a fearful thing, but the fear of death and hardship.' Because the possibility of physical danger does not frighten her, courage is not required. 'When a man tries to rob or assault me or when I find myself, as darkness is falling, utterly exhausted and waist-deep in snow, half-way up a mountain pass, then I am afraid, but it is the instinct of self-preservation, rather than courage, that takes over.'

During her travels in India, Dervla had heard about some of the unfortunate people from Tibet who had sought sanctuary over the frontier. As a result, before returning to Ireland, she had worked for six months at the Refugee Nursery at Dharmsala. This work had given her another aim in life and she desperately wanted to return. She read that a refugee camp had been recently formed in the Pokhara Valley where five hundred Tibetans were living as family units in tents with only one western volunteer to help them. In April 1965 she decided to fly out and offer her services. *The Waiting Land* is about her seven months' stay in the camp and gives a picture of her life in Nepal. Before starting work, she had an audience with His Holiness the Dalai Lama who was living in a heavily guarded bungalow near Dharmsala. They talked about the insoluble problems of the refugees in Nepal where the political difficulties of the host country created many special complications. The Refugee Nursery nearby where she had originally worked was being run by the Dalai Lama's younger sister who had transformed it from a squalid, infectious inferno into a model nursery full of rosy-cheeked children.

Although Pokhara, meaning 'lake', is Nepal's second city, it is still only a small town and lies in the Pardi Valley, directly beneath the snow-peaked mountains of Annapurna. Its sub-tropical vegetation is dominated by Machhapulchhara, the home of its tutelary deity. Dervla fell 'hopelessly in love with the place and was immediately conscious of the ancient, strong traditions that determine every action, thought and emotion of the local people'. Despite the perennial anxieties of debt, disease and political unrest, she sensed the basic stability and tranquillity inherent in the community. Living in a room twelve foot by fifteen with rats as her only companions, she seemed oblivious of the discomfort.

She and Kay, the other westerner, supervised the dispersal of provisions which arrived at sporadic intervals by air from Kathmandu. Once a German climbing expedition gave away the remains of their food and the entire population of Pardi were at the airport for the share-out. The camp was suddenly full of exotic delicacies. Dervla saw *pâté de foie gras* being tentatively mixed with *tsampa*, salad cream being added to tea and soup cubes being chewed like toffees. Howls of agony came from one small girl who had just been given a spoonful of neat mustard by her loving mother.

She and Kay organised the building of bamboo huts, hoping to install the refugees before the monsoon came. 'Between Nepalese procrastination and Tibetan laziness it wasn't the easiest of tasks.' The refugee nomads put up a form of passive resistance, preferring the seclusion of their traditional tents to the communal existence they would have to endure in the new shelters – not realising that, in their weakened condition, it was a matter of life and death to get them into suitable accommodation before the wet weather. Dervla was to find that many western workers became disillusioned, often dismissing the Nepalese as being stupid. 'But this is an over-simplification – the fact being that values are different and people operate on different principles.'

One of her first tasks was to trek with a group of reluctant Tibetans to Siglis, a village due north of Pokhara, where bamboo mats were made. Following the only path beside the paddy-fields, they had to make their way across a river which was rising rapidly. The only bridge was a narrow, slippery tree-trunk. The Tibetans, who trooped through the flooded river without hesitation, rolled about with mirth as Dervla sat aside the tree-trunk and cautiously propelled herself across it. Leeches were a constant irritation, and Dervla had to explain that they must never be forcibly detached from the skin, but salt or a lighted cigarette would get rid of them. As salt was too expensive to waste on leeches, she was constantly going from leg to leg with her cigarettes to burn them off. The Tibetans were unaccustomed to the pests and had to be reassured that, contrary to appearances, they would not bleed to death.

In spite of the physical discomfort, she found the mountain country 'too beautiful to be conveyed by words . . . none of the books or photographs had prepared me for such majesty. Truly this is something that does have to be seen to be believed, and that once seen must be continually yearned for when left behind, becoming as incurable a fever of the spirit as malaria is of the body.'

All in all, Dervla found her stay at the camp a rewarding experience. A less resilient human being would have been thoroughly debilitated by the conditions. Before the monsoon the heat was appalling, and she would lie naked on her bamboo mat, tormented by heat rash while rats scampered around her and millions of tiny, red-brown ants swarmed all over her, getting into everything. She tried picking them out of the rice, *dahl*, sugar and tinned milk, but in the end she gave up the battle, deciding that the ants would have to be her daily source of protein.

There was a total lack of privacy, and men and women would walk into her hut whether she was clothed or naked. One day a lama presented himself and asked simply if he could live with her. When she hesitatingly agreed, he smiled happily and went off to get his possessions. Soon twenty-two boys marched in, carrying between them the full Buddhist Canon – one hundred and twenty-eight cloth-bound volumes. Luckily the rest of his luggage only consisted of an incense burner, a prayer-wheel, a prayer drum, a *dorje*, a prayer-bell, a small photograph of His Holiness, eleven tiny silver lamps to burn before it, and for himself merely a dented kettle, a wooden spoon, a silver-rimmed bowl and an uncured stinking yak skin to sleep on. Dervla's life was now brightened by the scent of incense and ecclesiastical music. However, her enthusiasm waned when she found the lama was capable of praying non-stop for six hours without moving a muscle and often started at 3 a.m. with full instrumental support. Through an interpreter they had many interesting discussions, but when Dervla admitted she wasn't an orthodox Christian, he looked worried and said he hoped she wasn't a western-style Buddhist like the ones he met in Kathmandu.

One day she attended an uncanny ceremony – the exorcism of evil spirits by a monk magician. An acolyte placed a bizarre cockade mask of bedraggled peacock feathers on his head. After much chanting and shuddering, he went into self-induced trance, leaping to his feet and shouting loudly in Lhasa Tibetan – a sophisticated dialect far removed from his native Dholpt dialect. Frenziedly shaking his drum and bell, he roared his maledictions, and Dervla's blood froze as the complex rituals followed with the exorcism which included the ferocious biting of a baby between its shoulders. A motionless, coma-like trance followed with incantations and music. He eventually fell to the ground, groaning and twitching convulsively until the spell was broken. Dervla felt that his trance was undoubtedly genuine, but that only the faith of the sufferer could determine whether he would be healed.

The health of the refugees was a constant worry. Even the

toughest of them were afflicted with rheumatism, dysentery, abscesses, scurvy and stomach ulcers, caused by over-indulgence in *rakshi*, an even more potent brew than that distilled in Kathmandu and innocently labelled *Pineapple Wine*. Dervla had been warned against it by the doctor as it could produce sudden, total blindness.

When the time came for her departure, however, her new friends gave her a series of farewell parties. By the time she arrived in Kathmandu, the pain of her hangover was even greater than her pain at leaving Pokhara. 'In the course of a not abstentious life I have only once before had a hangover . . . but it was obviously the mingling of *chang* and *rakshi* that did the damage. Having gone to a Tibetan party and then on to a Nepalese party and drunk multi-racially, I can't reasonably complain of the consequences.'

In her book Dervla expressed strong views about the misguided ways in which the west help their 'less fortunate' brothers. She felt that by expiating our collective guilt merely by giving money, situations can arise in which problems are aggravated. 'The essence of the refugee tragedy is not disease, hunger or cold. It is the loss of emotional security, of belonging to a stable community, and the self-respect which can soon be destroyed by indiscriminate aid.' Perhaps the authorities in charge of distributing aid could do worse than listen to those who have actually had first-hand experience of living amongst those in need of help.

Having spent seven months in Nepal, Dervla had found herself trapped by its contrast of splendour and pettiness, indolence and energy, generosity and cunning, freedom and bondage. Yet when friends ask, 'Did you like Nepal?' she usually replies, 'Yes,' and leaves it at that.

Ten-and-a-half years and one small daughter later, Dervla returned to India. As Rachel was hardly five years old, Dervla decided to go to southern India on a trip that would not be too taxing. She would fly to Bombay and then wander south to Cape Comorin – the sombre tip of the sub-continent. When they arrived Dervla didn't flinch from letting Rachel see the horrors of Bombay street life. 'I must say this place seems rather shattered,' Rachel said as they passed through the jostling crowds, adding cautiously, 'you must be careful not to lose me.'

After a brief stay in Goa they travelled south towards Coorg, a little-known province in the south-west between the Malabar coast and Karnataka. During the bus journey, Dervla thought how superficial the westernisation of India really was. 'On the whole, British influence, like so many earlier conquerors, was being inexorably assimilated into India's *d'harma*.' The Coorgs were in fact the only martial race on the sub-continent never to have taken up arms against the British Raj, actually expressing a desire to live under the Union Jack. The welcome she and Rachel received from so many local people made Dervla reflect in her book, *On a Shoestring to Coorg*, 'For the ordinary traveller it is not only heart-warming but flattering to be made to feel immediately at home by people who, though westernized in many superficial ways, have so far remained emphatically a race apart.'

She was keen to visit Mysore in Karnataka for two reasons: to see the famous palace and to visit the hospital where Kay, the medical missionary with whom she had worked in the camp in Nepal, was now working. On their way they stayed at 'hotels', but as Dervla commented, 'one was no more than an ill-disguised brothel, but since I am above the age of provoking sexual assault, and Rachel below it, this detail is of no practical consequence.' While waiting on the verandah of the hospital for Kay to return from her jungle leper clinics, an elderly British missionary asked Rachel, 'Do you love Jesus?' 'Yes,' said Rachel, 'and I love Ganesh and Hanuman, especially Ganesh – he has such a fat tummy. He's Shiva's son,' she added helpfully. The missionary, looking shocked, asked, 'Does the child not know there is only one God?' 'Of course I know!' said Rachel quickly and rather huffily, resenting the slight on her theology. 'But he has lots of different names.'

After watching the *Huthri* festival for cutting the first sheaves of paddy, Dervla and Rachel travelled down to the tip of India by bus and train through the crowded villages of Kerala, where the Red Flag fluttered gaily, gaudy wayside shrines contained statues of the Virgin Mary, and the Hammer and Sickle was daubed on walls alongside Christian churches. Although Kerala was the first elected communist government to come to power, it still remained a stronghold of Brahman conservatism. Cape Comorin, the southernmost tip of India, was fundamentally a place of pilgrimage, and the

Hindu women taking their ritual baths fully clothed found Dervla a shocking sight in her Edwardian-style costume.

At Cochin they had a memorable experience watching a performance of *Kathakali* – a religious dance dating back ten thousand years. The technique was a language of gestures, so clearly developed that by using various combinations of twenty-four basic hand positions, over eight hundred words could be formed by the players. The movements of the eyes, the miming and the footwork all had specific meanings. The elaborate make-up, applied in solemn silence, took hours to put on; the fantastic, heavily jewelled brocades had been passed down through generations. 'These must be magic clothes,' exclaimed Rachel. 'Indeed,' wrote Dervla, 'without having seen them I could never have believed it possible to produce, through the controlled use of eye, face, hand and foot muscles, such an effect of ineffable beauty, adding up to what can only be described as a prayer in movement.'

On Christmas Eve during the train ride to Madurai, Dervla became really ill. She was also penniless after missing a visit to the bank that morning. During the journey Rachel also became stricken and was vomiting badly when they arrived. In spite of being semi-delirious, Dervla managed to find a traveller's bungalow near the station, where they collapsed in great distress. Luckily their water bottle was full and, while Rachel drank, Dervla dosed herself with fistfuls of codeine. From 10 p.m. on Christmas Eve to 11 a.m. on St Stephen's Day, no one even put a head around the door to see if they were still alive. Without knowing it, they both had brucellosis. Dervla was becoming delirious and Rachel suddenly took the situation in hand. She couldn't yet write, but she said, 'Why don't you write a letter to a doctor?' In a shaky hand Dervla wrote a note and off Rachel trotted, re-appearing with a rickshaw-wallah who said he would find someone. Less than fifteen minutes later a lady doctor arrived from the local maternity hospital.

They returned to Coorg to live in two rooms in a small, two-storied, empty family house. With no electricity or running water, it thoroughly appealed to Dervla. One of their neighbours lent them some basic utensils – a slop-pan, a basin, a jug and spoon, and two saucepans. As Dervla said: 'Anything in excess of what you need is luxury.' Reading to Rachel from *The Heroes* and *The Arabian*

Nights, it struck her that in future such stories were going to seem much more real to Rachel. 'Grinding the day's supply of flour, drawing water from the well, going into the forest to collect firewood to cook the evening meal, fetching bales of cloth home from the bazaar on one's head, yoking the oxen, shaping and firing bricks to build a new home, hunting for meat, trimming the lamps at sunset, making offerings to the gods – all these are commonplace activities here, though weirder than space travel to western children of the technological age.'

For Rachel these two months were the most exciting of her life, although she had strong reactions to some Indian customs. She was a little scared by her first sight of Moplak women, completely shrouded in their *burkhas*. She found the Hindu attitude to cows difficult to understand, but she was fascinated by the golden, painted horns on the enormous pure white 'sacred bullock' and was mystified at the sight of the sixteen-foot statue of the god Nandi being covered with garlands of flowers. She asked her mother, 'Do they believe bulls are gods?' She enjoyed her Indian playmates whom she dominated quite effortlessly. She was overcome by the life-size silver horse and gold chariot guarding the famous seaside temple at Tiruchendur and was blessed by the ornamented temple elephant. She acquired a Madrassi costume especially made for her by a village tailor's eleven-year-old apprentice. She saw the death of a thirty-six-year-old woman neighbour and said to her mother, 'I feel very sad, I hope you won't die before I'm married.' But when she was banned from the cremation, she wailed, 'I wanted to find out if burning human smelt like cooking meat.' Because of the need to look after her small daughter, Dervla had the time to research into the complexities of the country – its history, religions and the inexplicable caste laws, still so inbred in even the most sophisticated Indians. One morning when overhearing her mother discussing the Bhakji movement in southern India, Rachel had interrupted, 'I think I'm too young to understand Hinduism. Will you explain it again when I'm eight?'

She was to see Pakistan the following year, when she was still small. Dervla decided to take her daughter on a more arduous trip to a place she had seen but not explored. They would spend the winter in Baltistan (or little Tibet), a region containing the greatest concentration of high peaks in the world, the Karakoram Himalaya, and still one of the least developed areas of Asia. Covering an area of ten thousand square miles, it was part of the old domain of the Maharaja of Kashmir, now disputed between Pakistan and India.

While waiting in Rawalpindi for an aeroplane to take them to Gilgit, Dervla revisited Swat, where she had been so regally entertained by the President and his family on her last visit eleven years before. Sadly the palace was now empty except for the old retainers, who greeted her warmly. Recently all princely states had been ended, the numerous tiny chieftainships in Baltistan were now known as the Northern Areas. The other noticeable change was the enormous influx of hippies. Indeed Dervla's book, *Full Tilt*, had been held responsible for increasing the momentum. This troubled her conscience more than it flattered her vanity, when she saw 'groups of drugged wrecks dragging themselves around Asia . . . . However, the hippies are merely a source of local amusement – and of course profit for the many drug-peddlars in the bazaars.'

Flying to Gilgit over the snowbound Babusar Pass, Rachel remarked, 'You must have been dotty to cross that on a bicycle!' Dervla gazed down at the barren Indus Valley and saw Chilas, where she had collapsed with the 'sun devil' and remembered how the locals had looked after her with such kindness. But she did not contradict her daughter.

During the next ten weeks, they were to travel through five valleys, including the perilous Indus Gorge. They met no other westerners and lived on the customary Baltinese diet of dried apricots and nut kernels. They had been told by a pessimistic official in Rawalpindi that even the Baltis would not spend winters in Baltistan if it could be helped, and they were to find that, during the trek, the locals would stare at the *ferenghis* (foreigners) as if they were quite mad. But Dervla felt that, like many simple people, the Baltis delighted in exaggerating local dangers but were little affected by real tragedies.

On 25 December, nearly one month after leaving England, they were in Juglote. Both of them forgot it was Christmas Day until they were writing their diaries that evening. Their Christmas dinner consisted of *chappatis* and a *dahl* gruel followed by watery tea, but as this was their first meal in twelve hours at a temperature of minus twenty degrees, it tasted remarkably good.

Much haggling over the price went on before an ex-polo pony was found for Rachel, who named it Hallam after her favourite man-friend. They were already equipped with a saddle, which they had bought in Rawalpindi, because of Fillipo de Fillipi's account of his 1909 trek in *Karakoram and the Western Himalaya*. 'Anyone intending to take a long journey through Baltistan should provide himself with a good leather saddle . . . the primitive saddles were so uncomfortable that we usually preferred to walk.'

Hallam proved to be a valiant, sure-footed creature and only lost his nerve twice – once on a narrow track hewn out of a precipice directly above the Indus when several large rocks came hurtling down ahead of them, causing him to shy towards the edge of the track. Luckily he and Rachel both kept calm heads. The second time was on the same day where the track had been built up on stakes driven into a rocky wall rising sheer out of the Shyok River. Suddenly they met a jeep, which made Hallam snort with terror and rear up on to his hind legs. Dervla wrote in her book, *Where the Indus is Young*, 'There has been no nastier moment in my entire forty-three years.'

In spite of their padded suits and astronaut's blanket, the cold was intense and often kept them awake at night: at nine thousand feet, in mid-winter, the temperature was around 35 degrees below freezing point. The small rest houses where they stayed were unheated, and although they carried with them a small kerosene stove, the snow on the floor remained unmelted at night. However, the joys of trekking in such beautiful landscape more than compensated for the discomfort. Fillipo de Fillipi in 1913 had different views: 'The misery of the Baltis has often been described. But one was even more struck by it seeing them in winter, going about numb with cold, barely covered by their wretched home-spun shawls, and certainly undernourished. For three months in the year they live almost entirely on fresh fruit, for the other nine on dried – the famous apricot of Baltistan.' Sometimes even Dervla became disenchanted. Outside Khapaulu, while musing on the beauty of the mountain in all its perfection, the land glittering with new snow, the light crystal, the silence profound, she was interrupted by Rachel wanting to know what uranium was, how gems were mined, why different races speak different languages, where numbers were invented and when the Himalayas were formed. 'At times I itch to push her over the nearest cliff.'

Rachel's saddest moment came at the end of their journey when she had to part with Hallam. Dervla became extremely snappish, not having an outlet for tears, 'Therefore when she needed most cherishing she got abuse instead.' But their real sadness was leaving Baltistan. 'It will break my heart to leave the beauty, the silence and the endless variety of these mountains. Yet I shall be taking with me some of this strange, fortifying Himalayan peace. And it will endure. There is nothing ephemeral about the effects of a journey such as this.' Rachel on a more prosaic note commented that it was her favourite place where she planned to spend her honeymoon.

When Dervla was Rachel's age she had no such romantic notions. In fact she had been convinced that she would never marry. But then she had had a totally different childhood. Until the age of thirty she was virtually a prisoner in her own home. Within months of her birth in 1931, her mother was struck down with crippling arthritis and during the last years of her life she turned from being a warm and stimulating woman into a querulous and demanding tyrant, utterly dependent on Dervla for her every need. Later Dervla was to describe those years as 'hell on earth'.

She had been born in Cappoquin, Co. Waterford, of an incongruous alliance between a mother who was descended from a mildly Unionist family and a father whose whole background was strongly Republican. They had originally met while touring through Poland. Her mother was a beauty with waist-length chestnut hair and before her illness she had loved going for fifteen-mile walks. She smoked Turkish cigarettes, drank China tea and held exceedingly advanced views for those days. Dervla's father, on the other hand, was a lonely introvert, withdrawn, bookish and impractical. When he took the post of County Librarian at Lismore, the couple had arrived on their wedding day in the cab of the lorry which contained all their worldly goods. Their poverty, coupled with their eccentric bourgeois tastes, made it difficult for the Murphys to be accepted into the local community, but it was soon disarmed by their dedication to duty.

Dervla grew up supervised by a maid while her mother helped her husband in the library until the rheumatoid arthritis, which had originally threatened her when she was twenty-one, attacked her again, and she became a permanent cripple, unable to walk or wash or dress herself. With the realisation that they could have no more children, her parents resigned themselves as devout Roman Catholics to an unnaturally restricted marriage. All their parental emotions centred on their only child, Dervla, who as a result became precocious and egotistical, living in a fantasy world of her own. She created an intricate family of four generations of omnipotent teddy bears, who lived in the branches of an enormous elm tree in a nearby wood and meant more to her than any human friend. One of her chief amusements was telling herself interminably convoluted stories. When her mother tried to encourage her to make friends with other children, she could not disrupt her daughter's elaborate fantasy world. When Dervla was five, a formidable character known as Old Bridget moved in with them and purposefully set about controlling the whole Murphy establishment. 'It cannot have been easy to contend with a disintegrating house, an invalid mistress, a chronically vague master and a nasty child.'

Dervla went on to describe her first sexual experience when at the age of six 'with an acute sense of guilt I became a proficient and dedicated masturbator'. Her mother reassured her that it was just a childish habit that she would outgrow, which sure enough she did, only to 'supersede it by more cerebral sexual interests centred on scientific investigation of the male anatomy'. Luckily the small eight-year-old boy who lived opposite 'was a professional exhibitionist. He had perfected a variety of ingenious urinating techniques and his penis was public property. We were an ideally suited couple. He performed, I admired, and it occurred to neither of us that his penis could be put to other uses.'

At six-and-a-half she was sent to the local Catholic day school where she immediately showed her rebellious nature by screaming and kicking, to the amused scorn of the other children. One of the nuns, Sister Andrew, flayed her verbally and battered her physically, but Dervla set out to prove that she could withstand the adult world, however painful the consequences. The verbal abuse hurt her far more than the beatings, but she never revealed the humiliation to her mother and, paradoxically, Sister Andrew in later years became a very good friend.

Dervla took a delight in terrorising her contemporaries by telling them stories about wild animals which hunted on the rooftops of Lismore. When the local priest complained to her mother, her response was to advise Dervla to write such stories down instead. Thus began a lifetime passion. In fact even at the age of four, before she could read, Dervla had picked up a book, pointed to the author's name on the title page and said, 'When I'm grown up I'm going to write books and have my name there.' 'I think she means it,' her mother had said, 'she's a very determined child.' Dervla's father had been a failed writer and his study was full of returned manuscripts, but this left her undeterred. Years later, she felt that 'writing was not a career but a necessity. I was not thinking in terms of success or failure, prosperity or poverty, fame or obscurity.' Dervla had inherited from her bookish father a certain shyness and gaucherie which was aggravated by a sense of inferiority towards a mother who always seemed at ease in any situation. She hero-worshipped her mother's looks, poise and intelligence, which she felt she could never attain, nor her capacity to inspire devotion.

The outbreak of war in 1939 made little impact on the Murphy household. Her father resolved his inner conflicts by persuading himself that the evils of Nazism were a creation of British propaganda. Parcels of smart clothes from a generous French godfather in Paris ceased to arrive, ending for Dervla a period of acute misery when she was dragged off to Mass every Sunday 'looking like a cross between a damn silly doll and a circus clown. My mother, having longed for an elegant daughter to share her own enjoyment of beautiful clothes, had produced an uncouth little savage who only felt happy in shorts and shirts . . . a phobia which persists to this day.'

It was around this time that she was suddenly afflicted by an irrational terror of darkness, a fear that dominated her waking hours. As the days passed, her dread of bedtime increased. Pride stopped her confiding in her mother, and night after night she lay sleepless, telling herself that the terror would end if she could find the necessary courage. Then one night she did. Slipping out of bed stealthily, she went on a tour of the whole house, her hands outstretched to guide her in the dark. 'The thudding in my heart seemed to hurt my ribs . . . but it was worth it. When I got back to my bedroom my self-respect was restored and all fear of darkness exorcised forever.' This was one of the first examples of how she overcame her fear by her persistence. Another example was when she invented secret endurance tests. She regularly inflicted increasing degrees of pain on herself until she was capable of walking three miles with a sharp thorn embedded in the sole of one foot, striking and bruising the back of her hand harder and harder with a heavy stick, tying twine around her finger and pulling it tighter and tighter, and immersing her feet in boiling water. Her battle with Sister Andrew had continued, and she thought it worth cultivating the tolerance of any pain Sister Andrew might inflict on her. Later she embarked on more prolonged trials of herself, practising mental detachment from bodily sensations. She found she could, and she still can, repel pain at will.

When she was nine years old, her parents sent her to an Irish-speaking co-educational boarding school where books in English were forbidden – a rule which Dervla considered the utmost treachery. As she was not allowed to speak English, she decided not to speak at all, and to compensate for the lack of books she decided to write one herself. Demoralised by homesickness, she became a favourite bullying target for the more sadistic senior pupils, who considered her 'priggish, precocious, pedantic and pusillanimous'. In her letters home she greatly exaggerated her predicament, emphasising the health hazards of under-feeding and over-exposure. Her parents took her protests seriously as she developed severe bronchitis, and they arrived suddenly to sweep her away with the headmaster's disparaging remarks ringing in their ears.

Perhaps in compensation her parents gave her for her next birthday a second-hand bicycle. Soon afterwards she made a resolution to cycle to India one day. 'I have never forgotten the exact spot, on a steep hill near Lismore, where this decision was made. Halfway up I rather proudly looked at my legs, slowly pushing the pedals round, and the thought came: "If I went on doing this for long enough I could get to India." The simplicity of the idea enchanted me. I had been poring over my atlas every evening, travelling in fancy. Now I saw how I could travel in reality – alone, independent and needing very little money.'

Until the age of seventeen, the three most important male influences in Dervla's life were her father, her paternal grandfather, a doctor of philosophy known as Pappa, and Mark, a curate and the son of a retired country schoolmaster. Pappa spent each summer holiday with them and always arrived with a battered suitcase tied with rope and bulging with books. 'No one – not even my mother – could read aloud as Pappa did. He involved us until we were transported into other worlds that seemed to be suffused with a special Pappa magic, whatever the theme of the story or the author's style.' One day, walking back from their morning bathe in the Blackwater, Dervla had asked him, 'What is philosophy?' Pappa had answered simply, 'It's the study of how to live contentedly and how to die peacefully.' The holidays were spent in various seaside cottages, and it was only Pappa's presence that made up for the move from home and the surrounding countryside she loved so much. There she could enjoy herself as nowhere else, wandering alone, imagining the distant lands she intended to explore. The domestic cosiness of a seaside cottage was no substitute for dreams of adventures to come.

Mark Ryan came from a family who had for generations been involved in Irish politics and had a cultural integrity not often found in Dublin families. Dervla spent nearly as much time with them as at home, although their parents never fraternised. She hid nothing from Mark and never felt a need to project an image of herself that was an improvement on reality. It seemed quite natural to her that Mark, a Roman Catholic priest, should have adopted as his closest friend a female twenty-seven years his junior. He was so totally devoid of respect for any Establishment, clerical or lay, that he could almost be described as a Christian anarchist, and the only vice he despised was what he called 'humbug'. It was natural that Dervla would be influenced by him. Like her contemporaries she became deeply engrossed in preparing for her First Confession and Holy Communion, and she went through a phase of intense orthodox fervour. She never hesitated to take part in heated theological discussions whenever a particular inconsistency seemed to manifest itself, and she read widely about other religions.

Dervla's inability to communicate with her father came to a head when she refused to accompany him on their regular educational Sunday walks. Her mother was stricken, but Dervla was steadfast in her resolution, declaring, 'I can't stand it any more. Daddy's so boring.' This calculated cruelty tormented her for years afterwards. But there was no doubt of her love for him, which was proved a few months later when they were all in Dublin. Her father, usually so punctual, failed to turn up for family lunch, and Dervla was convinced he had been killed. When at last he arrived, she nonchalantly said, 'Hello,' and then slipped away to the lavatory where she was violently sick. Had she been able to show him how worried she was, their relationship might have changed. As it was, they grew further apart while retaining an almost uncanny gift for reading each other's thoughts.

Dervla was shouldering more responsibilities at home, and when she was sent at thirteen to board at Waterford's Ursuline Convent she soon found a freedom and happiness that she had never before enjoyed. The atmosphere was relaxed without being permissive. For the first time, she was leading a life appropriate to her age. But it was to be all too short. A year later she was to go home for the Easter holidays, never to return. The household was in chaos – her parents had no one to help them, her father's health had deteriorated after a bout of sciatica, and her mother had become a demanding and helpless invalid. After a family conference when all possible alternatives were discussed, the decision was left to Dervla. She declared emphatically that she would stay at home and take care of the situation. At the time the decision seemed inevitable but not intolerable. She would miss school, but she would be able to see Mark regularly; he meant more to her than her school friends, and she would have more time to indulge in her new passion – writing. Mark, in fact, strongly opposed her parents at the time, foreseeing how she would become trapped as her mother grew to depend more and more on her as a nurse.

Dervla wrote her first novel, a boys' adventure story, in three weeks and sent if off secretly to various publishers in England. When it was repeatedly returned with rejection slips, together with kindly words of encouragement, she was not disheartened. 'The literary world had taken me seriously enough to urge me on . . . and I came of a breed used to rejection slips – as it were – on the chin.' During this time she was reading avidly most of the works of the great English, French and Russian novelists. 'When I look now at those scores of volumes, I marvel at my idea of relaxation years ago. Many I have reread . . . and a few I am reluctant to return to, fearing disillusion.'

The domestic treadmill continued and by the age of seventeen Dervla was nursing her mother and doing all the chores in the house. She had four hours off-duty from 6 to 10 p.m.; occasionally her father took over, and she had a whole day to herself for long cycle rides of sixty to seventy miles. Sometimes she would take their Irish terrier Bran with her. One day, without any warning, he was set upon by a black and white mongrel. When his owner, a very tall man in his mid-thirties with a slight limp and a conspicuously scarred face, appeared, he scolded his dog severely. 'At seventeen I was abnormally shy, but my companion seemed even shyer. We exchanged no personal information and when we parted I did not think I would ever see him again.'

However this meeting was to be the beginning of a great love affair. Godfrey, an archaeologist, had been a prisoner in a Japanese camp where he had acquired his limp and horrific scars. He had married while still an undergraduate, but his wife had left him for someone else during the war. Although they were divorced, as a High Anglican he did not feel himself free to remarry. As their friendship grew into something deeper, he and Dervla spent a great deal of time together, but during the first three years of their relationship they never once expressed their affection by any physical contact. Religion provided the area in which they grew closest, and Dervla confessed that she could never be a sincere Christian, while Godfrey desperately needed his faith and was frightened to think of ever losing it. In spite of the differences in their ages, Dervla's domestic hardships had made her understand the different, but no less wearing, stresses and strains in Godfrey's life.

Dervla was experiencing all the emotions of first love, but she never imagined that it could be reciprocated. To love was enough. As she wrote of her love, 'Despite the apparent artificiality of its framework, it developed and matured and grew richer as the months and years passed. And for me it had – as I see it in retrospect – a most precious and irrecoverable beauty. For it was the fairest flower in the garden of youth; love without passion.'

But Godfrey, in his tortured way, came to return her love. The deep and strong friendship of three years became a physical passion. When this was eventually consummated, Dervla remembered her 'exultant sense of kinship with everything I saw . . . I felt that until this day I had been only half-alive, half-aware; now I had a new relationship not just with Godfrey but with all of nature.' The durability of their love was never questioned, but it was left unsaid between them that Godfrey would never consider himself free to marry. Even at sixteen Dervla had had a strong premonition that she would never marry, and now at twenty-one she accepted the inevitable. Although she thought his scruples about extra-marital sex were absurd, she loyally deferred to them, but she was secretly delighted when they occasionally ceased to be effective.

The emotional excitement of being in love compensated for the increasing demands made upon her by a mother who was determined to dominate her. Dervla might argue against scrubbing the hall floor every day and cleaning the windows every week, but she couldn't refuse the constant use of the bedpan or the endless changing of her mother's position as she lay in her bed. The atmosphere was deteriorating rapidly. Her mother's years of controlled frustration were taking their toll and, instead of expressing some sympathy with Dervla's situation, she behaved as if her daughter were merely doing her duty and began treating her like a skivvy. 'By 1955 we were both losing our emotional grip and, looking back, I can see how a grim spiral developed as she sought to punish me for adding to her suffering by exposing my own.' But strangely at this time there was still a strong mutual love and they shared the same sense of humour which kept them sane.

During this period Dervla wrote her second unpublished novel. It was in no way autobiographical, but it had a prophetic theme, the growing up of an illegitimate girl in a small Irish town. Seven years after her first meeting with Godfrey, they spent a whole night together for the first time while her mother was in hospital suffering from kidney stones. Cycling home the next day, Dervla felt a deep despair that she would never escape from the prison of her home. Her off-duty hours had been reduced to three; it was virtually impossible for her to enjoy the simple but exhilarating pleasure of roaming the countryside – a deprivation she felt more acutely than any other. For years to come her freedom would be unnaturally restricted.

Her father was now excluded from helping with the nursing. Her mother decreed that only Dervla could cope effectively. Mark condemned this as a form of moral blackmail, but to no avail. Dervla understood: after a decade of daily practice, it was her touch alone that her mother did not dread. But this was little comfort to someone who detested nursing even more than housekeeping. Dervla began to hate her mother for using her physical helplessness to wield such power over her. It became worse when she had to give up her own room to sleep beside the invalid. Mark could see that she was near breaking-point. Obviously Mrs Murphy's illness was not only physical, but mental.

For some time Godfrey had suffered from a bad cough, and when he suddenly announced that he was going to London and on to Peru to explore Inca sites, Dervla instinctively knew he was lying to protect her from the truth. For the next few months he wrote stilted letters from London, but when Christmas came, they suddenly stopped. On 3 January 1959 Godfrey's servant came to the Murphys' back door and handed her a small parcel containing a letter and diaries. He said that Godfrey had wished to be buried at sea. Neither of them showed any emotion and no explanation was given as to the cause of death.

On the surface Dervla remained composed, but inwardly she had a complete nervous breakdown. She remembers few details about the appalling months that followed, but she recollects picking up a heavy chair and flinging it across her mother's room in a paroxysm of rage. Then, five months later, she loaded her bicycle, said good-bye to her father and told him she wasn't coming back. After being looked after by friends for a while, she went to London and found a job working in a canteen in a home for down-and-outs.

When she did return home after a few weeks, the fact that she had been seriously ill resulted in the local doctor insisting they employ a daily maid to take some of the strain off her. For some months life became a little easier, but then her mother developed asthma and Dervla had to sleep in her room once more. They were back to the impasse of the previous year and, once again, Dervla was losing her grip. Several times the asthmatic attacks threatened her mother's life, and Dervla found herself longing for her mother to die. Soon she was nursing both her parents as her father had contracted severe influenza. She and her mother sat up drinking whiskey and, in the shadow of death, they talked once again as adult friends and savoured a relationship they had lost.

Her father died in hospital two months later and Dervla was left to look after her mother, who outlived him by eighteen months. Once again she was on the treadmill of attending to her mother's every need twenty-four hours a day. To preserve her sanity she put her mother into a nursing home, this time taking a job as a farm-hand in Germany. During six back-breaking weeks thoughts of her abandoned mother were dulled by the welcome drug of exhaustion. On her return she found her mother was losing the will to live. Dervla stayed with her until her death. 'As my mother drew her last breath, peace enfolded me. It was profound and healing, untinged by grief or remorse, or guilt, or loneliness. . . . A great burden was gone, the double burden of another's tragedy and my own inadequacy. I stood at the threshold of an independent life and I felt that night my parents' blessing on it.' She was thirty years old.

As the Far Eastern veteran traveller Ella Maillart has written, the only real thing is the here and now. For her, the past is dead and the future does not exist: the present is at once the past. Before Rachel's birth, and after Dervla's first journeys to India and Nepal, she became fascinated by the idea of travelling through Ethiopia. A British soldier with the Napier Expedition of 1867 had written, 'They tell us this is a tableland. If it is, they have turned the table upside down and we are scrambling up and down the legs.' Dervla agrees with him. When she is asked the two questions, 'What is the toughest journey you have undertaken?' and 'Where were you when you were in most danger?', the answer to both is, 'Oh, most certainly, without any doubt, Ethiopia.' Foreigners were not encouraged to travel through Ethiopia's remote regions in 1966, and it was against official advice that she planned her highland trek which was to take her from Massawah on the north-east coast and then

south across the Takazze Gorge, into the icy High Semiens, around
Lake Tana, over the plateau of Manz, finishing at Addis Ababa.
The stories she had read as a child had conjured up a picture of a
land synonymous with violence, beauty, peril, solitude and mystery.

She did her homework vigorously before leaving, reading countless
books on the country, and she was fully equipped mentally, histori-
cally and geographically; but on a practical level, her equipment
seemed almost perversely spartan: a rucksack, a pair of boots, a water
bottle, a Husky outfit, a few basic medical supplies, notebooks, ball-
point pens and a great many books to read. The only good maps were
Italian, which she found 'inaccurate enough to give me the gratifying
illusion of being an explorer in trackless wastes'.

On her arrival by boat at the Red Sea port of Massawah in mid-
December, she was immediately aware of Ethiopia's isolation and
felt more alien there than she had in any other country. The first
few days climbing up to Asmara made her realise how much she
missed Roz – she was carrying a load of fifty pounds while climbing
up thirty steep miles to the Eritrean plateau. Painful blisters formed
on her feet, and it was only her flask of emergency brandy that kept
her going. By the time she reached Asmara she was in extreme pain
and collapsed on a bed in an Italian-run *pensione*. When she pulled
off her socks, all the skin from both soles came with them 'leaving
what looked two pounds of raw steak ... undoubtedly, this is
where I forget "mind-over-matter" and sit around for some days
growing new skin.'

The British Consul and his wife, John and 'Peter' Bromley, asked
her to stay for Christmas and strongly advised that she purchase a
pack-mule, as it would be necessary always to carry a full water-
bottle and supplementary food supplies in the highlands. They
introduced her to Her Highness Princess Leilt Aida Desta, the eldest
grandchild of the Emperor Haile Selassie. She was going to prove a
wonderful ally and an 'open sesame' throughout the journey with
letters to the various district governors *en route*. The Princess also
found her a suitable mule which Dervla immediately named Jock in
honour of a friend 'noted for his kindness and dependability'. A
strong rapport soon grew between Dervla and Jock, and although
she was incapable of the intricate process of mule-loading, she had

her usual fatalistic belief that there would always be a kindly stranger at hand to come to her rescue.

Armed with a *dula* (stick), she bade farewell to the Princess who insisted that she should telephone her whenever possible, never hesitate to ask for help and never sleep in the open. She was warned, as many others had been, of possible attacks by *shifta* (bandits). Later in Arsum when the police forbade her to walk alone through the Semien Mountains, it was a telephone call from the Princess that over-ruled them.

The attitude of most highlanders to a *faranj* (foreigner) was a mixture of restraint, hostility, fear and avarice. Dervla was to miss the friendly, unrepressed interest aroused in Asia by wandering foreigners. But it didn't alter her theory that in remote regions it is best to show a total dependence on the locals. And, in fact, staying overnight in their huts, she found that once they had got over the initial shock and fear of the *faranj*, people were gracious and warmhearted, sharing with her their food and *talla* (an intoxicating grey-green brew) served in huge yellow-brown gourds. She was again mistaken for a man, and once two small boys offered to get her a 'good bad woman' for the night. Apart from the Italian occupation, the region had never been in touch with the outside world. It was no wonder that a wandering *faranj* with a mule caused such consternation among the people, which was mixed with awe when they heard that she was a protégée of Leilt Aida.

For the first few weeks of her trek, Dervla was accompanied by guides. When she approached the Takazze Gorge, no fewer than fourteen men (eight of them armed) were considered the minimum force for a safe passage through *shifta* territory. 'My would-be unpretentious one-woman expedition had now got completely out of hand . . . but instinct told me that beneath their dutiful solicitude lay a basic distrust of the unprecedented lone *faranj*. . . . For me such a situation is new. I have never before travelled amongst people who inspired sufficient fear to make me abandon my aim.' But soon Dervla became an 'honoured guest' instead of a 'damn nuisance', for the simple reason that her climbing speed was greater than that of her highland escorts, who admired physical prowess above all qualities.

The word 'precipitous' was to crop up frequently in Dervla's

account of her journey, *In Ethiopia with a Mule*. Indeed, the descent
to the Takazze Gorge was the toughest she had ever experienced –
'more like falling down a mountain'. Eventually her Tigrean guards
departed for home, leaving her with an unarmed puny youth from
whom she managed to escape without too much difficulty. 'It was
blissful to be on my own again – alone in a region that looked more
grandly wild and felt more remote than anywhere else I have ever
been.' That night she slept on the mountainside and, waking at
dawn under a sky of splendid beauty, she felt 'an almost intolerable
awareness of the duality of our nature. We belong so intimately and
joyously and tragically to this physical world, and by its own laws
we must soon leave it. Yet during these moments one knows, too,
with humility and certainty, that each human spirit is immortal –
for time cannot destroy whatever element within us reverences the
glory of a dawn in the mountains.'

Approaching the High Semiens, poor Jock had to be urged on
with vehement shouts and whacks with her stick, but the satisfaction
of reaching the point where at 13,800 feet she could look down on
countless craggy peaks, made her feel like a 'mini-Hilary, with all
Northern Ethiopia lying at my feet'. Her final climb was to Ras
Dashan, at 15,158 feet Ethiopia's highest mountain, with a group
of schoolteachers from Addis Ababa on a camping trek. The young
men could not understand why she would choose voluntarily to live
in *takuls*, while she deplored the idea of trekking through a country
in isolation from the people who inhabited it.

In the small towns through which Dervla passed, she would spend
the night in the local hotel – usually a courtesy title for a brothel
where 'harlots may be observed partially undressing truck-drivers
in the bar'. At Massawah she had found that, in the ill-lit lanes
behind the main street, most of the houses were brothels. Tigrean
girls sat in doorways playing with their toddlers or dressing each
other's hair in tiny plaits while smoking endless cigarettes – the
prostitute's trade mark.

After the arduous climbing in the High Semiens, and the exhausting ten-day trek south to Gondar, Dervla and Jock were both so
emaciated that she decided they should rest for a week before
continuing the journey. They had been met by a crowd of excited
people because, as she later learned, Leilt Aida had been telephoning

the Chief of Police for news of their arrival. Dervla was taken on a tour of the town, passing the market place where a public gallows – still in regular use – dominated the scene. The Italian invaders had planned to make Gondar the capital of their African Empire and featureless Fascist buildings remain as a monument to Mussolini's ambitions. Dervla observed that goodwill towards the Italians seemed to be universal amongst educated Ethiopians. It was based partly on gratitude and partly on the realisation that the construction of the roads and buildings and telephone communications, which took the Italians five years, would probably have taken the Ethiopians a whole century.

Dervla was robbed three times during her epic journey, but the first time was the most frightening. She was rounding the northwest shore of Lake Tana just before the incident. Treacherous swamps kept forcing her and Jock north, away from her destination of Dengel; in the distance she could see a group of *takuls*, and walked towards them, thirstily thinking about *talla*. Suddenly her path was barred by four men, led by a priest carrying his Coptic cross and twirling his horse-hair fly-whisk. The laymen were holding their *dulas* menacingly, and the priest's eyes were bright with greed: 'He used his cross to gesture towards me – and then towards the lake.' Immediately a ferocious argument started between the four men. 'During those brief long moments I was reacting on two levels, for beneath the seething terror was a strange, indifferent acceptance – a feeling that gamblers can't always win and that if this was it, it was it. . . . While the argument was going on and before it was possible to judge who was winning, I suddenly knew I was safe. . . . For an instant I was aware of being protected by some mysterious power; and to a person without definite religious convictions this was almost as great a shock as the unpleasant encounter itself.'

Dervla was convinced she had escaped death, but the men stole all her possessions including Jock's bridle and W. E. Carr's *Poetry of the Middle Ages*. However, they left her cigarettes and her traveller's cheques, which she wore in a belt under her shirt, so she shakily continued her trek. But she left the path and nearly lost her life for the second time that day by falling into a seven-foot hole in the swamp. By luck she was holding on to Jock's halter; the steadfast animal did not panic and she hauled herself to safety. That night she spent in a *takul* with an hospitable but pathetically poor family, who looked as if they would die either of disease or starvation. Throughout her journey she had been all too aware of the dreadful poverty and illness among the highland people. That night Dervla hardly slept, rats raced all over everyone, and she began to feel 'like a shipwrecked nonagenarian'. But she was determined to reach Behar Dar to report the attack to the police. The main obstacle was the muddy water of the Little Nile, which she had to persuade Jock to cross. Tigre mules have an aversion to deep rivers, and after all her efforts to persuade him had failed, Dervla looked in the other direction while some donkey-drivers tried to make him cross by brutal thrashings. As the poor creature plunged despairingly in, Dervla seized the halter and swam beside him to the far shore.

When they presented themselves at the Ras Hotel, she looked a sorry sight and the dapper Ethiopian manager only relented and gave her a room when she produced a damp, but valid, traveller's cheque.

Fortunately, the story had a satisfying ending. A week later the Chief of Police, together with seventeen armed men, took her back to the scene of the crime. Travelling by launch and following the shoreline, she eventually identified the swampy area where she had been attacked and found the compound and the culprits. Two had apparently recently been in jail and the 'horrified priest's eyes were an eloquent admission of guilt'. Most of her possessions were recovered – the most important being her flea-bag – but, more important still, she had wrought her Irish vengeance.

Dervla was to be robbed twice more, the second time by a youth who took her sun-hat and *injara* (food basket) which contained her compass, map, altimeter, torch, and water and malaria pills – a disastrous theft. The third time the loss was not so great, but the circumstances were particularly unpleasant. She had wrenched her knee, which was giving her extreme pain, and when a handsome young gunman, who claimed to be 'Police', asked her to stay in his family's *takul*, she reluctantly accepted. 'My host's family consists of his mother, a child-wife and two other women, and the atmosphere in this *takul* is unique. All the time I am being laughed at unkindly ... and payment in advance demanded for every glass of *talla* I've drunk, for my *injara* . . . and for Jock's fodder.' The next morning she realised her coin-box had been stolen, but as the young gunman started to prod her with his rifle she decided to say nothing, but to go on her way.

'Travelling in this country fosters an abnormal degree of fatalism, doubtless produced by one's own subconscious as a protection against nervous breakdowns. Tonight I'm past caring about untrustworthy locals, *shifta*, leopards or hyenas. The probability is that Jock and I will survive, the possibility that either or both might be attacked has ceased to worry me. . . . Loneliness never touches me in uninhabited country, where my solitude is complete, but I do feel twinges of it when people are unresponsive.'

Crossing the pathless drought area of Lasta, on their way to Lalibela without maps or a compass, they were both at their lowest ebb. Dervla's knee was becoming more painful by the day, and Jock was beginning to collapse. 'His expression was the ultimate in dejection . . . the miles that followed were the most trying of the whole trek. Had Jock behaved mulishly, his suffering might have been a little less heart-rending, but he struggled on – becoming hourly more enfeebled – with a faithful courage that I shall never forget.' At Lalibela Dervla fell ill with dysentery and sent an SOS to the Bromleys in Addis Ababa for a replacement of some of her stolen possessions. These came back the same day by diplomatic bag plus some 'extras' and a large load of mail.

Although Jock struggled on manfully for a while, he was suffering from severe malnutrition and Dervla knew with a heavy heart that he needed at least a month's rest and proper feeding. A kindly local herdsman agreed to exchange him for a donkey. Knowing by his treatment of his own animal that he would treat Jock well, Dervla realised how lucky she was to meet him at this crucial time.

Without saying goodbye to Jock, she made the final stage of her journey to Manz with the donkey who soon gained the name of Satan, through his devilish nature. Dervla found the scenery of the Manz uplands so glorious that the chasing of a demoniacal donkey was 'just another pleasure. If the highlands in general seem remote from the rest of the world, Manz seems remote even from the rest of the highlands. Its atmosphere is unique.'

Ending her journey in the modern city of Addis Ababa, Dervla looked at her pocket pedometer and realised she had walked 1,024 miles. 'A traveller who does not speak their language cannot presume to claim any deep understanding of the Ethiopian highlanders. But it is the gradual growth of affection for another race, rather than the walking of a thousand miles or the climbing of a hundred mountains, that is the real achievement and the richest reward of such a journey.'

She had seen many fascinating sights including the medieval church in Bethlehem discovered by Thomas Pakenham and Imrahanna Kristos standing in a deep cave and, like so many other Ethiopian churches, guarded by mercenary and immoral priests. Hyenas and leopards had crossed her path, and she had seen countless Geleda baboons, sometimes frighteningly near. She had suffered traumatic experiences at the hands of some of the people, but above all she had been captivated by the highlands. 'Yet it is not only through their beauty that these highlands have enchanted me. I love them, too, for their challenging brutality, and had I seen the beauty without meeting the challenging brutality, I could not now feel so attached to Ethiopia.'

Dervla was thirty-six and still unmarried. Nevertheless she decided to have a child, in spite of the fact that this would have been considered somewhat unorthodox for a single woman living in Ireland at that time. Her second unpublished novel was indeed prophetic. During her pregnancy she made a three-month trek round Turkey. Her friends tried to dissuade her, but she retorted, 'The food is very good in Turkey – just the job for building bonny babies.' She says that the day Rachel was born was definitely the happiest day of her life. Believing that small children need a regular routine in familiar surroundings, she decided not to travel during her first five years. Motherhood made up for the temporary loss of freedom, and as Dervla and Rachel lived very frugally, they managed to exist on the money she earned from her books and her regular reviews for the *Irish Times*. It was during this period that she wrote her autobiography, *Wheels Within Wheels* – the story of her first thirty years. 'I really wrote it for Rachel to read later and to help me unravel a lot of things, never dreaming of publication. It was, I suppose, a kind of therapy.' While Rachel was a baby, she feared their relationship might become too close, but she realised by the time Rachel was three that there was no danger as the child was developing her own distinct personality. Although she was temperamentally very different from her mother, they had a lot in common, both being book and animal lovers. 'Neither of us minds,' Dervla says, 'if the cat licks the butter, the dogs' hairs get into the soup or the goats come into the living room.'

The period of Rachel's first years at school allowed her mother to go away, but not too far away. She decided it was time to look to her home island. The Murphy family were strong Republicans, and when Dervla was twelve, the Chief-of-Staff of the Irish Republican Army had appeared at her home. He had been on the run for the killing of a detective-sergeant in Dublin. Sent by Mr Murphy's sister, Dr Kathleen Farrell, who was active in the cause, the family had taken him in, Dervla's mother wanting to cure his sick idealism. Dervla was thrilled at the time, thinking Charles Kerins a glorious patriot, though she commented later in her autobiography that he had never outgrown either the innocence or the ruthlessness of his youth. Her big moment was seeing his black automatic laid on the white pillow of his bed. He went back to her aunt's house and was captured there and eventually hanged, while Kathleen Farrell was put in prison. At the news of his death for a United Ireland and the cause, Dervla felt an hysterical elation. He had sent her a silver ring, made by another comrade who had been shot for the cause. She wore it constantly until her finger and her ideals outgrew it. She still has it, though she is no Murphy Republican now. Yet the 1916 myth of the Easter Rising, like malaria, is still in her bloodstream.

When she went to research *A Place Apart* in Northern Ireland in 1976, she had almost laid her Republicanism to rest. She was a lapsed Catholic – and no priest had tried to bring her back. On her travels in India and Ethiopia, when people asked her why Christians were fighting in Ireland, she replied she didn't know herself – and only noticed later that such a reply from an Irishwoman might seem stupid and unkind and irresponsible. She even caught herself saying, 'Why don't the Brits get out and let them all slaughter each other if that's how they feel? There's nothing to choose between them.'

But choose she did, when she finally reached the real battleground of Belfast. She had to use a British Army 'Tribal Map' of the city to get around. The ghetto areas were marked in orange and green for the warring tribes of the Prods and the Taigs. The ghettos shattered her. Although she had known worse slums in Asia, the sight of these undernourished wild children with sugar-rotted teeth playing vandals in the ten thousand abandoned homes of the city, the barricades between the rival areas, the jungle of the front gardens and the streets knee-deep in stinking litter, the rivers of broken glass and the bricked-up house windows – this was a journey in the urban wilderness. Because of her travels, she felt remote enough from her own land to look at it as a 'dotty Fourth World' country with the detachment she felt in Africa and Asia. 'The Brits versus Paddies feud', she says, 'frequently makes grown-ups behave like not very bright five-year-olds.'

She soon adapted to tribal life and confessed to feeling safer in Green territory than on Orange ground. She was more afraid of cycling at night on her trusty Roz along the 'Murder Mile' of the Antrim Road than wheeling across an Ethiopian plateau or in a Himalayan valley. And the senseless provocations got her down, the children kicking a football to each other and calling it 'The Pope'. Only in country pubs, where the men would ask, 'For who'll be fightin' over what?' or in the homes of the mothers bereft of their sons but forgiving the killer for the sake of his mother not having this sadness in her, or on the huge Peace Marches of twenty thousand Catholic and Protestant women, did Dervla feel common flashes of humanity. As always, she caught the right moment, the telling words – the Catholic girl marcher smiling at the British soldier and saying, 'We'd soon have yous out of a job!' and him smiling back and saying, 'I hope so!'

No more than anyone could Dervla see a solution to the sectarian war in Northern Ireland. The problems were not so much economic as emotional and ethnic and psychological. There would have to be direct rule from London for a long time to come, and the British troops would have to try to stop the secret armies of the Catholics and the Protestants from killing one another. The only sane policy was not to oppose violence to violence, but to oppose tolerance to intolerance and reflection to hysteria. But who would do it? How would it be done? Only by the traveller's example. That July and August riding her old bicycle once again, with her seven-year-old daughter following behind on her pony and their elkhound Olaf at the rear, they pitched their tent all over Ulster and never had a better holiday. Down in southern Ireland, her friends think her delirious and mad when she suggests going to Northern Ireland for a visit. It is the people and the place she loves, in spite of its holy war. She won't *have* to go there any more, but she *wants* to – and often.

For Dervla there have always been the journeys of the mind. In February, 1979, in a remote mountain village in Ecuador, she heard a question more difficult than those which had sent her back to examine her roots and the problems of Ireland. This time a young American asked her why she was exploring the Andes rather than the nuclear debate. What was crossing peaks compared with denying atomic fission? The great discovery had been how to explode the atom. Now a traveller like Dervla needed to explore the way out of that terrible invention that implied the destruction of all life on earth. So Dervla wrote about the nuclear debate instead of writing about Peru, which was postponed to a later date.

It went against man's exploratory nature to turn away from a supreme invention like the cheap energy released by splitting the atom. But Dervla realised it had to be done. It was as if Shangri-la had been discovered and it turned out to be the Abyss or the Maelstrom. After the dropping of the atomic bomb on Hiroshima, the survivors had to numb themselves psychologically to the horror of what was happening to them – decay by radiation. This 'psychic numbing' seemed to Dervla to become an Age of Numbing, in which people put aside their anxiety, because they could not live with the worry about a potential nuclear catastrophe. It was a necessary defence mechanism, but not a good one. Her book, *Race to the Finish? The Nuclear Stakes* was meant to galvanise people to get rid of the danger in their midst.

Dervla was thirteen when the bomb was dropped in Hiroshima. She was conscious that the Atomic Age presented a fearsome challenge to humankind; her father pointed out that Prometheus hadn't done too well after he stole fire from the gods. She quoted Eisenhower as saying, 'It wasn't necessary to hit them with that awful thing,' but as President of the United States, Eisenhower switched to an 'Atoms for Peace' programme, by which nuclear secrets would be shared so that all nations would produce cheap energy. But the danger of nuclear leakage and plutonium poisoning, and radiation deaths like Karen Silkwood's, turned Dervla with her love of nature into a fervent prohibitionist of all atomic fission. In India, England, Peru, France, America, Ethiopia and Ireland, she met people who accused her of being a crank or a freak in her opposition to *all* nuclear energy, but she would not change her extreme view. There was no middle of the road in that argument.

She wants to abandon the achievements of high technology because they destroy the environment. Yet mankind has never withdrawn from the far ranges of the mind. She happened to be riding on a Greyhound bus on the Pennsylvania Turnpike near Three Mile Island when the most serious nuclear reactor accident in America was about to happen. She wore a badge, 'Better Active Today than Radioactive Tomorrow', which got her into a bitter argument. The next day the reactor blew, radiation levels rose, a melt-down threatened, soon there was a mass evacuation of pregnant women and children. It was a prelude for Chernobyl, which happened after her book was written. But as on Ireland, Dervla is a prophet as well as a presenter of insoluble problems.

Dervla saw in the near-catastrophe at Three Mile Island a parallel between technological America and the stone-age culture of the Aztecs. Fearsome gods controlled the Aztec cosmos and could destroy the world, unless placated. American politicians believed such energy was necessary for the good of their world, and if these gods of fission became angry, they had to be kept quiet. President Carter himself flew in to prove all was safe – and he had served in a nuclear submarine, he was the man to know. So the crisis at Three Mile Island did not end in a bang, but a reassurance that did not convince Dervla. She joined an anti-nuclear crusade, which she agreed was quasi-religious. She felt she had to try to study this life-destroying technology, even though changing a light bulb gave her the tremors and after forty-five years of cycling she still could not mend a puncture. She agreed with her father, all subjects were interesting if taken seriously. And nothing was more serious to Dervla than the power of destruction within the split atom.

The real problem was that she came to realise nuclear scientists saw themselves as pioneers – as adventurers into the unknown.

They were clever, brave, persistent and imaginative; their qualities were repeated throughout human history. But she also saw them as victims of nuclear numbing. They did not want to think the unthinkable, to foresee the inevitable catastrophe – the Chernobyl that was to come after *Race to the Finish?* was completed. For as on Northern Ireland, Dervla offered no solutions, only that change was inevitable because of the limitations of the planet. The great nuclear adventure might be the climax of an era, not its end. She would not tell people how to stop nuclear power, but that it must be stopped.

Spurred on by her treks into the insoluble, Dervla later set out to examine the racial tension in the decaying centres of English urban areas. She subtitled her *Tales from Two Cities* as *Travels of Another Sort*. The idea had come to her nearly twenty years before she tackled the job, on a bicycle tour from London to Edinburgh, when she met many newcomers to Britain from the ethnic minorities. Nothing had prepared her for *residence* in deprived urban areas, particularly as she was a truly rural animal. But she persisted in her voyage to the heart of the colour problem. She found great similarities between Ireland of the 1950s and Bradford in the 1980s, when the reactionary influence of the Roman Catholic Church had been similar to that of some of the Mirpuri Muslim leaders. Ireland had changed in the past thirty years, as had the Mirpur she had known and loved on her first bicycle trip to India. Yet Manningham in Bradford, where the Mirpuris worked at the textile machines or were unemployed, had not changed. That was because exiles hung on to their traditions and did not want to alter them for the sake of self-defence. Some of these are the people now, Dervla says, who want Salman Rushdie's *Satanic Verses* burned, for they cannot learn the new island tradition of free speech.

Dervla hated the 'consumer-society deprivation' of the poor whites of Bradford. It was harder to take than Third World poverty. She was sorrier for them than for the displaced Mirpuris, who were better at coping with adversity and unemployment because they had low expectations and supported each other as the whites no longer did. The shock of the ghettoes of Belfast was repeated here. She saw a divided society in 'a European deprived area'. She found some of the have-nots condemned for life to remain so. They were tragic and dangerous because, even if they had food and shelter, they had no hope.

In Handsworth, Birmingham, a black friend of Dervla's told her that the blacks were not going to tell her what they felt or thought. They were sick of Whitey studying them. 'You don't want to understand, you only want to have *theories*.' She should go home and study problems in Ireland again, there were enough of them there. Dervla began to wonder if race relations could be studied. It made her feel like someone trying to untie a multiple knot in the dark, particularly the problem of colour. It was not made easier by her being white, when lightness of skin was admired in so many cultures of other colours. She would not judge. And after being present at a confrontation that turned into a riot, between the local police and the Rastafarians, she felt that she had ceased to study race relations, she was 'hanging in *surviving* race relations'.

Hanging in surviving was just what Dervla did in her deprived and difficult months in the urban jungle. But *Tales from Two Cities* is unique in its honesty and refusal to call black white or brown beige. Dervla has no time for liberal niceties. She tries to present the facts about the persecutor and the victim. And these travels of another sort reveal a fearless woman, searching for the unknowable. She is no expert, but she is persistence itself. As the saying goes, the difference between two of the social sciences is this: when we are looking at 'them', it is anthropology; when we are looking at 'us', it is sociology. When she is looking at them as us or us as them, it is Dervla's enquiry after human truth.

While Dervla was writing her book about Northern Ireland, Rachel spent three years at the primary school at Lismore. But Dervla wanted a last trip with her before boarding school and short holidays prevented any further adventures together. So she planned to walk the route of the Spanish conquerors of the Incas, thirteen hundred miles up and down the Andes from Cajamarca to Cuzco. She found the Peruvian Indians friendly and very like the Tibetans, supporting the theory that they had walked there long ago from Asia across a now-sunken land bridge. She bought a pretty but temperamental mule called Joanna for Rachel to ride on, then set off with her familiar sense of unreality into the unknown. And unknown it was, because she had been told that no Peruvian Indians could or would tell her the right path. 'It's better to get lost your way than theirs.' Dervla did get lost often enough, even on the old Inca trail, the Camino Real. And sometimes nine-year-old Rachel had a better nose than she did. 'Bitter experience has taught her that her mother, though allegedly an Intrepid Traveller, has no sense of direction.'

The grace and stillness of the mountains made Dervla launch into tirades against the acquisition game of the modern world with its technocrats and tycoons demanding constant, meaningless change. Who could stop the multi-national *Conquistadores* any more than the Incas had stopped the Spanish invaders? She loved the simple freedom to walk the mountains with her daughter and her mule. But the way was rough and thorny. And Joanna would sometimes do the worst thing a mule could do – go down on her knees and roll over on her rider and her loads. Dervla gave her a good walloping for that, but loved her for her courage in charging up slippery sand slopes and across rotten, wooden bridges over roaring rivers. In spite of mulish obstinacy and fleas, poisonous cactus spikes and thorn bushes worse than barbed wire and nails in her boots, Dervla felt herself '*absorbed* by the Andes. . . . The boundless glory of mountain beauty [left] a memory forever, an indelible imprint on one's whole being.'

The wonder of the landscape did not prevent Dervla's pity for the Indians of the Andes. As one young man told her, they were stranded by history. Nominally Roman Catholics, but still with their ancient animist beliefs, they did not have the spiritual power of the people of India and Pakistan. They had no hope. Even the reforms which had given them their own land had done little good. And with the same bleak vision which made her refuse to make easy solutions for the problems of Northern Ireland or English city ghettoes or nuclear fission, Dervla consigned the Peruvian Indians to slow oblivion. Their doom had begun with the Spanish conquest of the Incas 450 years before. 'Outside aid' to them would only prolong their agony, even if they were now half the population of Peru. Sick-drunk or fighting-drunk on *chicha* at their fiestas in the mountain towns, or sullen on chewing wads of *coca* leaves, the Indian men were defeated and had no future. Of course, when her

friends all asked her what she felt about chewing *coca*, she said she
was already addicted to alcohol and nicotine, and that was quite
enough.

Such Irish fatalism about others had no effect on Dervla on her
journey with Rachel and Joanna in the steps of the *Conquistadores*.
Perversely, she even came to admire the Spanish invaders for their
courage and endurance in getting to Cuzco, fighting innumerable
armies all the way, when she and her daughter and her mule were
only fighting for alfalfa and tinned sardines to eat, and somewhere
warm to sleep at night. That self-mockery which is Dervla's great
quality made her play down the many trials and deprivations of
their journey, even crossing one pass at 16,000 feet with the air so
thin it hurt. Compared to the daily suffering of the poor mountain
Indians, Dervla said that their adventures were merely 'interesting
experiences'. 'Our treks are just playing with hardship.' Yet it was
some game – almost as fatal on precipices or in gorges as the game
of football, which a fanatic in Janja claimed the Indians had
invented by wrapping an enemy's skull in his skin and kicking it
around.

It is that understanding of the hardship of the lives of other
people that has made Dervla travel with such unconcern for danger,
and even risk the life of her nine-year-old daughter, amongst
tarantulas and icy torrents and sheer drops ten thousand foot down.
Rachel seemed to share her mother's lack of fear and her diary was
very funny, particularly on her mother losing the way. Although
sometimes Dervla does seem like that tireless Victorian traveller, Sir
Samuel Baker, who spent three years followed by his devoted young
Hungarian wife, whom he had bought as a slave, through darkest
Africa to the source of the Nile, commenting later that 'she was no
screamer!'

The Murphys do not scream, they tell a joke and wander. And
they do not care what they look like as long as they get there in the
end. Dervla's description of herself in the midst of the Andes is a
typical statement of self-awareness. Confronting a mirror for the
first time in months, she saw an apparition and wrote in her diary:
'By now I scarcely look human, never mind feminine, with hideously
bloodshot eyes (dust and wind), a dirt- and sun-blackened face,
thick cracked lips and hair like a gorilla's mane. Add to that my

Peruvian army boots, bulging bush-shirt, ragged jeans, broad shoulders and deep voice – it's no wonder I'm addressed more often than not as *Señor*.'

At least, when Dervla went off *Muddling Through in Madagascar* with Rachel at the age of fourteen, she was not taken to be a man. But a fine old muddle it turned out to be, in a Great Red Island full of contradictions. Not only was it a Christian Marxist state inhabited mainly by Polynesians, but was stuck off Southern Africa; it also, as the guide book said of one resort, 'was pretty dormant for the now being.' So wandering through on foot or by bus was the best and only way about the place. Although the Madagascan tribes were nominally Christian, they were full of superstitions and taboos (called *fady*), which prevented almost any kind of help being given to them. 'I'm just another expert,' one of the few European women she met said gloomily to Dervla, and only the Chinese seemed to have enough faith to be building an unnecessary highway through the bush. Dervla again responded to the savannah and the mountains, 'far from the distorting pollutions of Technological Man. There must still be an animist in each of us,' she declared, and the occasional beauty and solitude of Madagascar still brought it out in her.

The oddest thing about the Madagascans was their ancestor-worship. They had a cult of the tombs of the dear departed and spring-cleaned them from time to time. The corpses were shifted back to the houses and parties were held in their honour, not really like an Irish wake but a reawakening. Poor people squandered most of their money on these feasts and on wrapping the dead bones in new scarlet shrouds. Dervla and Rachel met wild drovers using zebu cattle to drag great tombstones down from the mountains, and later Dervla admired tombs covered with zebu horns and decorated with high-spirited and comical carvings, 'the creations of people who believe the Hereafter can also be fun.' The crosses on top of some of the tombs seemed perfunctory, 'nods in the direction of a more sombre theology.'

Eating caused its usual problems. Dogs seemed loved everywhere; there was a *fady* against eating them, but not cats. To Rachel's disgust one acquaintance said that he fancied baked cat; it was similar in taste to baked lemur, like the Sifaka lemurs so admired by Dervla in their hallucinatory reserve at Isalo. And Rachel simply could not swallow a prized local delicacy – rotten fish. Dervla got rid of it by shovelling most of it into a plastic bag, concealed on her person for just that purpose. But perhaps the best remarks on Madagascan feeding-habits came from one of a pair of world-weary English undergraduates met on the journey. Of a baby vomiting copiously all over Dervla in a bus, when not being given the breast by its mother, the young Englishman commented, 'Too much of the milk of human kindness.'

Too much for Dervla were the crushed and jolting bus journeys at an average speed of twelve miles an hour. She broke her ribs for the fifth time in her travels. She tried to ignore the evidence: 'Pain usually goes away if not encouraged by being brooded on.' This time it did not, and she bought a half-litre of hooch with repellent fumes. After a few swigs of this brew, she nearly cut off her thumb while hacking at some sugar-cane for Rachel. Later her wrists swelled up and became so painful that she could not use her hands. Luckily a French doctor was found to look at her. He was not at all amused. She had gout from drinking the hooch, which was made from the sap of 'the Man-eating Tree'. That stuff had been killing Frenchmen on the Great Red Island for years. 'Gout is the best thing it does for you,' even if it was gout in the wrists and not the ankles. The doctor would take no fee from Dervla for giving her some gout-curing capsules, because she was such a 'foolish Irishwoman'.

Finally Rachel contracted hepatitis, and they had to go home. Dervla is as cheerful and courageous about the journey as usual, and as pessimistic about the hope for change or improvement in the local people as always. There has been an explosion of births. One-third of the population is under ten. There are no teachers in the schools. The forests, which covered the whole island, only cover one-fifth now, while a quarter of the island is burned over every year for crops. It is what one lecturer in Madagascar called 'our suicide by fire'. For once, Dervla's fatalism seems to overcome her ineradicable faith in people and in muddling through. Perhaps the truth of her journey to Madagascar lies in the words of one of the few survivors of the first English colony there three hundred years before. It was such an island, he wrote, 'from which place God diverts the residence and adventures of all good men'.

But their tribulations in Madagascar could not keep the two Irishwomen from returning to Africa again in March 1987. They were told in the Cameroonian Embassy in London, 'Nowhere need you fear *people*, in the bush we have no criminals, no bandits, no bad men.' The advice was unnecessary. Dervla has never feared people, only trusted them, and with her faithful Rachel as her human compass and commentator, and with a splendid Fulani bay stallion named Egbert with four white socks and a congenital hernia, she saw Cameroon after finishing her race relations book on England, *Tales from Two Cities*. Race was no problem in Cameroon, only gender. As in Peru, where she was often called *Señor*, she was thought to be Mister Murphy travelling with his junior wife, Rachel, and she had to bare her breasts all over the place to prove she was a mother. When she proved this to one African village barkeeper, he crashed his fist on the counter. 'Why no husband?' he asked. 'Now you are old, worn out, grey and finished. But when you are young you must be like this fine pickin – you must have husband paying *so much* brideprice!'

It wasn't like that in Europe, Dervla explained. Lots of women didn't marry. 'And a few who have no husband do have pickin.' She found in Cameroon that many families sent out their *fat* daughters to act as prostitutes for a while when the crops failed – and it was not considered too bad, it merely lowered the later brideprice. Communications were difficult, because the customs were so different; but all the same, Dervla felt the usual similarity between Irish village life and village life anywhere. The weather in Cameroon was often 'Irish-capricious' and Irish potatoes grew well locally, though she couldn't explain that two 'Murphies' like herself and Rachel meant two potatoes in Ireland. Her oddest encounter was meeting a fan of Jane Austen in the bush, who declared that her books were easy to understand because they were about village people, 'though English villages are rich and ours are poor'.

The climax of the expedition came when they lost Egbert (because of theft or his *penchant* for female donkeys); and a trek by foot through a Restricted Zone to the infamous jade-green Lake Nyos, which had exploded a year before, releasing a cloud of poison gases and killing more than two thousand people. They met in the deserted compounds of Nyos one robed figure, who declared, 'There is nowhere to go. Everyone is dead.' But they did get to Wum, where they were arrested for going to the scene of the disaster.

A woman's role in African society was illustrated by a wonderful sign held up by a local street-doctor called Ngahbouba:

TREAT – STOMACH DISCOMFORT, FAINTING, REMOVE POISON, SIDE PAIN, CHEST PAIN, FELERIA, *UNPRODUCTIVE WOMEN MADE TO BE COMPETENT*, WIZARD AND WITCHES, GONORIHEA, BACK-ACHE, SLEEPING-SICKNESS, MALARIA-FEVER, UNPRODUCTIVE MEN, EYE TROUBLE, GENERAL COUCH, WAIST PAIN, DIERIA AND YELLOW FEVER

There had been a recent population explosion in Cameroon with three in five people under the age of sixteen. The truth was, as Dervla found out, that the villagers were worse off under independence than before. Deforestation and erosion were ruining their agriculture, with too many people on marginal soil. 'Stripped of vegetation, Africa will die – both the land and the people.' The tsetse-fly, which killed cattle and caused sleeping-sickness in human beings, and the mosquito, which gave Rachel bouts of fever, were coming back resistant to new methods of pest control. Again, Dervla was fatalistic about attempts to change traditional ways into modern methods of farming. Most major agricultural aid projects failed; the few modern towns looked 'like wounds inflicted on the country by some alien force'. Africa was rightly not inclined to be dragged into the modern age. That was her opinion as well as the opinion of most of the foreign aid experts she met, including a Swiss one who summed her up very well. 'You are an old lady of the world, yes.'

Cameroon with Egbert is also a tribute to the common sense and resilience of her daughter Rachel, who knew her mother wonderfully well. In all their weary wanderings, they only had two quarrels or 'emotional harmattans', the hot desert winds. When Dervla gave way to a rare fit of self-pity, saying she wanted to lie down and die, Rachel said, 'You might as well go on and die. There's no point in lying down here . . . I wonder why you're so feeble about heat.' And when Dervla was on one of her usual mountain rhapsodies about the view, Rachel asked, 'When you've quite finished being ecstatic, maybe we could have something to eat?' Her only comment on huge leopard pug-marks was 'Some puss!' On the eleven hundred miles covered on foot in the Cameroon, mother and daughter found they were the best of companions, if occasionally caustic.

Dervla tells such good traveller's tales that the flashes of insight which come through her accounts are even more rewarding. She says, for instance, that Europeans are uneasy about Cameroon because it has no history for the two thousand years after Hanno, the Carthaginian general, discovered a volcano there, which he called 'the Chariot of the Gods'. She makes it clear the Africans themselves were as enthusiastic slave-traders as the Europeans and the Arabs, and that colonialism was no bad thing, even if it brought an unhelpful modernism with it. In her most telling interview of all, she was told that colonialism was like the zebra. 'Some say it is a black animal, some say it is a white animal and those whose sight is good, they know it is a *striped* animal.' Dervla's sight is excellent, and she found independent Cameroon a striped animal, with generous Fulanis running free milk-bars from foaming bowls during her highland travels, while down in the cities the necessary bribery, called *dash*, and the African sense of time with its long past and present and little future meant endless frustration and delays. But then, another journey and another book of extraordinary adventures, which ended with one of the few survivors of the Nyos catastrophe sitting on her lap, a little girl with dead eyes, who was found after three days strapped to her dead mother's back. She had lived because she ate 'Mamma's neck for chop'.

For the time being Dervla and Rachel have decided to go their separate ways. Although they are close, theirs is more a meeting of minds and feelings than an intimacy. They always showed a great respect for each other's privacy, even if they were naked in a tiny tent together. Perhaps as a result of her childhood confinement and virtual imprisonment, Dervla needed solitude to feel the extreme joy of Andean mountains and Himalayan streams without the voice of a daughter telling her to give up her beatitude and get on with dinner. But she has said that she is never lonely on her travels because she shares her experiences later at the end of the day when she writes her journal.

People have constantly asked what motivates Dervla's drive for seeking out remote and often dangerous places. She has been accused of masochism, of purposely looking for risk and discomfort. She firmly denies this image of the dauntless Dervla defying danger and insists that she always proceeds cautiously. There is no doubt that she has a tireless urge to search for the truth behind pre-conceived concepts and has no tolerance for the views of the extreme right or left.

There is no challenge more fascinating to her than an inquiry or inquest into a situation with no easy solution. Her forthright examinations are as tireless and engaging as the accounts of her journeys. She is a voyager among dilemmas as well as deserts and mountains. To her, nuclear fission is more important than the recesses of Peru or Ethiopia, it may kill off the planet which we will then be unable to explore. But she is only the seeker and the explorer, never the dictator and the judge. In her opinion, mankind may still escape from the annihilation it has invented to better itself.

She had already begun her travels during her childhood in Ireland in the attic, where she was safe from the real world. She would pore over volumes of nineteenth-century engravings of the wilder parts of Scandinavia, climbing mountains, swimming icy lakes and fjords, crossing narrow footbridges over deep gorges and always stopping for imaginary chats with the local people. At the end of these three-hour sessions she would be as exhausted as though she had been on a real journey. She has spent most of her adult life living out these expeditions of the mind.

With the need to escape from modern materialism and the curiosity and capacity to understand the people from so-called primitive cultures she has needed to live with them on a local level, sometimes even going too far. In Nepal she shocked the villagers when she chose to wash herself and her clothes in the river and sleep on the floor, living below the standards of the poorest families. Dervla found that in such a class-conscious and conservative society the sight of the English *memsahib* 'going native' was the longest way round to integration. But in Afghanistan she felt she had been privileged to see 'man at his best – still in possession of the sort of liberty and dignity that the west have exchanged for what it pleases to call progress'.

Dervla has said that, more than anything else, the sole aim of her journeys was the enjoyment of life. Once in Bara, Baltistan, she wrote in her journal, 'I wish today's trek would go on forever. I have never enjoyed a day more.' Along with her need of solitude is her gift of communicating and making friends wherever she goes, which is proven by the many guests from all parts of the globe who suddenly arrive unnanounced at Lismore where they are given the same shelter and hospitality she received in their countries. But her restless and inquisitive nature will not allow her to remain in one place for long and she will soon be off on her own again.

Monica Kristensen

When you have gone so far that you can't manage
one more step, then you're gone just half the
distance that you're capable of.

Greenland proverb

'Antarctica is the world's biggest wilderness, as big as Europe and
the United States put together. Nature is shrouded in white and
only the light of the sun or the moon can lend brief colour to the
elements .... It is the light which defines the landscape. Nature
herself has nothing else to offer but ice and stone. This is the
greatest icy waste in the world and there is nothing to live on.
Clothes, food, warmth – you must take everything with you. If you
lose anything of what you need to support life, you must manage
without it. If you cannot do that, then it is death you can hear in
the wind round the wall of your tent.'

But to Monica Kristensen Antarctica is also the last great space
laboratory. She is at present the co-ordinator of a team of scientists
involved in an international research project being conducted on a
West Antarctic ice shelf. She believes that because the area has a
rapid response to climatic changes, signals of change will be detected
earlier than anywhere else.

'In future years satellite remote sensing will become an important
tool in the monitoring of the environment, but the retrieved data
will still need to be calibrated against ground truth data. The official
scenario from the Organisation of Meteorology is that an acceler-
ated greenhouse effect is certain because of man-made pollution. At
the moment the prognosis is that it's not going to be severe for the
next hundred years, but that's based on very little knowledge of the
polar regions and how they are going to respond. It could be that
the greenhouse effect is accelerating much quicker than people

think. If that is the case, will it be possible to change the way we pollute nature? I think there's still time to balance the system again. In prehistoric times (about one hundred and thirty thousand years ago) the ice mantle over West Antarctic disappeared and the sea levels were six to seven metres higher than today. If the same rise in sea level occurred today, it would have dramatic consequences for the world's biggest cities. The time for complacency is over.'

Dr Kristensen is well qualified to talk on the subject. Her awards and citations of merit connected with Antarctic research are numerous, culminating in the Founder's Medal awarded by the Royal Geographical Society for 'leading the 90° South Expedition of 1986–87, which was a gallant Norwegian-British attempt to recreate Roald Amundsen's first expedition to the South Pole, using a four-person team with dogs. Although the expedition did not reach the South Pole through bad weather, it did achieve notable scientific research.' 'Nothing can compare with that,' she says. 'Not only is it such a high honour, but it is given by friends and colleagues, whom I respect so much and who really understand what I have done.' Apart from her exploratory work she is a senior scientist at the Norwegian Meteorological Office and is on the Board of the Norwegian Space Centre and the International Foundation for Environmental Policies which has the former Prime Minister, Mrs Brundtland, as Chairwoman.

Looking at the photograph taken by Lord Snowdon in the book *Toward 90° South*, all this is hard to believe. Swathed in a fur-trimmed anorak, the face is of a young woman smiling at the camera. The pale grey slightly slanting eyes shine out of a sun-burnt face and the teeth are perfect. In reality she is a tall natural beauty with cascades of wheat-coloured hair tied back with a knot, although she usually wears severe steel-rimmed spectacles. But when she laughs, and she loves to laugh, she is transformed. She talks rapidly with a faint Norwegian accent and has a disarmingly frank and unaffected manner without any academic pretensions. But she also has formidable determination, which sweeps obstacles aside, and an abundance of energy. 'I always have about four levels of projects occupying me at any one time. There's my current project, my next project, my secret project and my secret-secret project.'

Born on 30 June 1950 in Torsby in Sweden to a Swedish mother and a Norwegian father, Monica grew up in Kongsvinger, a small town near Oslo where her father was the station master. He had a great love of outdoor activities and used to take her and her two younger brothers on long treks into the mountains. Brought up as a strict Calvinist, she was a strong-willed child, used to getting her own way, and when she was disciplined and reprimanded, she would simply laugh and continue on her happy-go-lucky course. She started reading books on exploration and science at a very early age. 'I read everything I could get my hands on – at the library they let me read anything and when I read popular science like Albert Einstein's *Theory of Relativity* when I was eight and obscure Russian authors, no one explained that these were really meant for grown-ups and that most children would consider them boring.' She loved the Jack London stories and the books by the great polar pioneer Fridtjof Nansen who was to be her inspiration. She keeps a signed photograph of him, and the logo of her future expedition was the sledge which Nansen developed and which she would later use. She also loves animals and has her own team of huskies which she keeps in the country, with the exception of one called Zoë. 'He is the son of Sennep who travelled in 1968 with Wally Herbert across three thousand miles of sea ice in the first trans-Arctic crossing. Zoë comes everywhere with me and he's become quite a star and loves being photographed.'

After attending the local day school, Monica was sent to a 'type of finishing school for young ladies' to bring out her more feminine qualities. 'I found it extremely boring and in the end one of us had to break.' It was not Monica who broke, and at eighteen she got her own way and went to the University of Oslo where she spent four years taking a degree in Mathematics and Quantum Physics. She had many interests apart from her degree work and once arranged a seminar in metaphysics with some other students. 'I was amused when I went back to discover that this has now become a proper lecture series and you can now take a degree in metaphysics.'

Once, she persuaded one of the professors who was an adamant disbeliever in astrology to set up an experiment at the Solar Research Observatory. It was a time when some believed that living under the shape of the Great Pyramid or cones would improve health and even sharpen old razor-blades. 'We put some little cones of paper into a solution of silver and watched to see if the passages of Mercury behind the moon would signify something. As the night wore on we got more and more lively and at midnight we looked at these papers, and there was a significant change when Mercury passed behind the moon. So we put papers in every half hour and every time the pattern was totally different. In the morning the professor got up very early and destroyed all the evidence. Although I wasn't totally convinced, I found it amusing – like the Queen in *Alice in Wonderland*, I do believe in a lot of impossible things.'

Moving on to the University of Tromsø in north Norway, she spent three years there acquiring a degree in theoretical plasma physics and then continued to work at the university for a year. But she was becoming bored by purely theoretical work and her love of outdoor life and ski-ing took her to the Research Station of the Norwegian Polar Institute in Ny Alesund, Svalbard (Spitsbergen) (79° north) on the edge of the Arctic Ocean, where there are four months of complete darkness in the year.

In 1582 a Dutchman, Willem Barents, discovered some small islands with a cliff-like coastline which he named Spitsbergen, thinking they were part of Greenland. He died of scurvy on the expedition and other members of the team told of the discovery. But it was not until 1607, when the English explorer, Henry Hudson, arrived on the shore of West Spitsbergen and reported seeing large colonies of walrus and Greenland whales, that the bloodiest period in the history of Svalbard began and lasted for two hundred years. Great fortunes were made and great suffering endured by hunters and sailors. The result was that the whales disappeared from the shores and the whaling industry was abandoned.

'I had been told no woman could go there, only men, who were isolated for the winter. I wrote off at once listing the things I had done and got accepted.' Doing research on the Aurora Borealis and ionospheric investigations at this Arctic base, she was also learning the skill of sledging with Greenland huskies. 'Controlling the sledge of dogs is a dying skill. There are no instruction books because it has been handed down from driver to driver.' She spent two winters alone with six men in this isolated region (where polar bears would walk past their huts and occasionally smash in the windows). As she has said of her study of the Northern Lights, 'You can't really explain how beautiful they are – they defy description. Even as a scientist when you know the explanation you think "this can't be real" – you see this fantastic pulsing light in the sky and think it must be some sort of miracle.' Those two years she spent on the edge of the Arctic Circle between the ages of twenty-five and twenty-seven had a profound effect upon her. 'I totally changed – at one time I felt I was going completely under and my personality was being destroyed.' As a therapy she wrote *The Magical Land*, a self-portrait in the form of fifteen short stories about the development of a young woman over two years in Arctic conditions.

The book gives an account of the Arctic landscape in terms of Monica's experience between 1976 and 1978. It tells of how she managed to survive both physically and mentally. The book is dedicated to Sennap, a wild husky she tamed and befriended during her first weeks at Ny Alesund in Spitsbergen, and called after Wally Herbert's dog. She had several times caught sight of the dog wandering in the distance and thought it must be a ghost. Although there were three dogs at the station, no one had mentioned a fourth. Thinking she would be accused of seeing things before even starting work, she did not mention it at first. The animal was too small to be a polar bear and its yellow shadow disappeared when she went closer. Every day she secretly put out food for it and eventually seduced it with some liver pâté. She named it Sennep and they became inseparable.

'The winterers' (as they were known) were a team of drillers employed by the King's Bay Mining Company. They were a macho gang of men who treated her arrival with great scepticism and showed off their physical prowess by racing along the icy precipices on their snow scooters and then accelerating to jump vast crevasses. Monica was determined to prove she was no mere academic, and she followed suit, skidding along the ice precipitously in their wake.

One of their occupations was setting traps to catch foxes. She felt sorry for the animals and one night went off alone on her scooter and dismantled them all. It was a dangerous expedition and the men were astounded. She had eventually proved her worth in their eyes and won their respect. They were even more impressed when one of the rare parcels delivered by plane to the station contained a .357 calibre six-inch-barrelled revolver with a walnut handle. As a member of a shooting club in Oslo, Monica was entitled to a licence. The men told her that shooting polar bears was forbidden as they were a protected species, but she would be allowed to go after foxes. Monica, though, had no intention of shooting any animal except in self-defence.

She was there to study the Aurora Borealis and immediately set up her instruments on the roof of a small wooden hut built on stilts and insulated with fibreglass. This would eventually become her sleeping, living and working quarters. In the daytime, she had only Sennep and the cook for company.

The Northern Lights are created by a drift of electrons and ions from the sun, caught up in the magnetic field round the earth. When they hit the atmosphere, they collide with atoms and molecules which have already been caught into the gravitational field of the earth. When these particles collide they give off energy sparks and these create the Northern Lights. Monica was measuring the intensity of the different colours of the spectra in order to find out what kind of atoms had collided and the degree of impact. She was monitoring what was already known, but she was keen to discover new information.

By the end of October the sun had disappeared below the horizon, and the nights became longer, the cold more intense and the sense of isolation more frightening. 'In the winter, there is no other light but the moon, the stars and the Northern Lights, also a weak glow where the sun has disappeared beneath the horizon. The bitter cold makes the light seem cold, too, like the reflection of the ice. In the distance across the icy snow, there is a glow from an oil lamp in the window of a whaler's hut, and it shines like hope – reminding us we will return home when the winter is over. But the hut is small and the time endless. Our eyes gradually became used to the darkness and soon we turned down the lamp indoors. When the full moon was shining the snow became a glittering dark colour – the contours of the landscape were sharply etched and the shadows crossed our faces. We looked different – a colder race of people with pale eyes and bright white faces. We were slowly turning into ice fortresses, entombed against the polar night. The inner emptiness, too, was growing blacker and greater every day, and the sky was hanging steel-grey above our heads with the promise of snow.'

Monica was beginning to sink into a state of depression not uncommon in people living so far north where no sunlight is seen for over four months of the year. 'The apparently everlasting winter is like an abyss of darkness – your thoughts die down and your mind becomes still – the hours stretch out towards a morning that never comes – there's an eternity of time to stare into an inner abyss until in the end you get the glimmer of a face, and if you are lucky it is your own face you see.'

To break the routine one day, a few of them took a small boat on what proved to be an extremely hazardous journey to Kvitøya (White Island). Because it was so late in the year there was a danger of getting caught in the ice. 'We saw the light long before we saw the island itself. The sky was grey, the sea a mass of white horses and the light between cloud and sea looked as if white crystals had risen from the ocean. As ice reflects seven times more light than the ocean, the clouds above the ice appeared much brighter than over the sea.' Polar bears were known to inhabit the island, and Monica had read stories of explorers who had died of hunger and been devoured by them. They are known to be one of the world's most dangerous mammals because of their great strength and unpredictability. They are also the world's fastest predators over short distances with a leap of over ten metres, while one blow of a paw in the face can be fatal.

As they were exploring the island, the cold became so intense that Monica began to lose the feeling in her feet altogether. Suddenly one of the 'winterers' said, 'Don't turn round, we've got visitors.' And there on a low mound about a hundred metres away was the yellowish-white outline of a polar bear and, in the opposite direction, the head of another. They were stretching their necks and sniffing the air. 'They're a bit unsure of us but it won't last long. It's best we beat a retreat.' They calmly retraced their steps as about five more bears appeared to their left. One of the men was armed. 'They're trying to surround us,' he said. 'We must increase our speed. If they get any nearer, start dropping pieces of clothing to distract them.' Monica's feet were very painful. 'I was moving, but I felt motionless. I could see the yellow fur round the neck of the nearest bear. They were all so thin that their fur was hanging round them in folds, and I could smell the strong scent of wild animals and see the yellow lights in their black eyes.' Polar bears have been known to attack people even in the water, and it was only when the 'winterers' had their tiny dinghy well out into the fjord that they felt safe.

As the darkest period of the year in early January enveloped them, the days were only divided by sleep and wakefulness. Monica was now totally engrossed in her meteorological readings and was sleeping in the hut under the laboratory. 'My alarm clock would ring. I'd stumble up the steps to the roof, turn on the red light to read my instruments. I'd sit there half-asleep and half-awake, shivering uncontrollably. Then down the steps and back into the sleeping-bag. "I must sleep a little," I'd tell myself, but then a few minutes later I'd be awake.' Time became divided into three-hourly intervals – two-and-a-half hours for sleep, washing and putting on clean clothes and routine work, then half an hour for monitoring the Northern Lights. Monica was putting herself through a punishing schedule. 'The days turned into an unending night. I couldn't sleep, I wasn't truly awake, I was like a zombie. Meal times became muddled – I'd be eating bread and cheese for dinner and then meat rolls for breakfast.' The cook became worried about her. Her lips had become blue, but she joked that it was only the colour of her lipstick. In reality she had virtually stopped sleeping and while the other 'winterers' slept, she would sneak to the library and read everything she could find on psychology and philosophy. 'One philosopher wrote of apparently unexplained cases of suicide, which can only be understood as the very beginning of a hope which is so terrible that it is unbearable. I felt that a fight was going on in the shadows of my soul, but I didn't know it. I was aware of an eternity that was empty or perhaps an emptiness that lasts forever. There is a magical land on the border of the external landscape of man's mind. Only when hope and longings loom like cliffs over the grey sea of everyday life can reality turn into experience. Man is a lonely creature guarding this border of sanity.'

It is now known that deprivation of natural light can have severe consequences on man's psychological and practical behaviour. The people who live in a summer without darkness and a winter without light can suffer acute mental disorders. Monica was going through an immense inner struggle. She was also becoming obsessed with the passing of time. The faint golden-pink colour that appears on the horizon in the middle of the day was enough to interfere with her recordings. As she told the cook, 'The earth is surrounded by several layers of magnetic fields rather like an onion.' She insisted on keeping her hut completely dark and made the 'winterers' turn the lights down outside because they interfered with her recordings. 'Even the weak shimmer of the Northern Lights can throw a shadow. When the full moon came up, we thought it was like a sunny day. But it was a dead light without the vitality or power to renew life in us. I became paler and paler and more lonely and more scared.'

The time was approaching when her scanning and recording of the radiation spectrum would no longer have any value, as the sun had come too near the horizon. But she struggled to keep awake by drinking coffee. She had become ill-at-ease and shy with the others and for several weeks had isolated herself from them. At one time the atmosphere clouded over, and she could not take her recordings and fell into a sleep so deep that she had difficulty in waking. 'Better to keep awake all the time, standing on the roof watching the Northern Lights. The faint glow filled the space between the glaciers and mountains. It seemed as if the light took on contours and movements, and I no longer saw with senses that I could describe or explain. I might as well have said that I could hear the light as music or that it had a sense of colour like flowers.'

On one of the last days possible to register the readings, she discovered when looking at the print-out a small bump where the lithium lines would normally be and over the next four minutes the bump increased in size. 'The sun was still under the horizon and the lithium lines now had such great intensity that I wondered if there was a mistake or a fault in the spectrometer. But no, this was a real registration of a dramatic occurrence in the lithium strata ninety kilometres up in the stratosphere. At long last and almost at the last moment, I had achieved my unique reading.' Monica's persistent research work on Spitsbergen for the Norwegian Polar Institute on Ionospheric Physics was to add another feather in her scientific career.

In 'The Grave Below the Glacier', one of the essays in her book, she quotes Michelangelo: 'I thought I was learning to live. But I was learning to die.' Her faithful old companion Sennep had reached the final stage of his life. Twice he had hidden away to wait for his end. 'The first time I had found him under the hut and cajoled him back to life. He could neither see nor hear me, but his sense of smell was strong, and as I held out the liver pâté under his nose, he put out his dry quivering tongue and licked my hand. His eyes were moist and the pupils refused to focus. I crawled along the frozen ground close to him in the dark. "Don't leave me yet – stay a little longer, Sennep."' He lived for two more days, but was slowly slipping away with deep dignity. Finally she took him away to be shot. 'Afterwards I stayed with him for a long time, taking in every detail. I had to remember everything because these moments had to last forever.'

When the time came finally to leave Spitsbergen, she looked back at the bleak landscape. 'The seconds were like an eternity. I had become obsessed with the clarity of the light and the landscape without reference and I remembered everything with great precision – but who knows how long a thought lasts when action is not possible and all other impressions are so sparse.'

On their way back the vessel was stuck in the fog by the edge of a glacier, and when the fog lifted a polar bear came right up to the deck where she was standing. 'It stood on its hind legs and leant on its forepaws. I bent forward curiously. I'd never been so close to a polar bear before. The nose was black and ridged like a car tyre. I felt like putting my hand out and stroking it. There was a strong smell and a warm breath on my cheek. The eyes were black and shining, and far, far inside them a white light glittered. The bear looked at me. I looked at the bear – our eyes met and held fast – both of us, woman and animal, met on the borders of two worlds. I looked into that strange landscape and was completely lost.' She was so engrossed that the man behind her had to insist, 'Now you must do as I say. Get up carefully, as slowly as you can. One fast movement and it will have your head off.' 'I felt no fear for this strange creature, just a longing to stroke him and lean my head against his.' But the man pulled her away, saying, 'Are you trying to get killed?'

Later, when describing the experience of wintering in Spitsbergen, she wrote, 'Imagine that you are in solitary confinement in a prison or that you have been shut up in a dark grotto or cave for many years, and that you must keep your thoughts and personality intact until your release. Under such conditions, you cease to feel the passage of time. This is actually what is called "barrack-room fever". You have so little to absorb from your surroundings that your soul feels ill. It's practically like a deficiency of the mind. At last, in the end, you become so used to the loneliness and the mental stillness that you grow fond of it, and then you don't want to return to be amongst other people – and even in the middle of the most cheerful gathering you are surrounded by the memory of that silence.'

Monica claims that her four years at Cambridge changed her even more than Spitsbergen. At the age of twenty-eight, she arrived at the Scott Polar Research Institute. At the time it would have seemed inconceivable that eight years later she would be leading an all-male expedition to the South Pole. In fact, the idea was conceived when in May 1979 a group of friends said they wanted to try to retrace Amundsen's pioneering route of 1911. 'I sat in the library and wrote in my diary, *I'm going with them*.' But it was not until she met the young, good-looking Neil McIntyre, who was working for his doctorate in Antarctic ice-sheet glaciology at the same institute, that the idea started to take off. Eight years her junior, Neil was a charismatic and brilliant student, and they soon became firm friends. He describes her as retiring and dedicated to her work, but the life and soul of the party within her close circle of friends. Monica recalls, 'I had no great romance at Cambridge – I was working too hard – and my very strong friendship with Neil probably sublimated much of my need for a deeper relationship. In many respects it was like we were married – we were together from seven in the morning until twelve at night and shared almost everything. He's an extremely good person.'

While the idea was still in its embryonic stage, Monica made use of her vacations to do some practical work on her thesis on the nature of icebergs. She went on two expeditions to the Antarctic in HMS *Endurance*, the Royal Navy's ice-patrol ship which played a prominent part in the events leading up to the Falklands conflict. Both times she was the only woman among one hundred and twenty-five men. Participating in all the naval life of the ward-room and being 'one of the boys' sometimes entailed taking part in some dangerous escapades. But it had its lighter moments, too. Crew members recall the night when she danced on a tabletop in Montevideo surrounded by naval officers, while the local ladies watched incredulously. 'Once,' Monica says, 'we were all invited by some rich people to a very smart party and one of the officers spilt a glass of champagne into his lap. The Captain was just going to tell him off and I felt very sorry for him. So I tipped my glass into my lap, too, and then everyone followed suit.' She never found it difficult being one woman amongst so many men. 'There was an unwritten code of honour not to make a pass. But I do think that the sexual desire becomes diminished in the extreme cold of the Polar regions – you don't think about it all that much, keeping alive is more important.'

Then in 1981 she and Neil started to plan the expedition which would combine the main elements of both Roald Amundsen's and Captain Scott's race to the Pole. (Amundsen claimed the prize and Scott got there a month later, but he and his four companions perished on the return journey.) Like Amundsen, their team of four would combine travel with ambitious scientific research – 'We are scientists so science had to come first.' No one had retraced Amundsen's route since 1911, although Wally Herbert had sledged in the Antarctic for three years mapping the area round Hope Bay, and in 1962 he had covered part of the route where he descended the Axel Heiberg Glacier with dogs.

Before being able to promote their plans, they set forth in detail their combined ambitious scientific proposals. These included using Monica's experience of icebergs to explore the way in which waves and tides affect the seaward margin of the ice shelf and to investigate whether particular sizes of waves are important in the creation of bergs. Neil, with his background of mapping and analysis of ice-sheet topography, could collect information to help the interpreta-tion of satellite data of the ice sheet. They would be able to take measurements over literally thousands of miles, and they arranged a consultancy contract to carry out microwave measurements for the European Space Agency. They would also be collecting samples to examine the chemistry of the snow on the polar plateau, and to shed light on the climatic record of the Antarctic ice sheet. But they needed recognition and financial support and decided to form a British Advisory Group which included experts in many fields. Among its members were Sir Vivian Fuchs, Rear Admiral Sir Edmund Irving and Lord Shackleton, all past Presidents of the Royal Geographical Society.

In 1983 Monica left Cambridge with a Diploma in Polar Studies and a Doctorate in Antarctic Tabular Icebergs. The members of the expedition decided to set up their base at a rented farm near her home town of Kongsvinger. Nick Cox, a dedicated member of the original team and an experienced polar all-rounder, began to train the Greenland huskies – chosen, as Monica ironically remembered, 'mostly for their sweet natures'. Whereas Amundsen had set out with ninety-seven dogs and came back with thirty-nine (the rest having been killed or eaten), they would take only twenty-two and had no intention of using them for food. 'The lead dog must be selected with great care; it must have fierce pride and be very attached to humans. I will use a whip like the Eskimos – not to beat the dogs, but to keep contact with the leader.' A team of eleven dogs would each pull two sledges, and Monica and the three men would ski, holding on to the end pole of a sledge or to the rope attached to it. From their base, they practised with dogs and sledges, using the wide-open spaces of central Norway, meanwhile putting themselves through an intensive training programme devised in conjunction with the Norwegian Athletics College. At the same time they were trying to raise sponsorship for the expedition. In the final event the cost amounted to over £2 million, but mainly in services and equipment. £240,000 was raised in cash from diverse sources, such as the European Space Agency, Norwegian Department of the Environment, various banks, a Japanese magazine and thousands of individuals. They estimated the return journey across more than one thousand miles of the Antarctic would take eighty-two days, about twenty of them devoted to research.

There had never been any question as to who should be the leader. 'She is the only one in the team with an all-round skill,' Neil McIntyre said. 'She understands science, understands logistics and has driven dogs in the Arctic. I would never go with someone I did not know and trust completely.' Later Monica said, 'I have some qualities which are different. The others had their specialities and were better than me in certain areas, but I could get the group to communicate, analyse their views and put them into a whole picture and reach a consensus. Also I have a certain recklessness which makes me set some almost impossible goals – and sometimes, not always, achieve them. I don't regard it as a fault to be wrong or to admit it to others – I don't have much prestige to be careful about, so I could run the expedition like a military system, but without any pretence or false pride. I tried to listen to everybody, but insisted on the complete truth. As a child I was very placid, but I've changed – I worry more now because I know more – you learn to be pessimistic.' Neil put it slightly differently, quoting David Lloyd George: 'We mustn't be afraid to take a big step from time to time. You don't get over the abyss in two short jumps.' This was the way he felt Monica tackled life.

In the autumn of 1985 they at last felt they were ready to make the attempt. They had twenty-two fully-trained Greenland huskies, the equipment and food was ready to be packed, and they had discussed the charter of an American-owned DC-3 aeroplane fitted with skis to transport them to the Bay of Whales in the Ross Sea, from where they would begin. Then came one shock after another. The Americans flatly refused to co-operate in transporting the expedition to the Antarctic, and when Monica and Neil flew to Washington to plead their case the answer was an unequivocal 'No': no dogs would ever fly in a US National Science Foundation aircraft, irrespective of availability or the quality of their scientific investigations. The decision was taken despite representations from British and Norwegian foreign ministers and a letter of support from Mrs Thatcher. Later Monica said, 'I felt they were completely inflexible. I believe that times have changed: the Antarctic is not a club of nations any more. There must be a looser structure to let in a whole range of different expeditions. But their behaviour towards me was no different than that towards others – it was a belief founded on superstition.' And also on a certain jealousy.

At about the same time Neil went down with a severe case of glandular fever, while Monica was involved in a serious car crash. At the wheel was a young Norwegian, Arne Solas, aged twenty-eight, whom she had met just after leaving Cambridge when she was on an expedition in Antarctica with the Norwegian coastguard ship KHV *Andenes*. He had been assigned as her assistant. Although very different in temperament they fell in love and were actually engaged at the time of the accident. Monica's knees were badly damaged and she could not walk for some time.

The whole expedition seemed to have come crashing down round their ears in a matter of weeks and the temptation to give up was almost irresistible. For Nick Cox there had been too many vicissitudes; he was emotionally worn out and decided to return to his career in Britain. The fourth member, the Norwegian Bjørn Wold, also left.

Monica had been afraid that Neil might have wanted to give up after all the disasters, but the question never arose. 'There comes a point in a project such as this,' Neil wrote in his report of the final journey, '. . . when too much momentum has been built up for an early and gracious withdrawal. There was also an unknown continent and an unparalleled adventure to lure one back.' They comforted themselves that the delay had one advantage – they could go through the planning yet again. But first the two missing team members had to be replaced. They were lucky enough to find two highly trained Danish servicemen from the Sirius Dog Sledge Patrol – Jacob Larsen and Jan Almqvist.

Their transport problem was more difficult, but it was suddenly solved by finding they could rent space on a ship taking another expedition to the Antarctic. When they arrived they would store their equipment at the Scott Base belonging to New Zealand. But time was short and they had to build from scratch in about twelve days their five supply depots and pack them with hundreds of boxes of food and equipment. By working day and night they had their 4.5 tons of supplies ready an hour before the deadline. 'For two weeks,' Monica remembered, 'my parents' home had been turned into a warehouse.'

They eagerly followed their equipment's progress down to Antarctica and congratulated themselves that at last their gamble was going to come off. But they were wrong. In early January 1986 Neil telephoned from England to say that the ship had sunk, crushed by ice, only fifty miles short of Scott Base. A few days later, in despair, Monica went to her office at the Meteorological Institute in Oslo intending to ring Neil and call the whole thing off. Whilst waiting for the call to come through, she opened her mail, amongst which were two letters, one from Australia and the other from Oslo. She opened the letter from Australia. 'I've been following the plans for your expedition in the papers and I hope that things go well for you. It said in the papers that you were short of money, so I'm sending you fifty dollars. I cannot make it more because at the moment I'm unemployed. All the best, Bill Burgess.'

The second letter was from a lady of eighty-three. She and her friends were studying Amundsen's route to the South Pole and wondered if Monica would like to meet them. Her name was Nelly Lundin. When her call to Neil came through, Monica said, 'I've thought of the names for the sledges, Neil. We'll call them Nelly and Bill.'

Having decided that nothing could now deter them, Monica and Neil set about rethinking the problem of transport. Eventually they were left with no option other than the seemingly unattainable: of buying their own ship and chartering an aircraft to drop their supply depots along the route to their final goal.

Soon after, they heard that a thousand-ton Newfoundland ice-breaker was for sale in Canada. The asking price was nearly ten times their original budget for the whole expedition, but Monica, by now both determined and reckless, managed to arrange the purchase of the ship with the help of a grant from the Norwegian government which was later repaid by leasing her out. While the boat was being renovated and refitted for the Antarctic cruise, she was based in Oslo, where the captain and crew of ten were recruited. One important crew member – at least in Monica's eyes – was the young Arne Solas, her fiancé. The ship was then transferred to the Norwegian flag and renamed *Aurora*. She was to be the key to the entire venture and proved herself beyond anyone's wildest dreams. They also chartered a ski-equipped 'Twin Otter' plane from Green-land and hired the service of a New Zealand helicopter.

The team members and twenty-two huskies left Oslo in October 1986 in a chartered Bristol freighter and transferred in London to a BA 747 for the flight to New Zealand. Before the departure there was the final press conference opened by Lord Shackleton and Sir Vivian Fuchs. Monica was completely exhausted and could hardly focus on the questions. 'What distance were they going?' 'Was it difficult for a woman to lead a team of men?' She answered curtly that she had no experience other than being a woman. 'What sort of food would they eat?' 'What perfume did she use?'

After stops at Bombay, Perth and Sydney with further press conferences and television interviews, they boarded *Aurora* at Auckland. Twenty-seven hours later Monica sank into her bunk to the sound of barking dogs and slept soundly for the first time for weeks. During the next few days the expedition's helicopter and supplies were taken on board. After flying from Greenland to Sweden the Twin Otter arrived, transported on one of the world's largest container vessels. There were still two thousand nautical miles between them and the Antarctic continent, but at last they felt they were truly on their way. 'You know what?' Monica commented. 'I'm a little bothered there's nothing to be bothered about.' She had spoken too soon. While she was talking, two thousand gallons of diesel fuel overflowed into the hold containing food, equipment, supplies and half a ton of explosives. It was only by some very swift action by all on board that a potentially serious accident was averted, although some of their supplies were irretrievably damaged.

While *Aurora* made her way to Christchurch, Neil and Monica flew ahead to discuss their plan with the New Zealand Antarctic Division. On 27 October, with all on board, they finally left for the ice of the Antarctic and were soon into the Roaring Forties, where they hit some severe weather. Seven years previously Clare Francis, sailing in the Whitbread Round the World Race, had experienced the unpredictability, harshness and isolation of the Southern Ocean. Monica and her team in *Aurora* battled through a raging storm and Neil suffered such severe sea-sickness that he lost a stone and a half. They decided to take refuge at Campbell Island (50° S) and in those calmer conditions Neil recovered.

They were increasingly worried about the time element. It was important to reach the edge of the ice at the right moment: too early and they would be unable to press far enough down into the Ross Sea, too late and it might be impossible to find a suitable landing strip for the Twin Otter. At the time of their first encounter with an iceberg they had to use explosives to blast their way through the heavy pack ice, while the helicopter made reconnaissance flights to find an iceberg on which the Twin Otter could land. With time running out, they were becoming desperate when suddenly a berg lying level with the water with an even, smooth surface came into view. Monica left the ship to look at the conditions, then sent a radio message for the Twin Otter to begin its ten-hour flight from New Zealand, four hours of which were 'past the point of no return'. The aircraft made a perfect landing. After refuelling, it flew on to Ross Island to await the rendezvous with *Aurora*. This was the first time in history that the technique of landing and refuelling on an iceberg had been used as a means of getting an aircraft into the Antarctic.

But morale on board was not good. While the plane had been waiting for suitable conditions for a safe take-off, the *Aurora* had become frozen into an area of heavily ridged ice and southward progress was delayed for ten precious days. Monica wrote in her book *Towards 90° South*, 'The crew and the media teams wanted to know what the consequences of the delay would mean for the expedition. I gradually developed a dozen different ways of saying, "I don't know". One day drifted into another. We tried to blast a way out with dynamite . . . . *Aurora* forced herself forward a metre at a time . . . . We were using too much diesel. The main engine had to be switched off and the ship fell silent. The only thing to be heard was the distant hum of the auxiliary motor which took care of the electricity supply – and reminded us that we were not a ghost ship . . . . We were alone and isolated in the middle of the most desolate sea on earth. . . . I was more despondent and worried than I had ever been, but I didn't feel I could show my real feelings to the others. At least they were able to give the dogs some exercise and the crew occupied themselves by going for rides on the helicopter, learning to ski and playing chess and bridge. At last on the morning of 25 November there was a movement in the ice, a channel opened up in front of *Aurora*'s bows and the ship pushed gently forward.'

Nine days later they caught sight of the Great Barrier on the seaward edge of the Ross Ice Shelf. 'It stretched out like a band of silver and white the whole length of the horizon, towering a hundred feet above the sea – an impregnable ice fortress. Under the water it goes on down to a depth of about nine hundred feet and from a distance the ice looks like a wall, a structure on such a scale that the mind has difficulty in grasping what the eye can see . . . . We sailed eastwards along the Barrier all day and at night came into a vast empty place. We had arrived at the Bay of Whales . . . the midnight sun sparked on the glossy water. On the sea-ice stood groups of penguins, stormy petrels circled the ship and further away we could see some seals sunning themselves. The surface of the water beside the ship was broken by a black and white back. It was a killer whale playing round the bows. I stood by myself on the bridge and was struck by how peaceful it was . . . and by these animals and birds who were so unaffected by our arrival. It was the first moment of peace and quiet since leaving Norway. I felt as if I'd come home.'

On 5 December *Aurora* moored next to the fast ice at 79.5°S 165°W, the most southerly ship in the world, and the earliest that a ship had made it to the Bay of Whales. The unloading of supplies began immediately and a base camp, Amundsheimen, was established on top of the Ross Ice Shelf about two miles south of the ship. The television film crew which had accompanied them from England were impatient to start filming, but Monica first insisted on establishing that the depots were in place along their route to the South Pole. Packed in black painted boxes, these depots contained essential supplies and were transported by the aircraft which ski-landed on the ice. Red flags on bamboo poles about nine feet high would be set out east and west of them to a distance of about a mile – the position of the depot was established by the areoplane's satellite navigation equipment. She felt they should not move until this had been safely achieved, and the Twin Otter could start making her way back to Greenland – a complicated journey via Terra Nova Bay, Cape Hallett, New Zealand, Australia and the Far East. Neil and Monica and Sven, the pilot, stayed up most of the night planning the strategy. Depots Four and Five could only be set out once an intermediate fuel dump had been placed at Depot Three, some seven hundred kilometres inland and within sight of the Transantarctic Mountains.

Meanwhile the helicopter shuttled tons of equipment, all the dogs and a quantity of fuel from the ship to the camp. While the depots were being dropped, the filming began in earnest. Some of the team were impatient and critical that precious time was being taken up. But a great deal of money had been invested in a film of the expedition, and Monica had to use all her powers of diplomacy. Finally the film crew got their footage, which eventually resulted in an hour-long documentary made in conjunction with Channel 4 and the National Geographic Society.

At last, on 17 December, they were ready to leave. After their long confinement in *Aurora*, the dogs were impatient to be off, the sledging equipment was all packed, and Monica bid an emotional farewell to all the people who had helped them to reach this stage of their journey.

'"All set," Jacob Larsen shouted, tightening his bindings. I nodded, but my words to the dogs were drowned by their delighted howls as they threw themselves forward in the traces. The sledge jerked hard and the journey to the Pole had begun.' Monica and Jacob's 'Nelly' team led with Larm as the leader dog, followed by Neil, Jan Almqvist and the 'Billy' team. After only a few miles some small dots appeared from the direction of the camp, and they realised that three members of the film crew on snow scooters were determined to get their final action shots. At the same time the helicopter flew over them, the pilot leaning out with his camera and waving a last farewell.

Finally they were alone. 'In front of us we had five hundred and thirty miles on the flat across the enormous Ross Ice Shelf and then a climb of nine thousand feet up the Axel Heiberg Glacier . . . We would then have to cross the feared polar plateau and travel the last three hundred miles to the pole. At that point we would be halfway there and so would turn round and go back. We had seventy-three days and, taking account of rest days at each depot, that would mean an average distance of twenty-four miles a day. As Jacob put it, we would have to be more than lucky . . . compared with the agreeable eighteen miles a day we had planned, the journey would now be more demanding, both physically and mentally. There was a chance we could do it, but no guarantee of success. Amundsen had a race with Scott. We had a race with time.'

Their schedule was dictated by the fact that they would have to return to the *Aurora* by the end of February, because any later than this there was the danger that she would be frozen into the ice and the whole expedition marooned there for a further ten months.

'The hours went by and the stillness fell slowly over us like a soft blanket. Skiing beside a dog sledge has its own rhythm. One hand rests lightly on the handle and from the other dangles the rope which is attached to the front of the sledge . . . . The dogs who had set off at such an impressive speed, quickly settled down to a slower tempo. The going was slow and even, and our skis swished soporifically through a layer of soft new snow.'

At the end of the first day they had only covered fourteen and a half miles. Setting up camp was an organised ritual. Each sledge team worked independently, first laying out the night-chain for the dogs – forty-five feet long with short side chains attached at regular intervals. The dogs were clipped on in the same order as they had been on the sledge with Larm, the leader, taking his place last. Next the pyramid tent was put up, the sledge unpacked and the foam mats, reindeer skins, sleeping bags, food box and primus stoves all put into position. Leaving the dogs for an hour or so to settle down so there should be no danger of intestinal obstruction by eating too soon after exercise, they cooked themselves a meal before giving the dogs their pre-packed high-energy daily ration.

Within a week both teams had settled down to an organised routine and Neil and Monica were able to devote some time to their glaciological investigations. But the temperatures remained high, making the going difficult, and they decided to switch to sledging at night. Although they were only averaging fifteen and a half miles a day they felt that at least this would mean they were breaking the dogs in gradually and safeguarding their stamina in the long run. It took them eight days to reach Depot One – just in time to celebrate Christmas.

They had taken care to avoid the enormous crevasses Amundsen had encountered in the area, but as the Ross Ice Shelf is the size of France and also the longest floating mass in the world, they could not be certain that the crevasses would still be in the same places. When they had caught sight of the first one, they saw ragged cliffs of ice descending on either side 'with the overhang of snow sticking out like frozen waves. Down below it gleamed blue, which got

darker the further down you looked. Smaller, snow-covered crevasses spread out from the main one. We had no wish to take the
risk of driving through this area and ending up in the same situation
as Amundsen when he almost lost his men and sledges.' When the
big abyss petered out into a mass of smaller crevasses, Jacob skied
ahead of Larm leading him over the network of snow bridges while
Monica went back to the brake to control the speed. As the sledge
crossed, Monica's relief spilled over to the dogs, who raced up the
far slope.

The first stage had gone remarkably smoothly except for a near
disaster on 20 December. Neil, Jan and the Billy team had gone on
ahead and had disappeared from view when a vicious dog-fight
broke out on the Nelly sledge. Taking his job seriously, Larm had
become furious when one of the dogs behind him started snarling
and tugging on the trace. He turned on the culprit and bit him
fiercely in the groin. The other dogs all joined in – an eleven-dog
fight. The victim whimpered in the blood-covered snow and had to
be treated for some fifteen deep gashes. After clipping the other
dogs onto the night chain, Monica and Jacob put up the tent, got
the primus stove going and took off the First Aid Box. They gave
the dog a local anaesthetic and while Monica held his head, Jacob
stitched the cuts. They were many hours behind the others when
they set off again with the invalid lashed securely onto the sledge.
Jan and Neil had already set up camp and were relieved that nothing
worse had occurred.

Christmas was a lively affair with Jacob decorating their tent in
traditional Danish style. Gifts were exchanged and even the dogs
got extra rations of frozen meat. But for the humans it was a feast
of salmon and Christmas pudding and the party did not break up
until early in the morning when Neil and Jan returned to their tent.
Monica lay awake listening to the dogs moving on the night chain
and the wind rustling the canvas and felt that 'even here, out on the
Ross Ice Shelf, Christmas was a blessed time'.

They knew they would have to do something to increase their
speed. Monica decided they must jettison some of their equipment
to lighten the load on the sledges. It was difficult to decide what to
leave behind, and she felt wretched at leaving some of her heavier
scientific equipment. Before setting off the next day, they repacked

the black boxes at Depot One with food and clothes to be used on the return journey.

The one hundred and forty-six miles to Depot Two took them a further eight days. They passed the crevasse of Steers Head without problems, but they could see day after day the mirages of the chaotic zone of broken ice. As they skied over the endless expanse of white, it was impossible to distinguish snow from sky – a condition known as 'whiteout'. 'Occasionally the sun cut through the cloud and lit up the tiny ice crystals, making them glitter like diamonds. It was one of those tricks of light which will always be the Antarctic's special gift – a few moments later the fog closed in round us again.'

Their basic working day was at least twelve hours long, and Neil and Monica often put in a few hours extra on their research and kept up their scientific log book. They all kept personal diaries, while each tent had a sledge diary, a dog diary, a navigation log and a radio log. They managed to make radio contact with *Aurora* and found she was well on the voyage back to New Zealand.

They had hoped to be at Depot Two by New Year's Eve, but it was 2 January before they arrived. Neil decided to hold a celebration in his tent, producing a feast of pancakes with Monica's Christmas present to him – a few strawberries. To mark the occasion, they opened the only small bottle of brandy they had with them and drank a toast to the New Year and family and friends at home. But Monica was becoming increasingly worried about the time factor and suggested scrapping that rest day and continuing straight on to Depot Three. Jan and Jacob were against the idea, knowing from their experience that if the dogs were pushed too hard at this stage, they might be unable to complete the journey.

The distance to the next depot was one hundred and thirty-one miles, and they hoped to get there in six days. The weather and snow conditions improved dramatically – the surface was as hard as ice and the sledges raced along, swerving and twisting over the bumps. During the next three days their spirits soared as they approached the Transantarctic Mountains. When they were only fifty miles from Depot Three, they thought they might reach it in two further nights' travel and make up some valuable time.

But once again luck was not on their side. When Monica opened up her tent after a few hours' sleep, she was horrified to find that the horizon was a white wall and the visibility only about three yards. In spite of the appalling conditions, they managed to struggle on another twenty-five miles. The following day the fog lifted occasionally, and they glimpsed the blue peaks of the mountains, but after thirty miles in continuously deteriorating conditions, they still had failed to locate the elusive Depot Three. In the end they were forced to stay in the same spot for four days, while they went out searching individually and in pairs. 'What on earth had gone wrong?' wrote Monica. 'We hadn't been able to determine our position by sextant because of the bad weather but we couldn't believe that our navigation had been so bad in the last few days that we were very far from the depot.' By the third evening they had still not found their supplies and were being forced nearer to the decision that they would have to give up the search and return. Their two days' supply of food would have to last the one hundred and twenty-five miles back to Depot Two. Jacob argued for turning back straight away. 'I said I realised that if the worst came to the worst, we might have to kill the weakest dogs to feed the others . . . these were dogs we'd known and been fond of for nearly three years . . . . I thought that this was one of the few times I would have to make a decision alone. As it could be a matter of the dogs' lives, I didn't want to burden the others. 'We stay here one more day,' I said. 'As I see it, it's foolish to leave an area where we know for sure there's food and fuel . . . . We must have confidence in ourselves and in our navigating. Depot Three is somewhere close by. It's just that we haven't found it.' 'And if we don't find it tomorrow?' Jacob asked grimly. 'Then we go back,' said Monica. While Jan and Neil shuffled over to their tent, Jacob got into his sleeping bag without a word. For Monica it was one of the most painful moments of the whole expedition.

The next day's search once again proved abortive. Heavy-hearted, they decided to abandon the whole expedition and start back the following morning. As Neil and Monica began to prepare for the journey, digging out the sledges which had become covered with a thick layer of wet, hard-packed snow, Jan and Jacob suggested that they ski out the last time towards the mountains, which were now just visible through the driving snow. It took Neil and Monica four hours to dig out the Nelly sledge and before tackling the Billy sledge, they warmed themselves with a cup of tea in the tent. 'Even in this desperate situation our close friendship was one of the most important resources we had. "We just have to find that depot," I said. "I can't bear to see the dogs go hungry." But Neil didn't reply. He was standing looking out over the ice. "Here come Jan and Jacob," he said. "They're moving at a tremendous speed."' Monica couldn't bear to look as they swung up beside the sledges, took off their skis and stamped the snow off their boots. 'You owe us a bottle of champagne when we get home,' said Jan. 'Jacob found it.' It had been hidden in a slight depression and only became visible with the improved weather conditions.

'It was almost impossible not to feel that we'd been put through a sort of mental endurance test. Now that the depot had been found, suddenly the sun shone and the mountains stood out through the fading blizzard in all their majestic beauty. But it would be dangerous to believe that Antarctica offers any rewards for endurance. It is an impersonal place and nature doesn't change in response to human courage and determination. In this landscape the best defence is realism, common sense and caution.'

Everyone was in good spirits and began planning the next and most difficult part of the trip. Amundsen had chosen to go up the Axel Heiberg Glacier, the steepest in the vicinity, because it lay along the shortest route from the Bay of Whales to the South Pole. They had spent hours poring over old notes and photographs studying the best way on to the glacier. Wally Herbert's last piece of advice had been both serious and alarming: they had to find the right flow line up the glacier; if not they could get themselves into such heavily crevassed terrain that it would be impossible to turn the dog teams.

'The sledge was heavy when we set out for the mountains the next night. All the same the dogs ran so fast on the hard, icy crust that it was difficult for us to keep up . . . our skis slithered this way and that and we had to brace every muscle to stay upright.' They travelled twenty-four miles before setting up camp where, for the first time for days, they managed to make radio contact with *Aurora* – which reported worldwide concern about them. The next day was overcast and misty with a bitter south-easterly wind blowing straight into their faces, but Monica found it most exhilarating. 'We encountered one of those tricks of light which I wouldn't have believed possible if I hadn't seen it with my own eyes . . . a few rays of the sun found their way through the cloud and were reflected round the dog team, with the effect that, from the dogs' feet and forward to Jacob's skis, there stretched a rainbow, like a bridge up towards the sky. It was so beautiful it took my breath away. The dogs' paws no longer touched the snow and seemed to be moving over a thin band of colours . . . I so badly wanted it to last. And unbelievably, it did. We drove along the rainbow bridge for more than two hours before it disappeared as swiftly as it came . . . I was deeply grateful that for once in my life I had been able to ski on a rainbow.'

They crossed the ridge into the valley of the Axel Heiberg Glacier on 18 January. 'And what a glorious view . . . this was our gateway to the interior of Antarctica and the ladder we would use to climb up onto the polar plateau.' The following four days were full of sweat and toil, and the hardest of the trip, but Neil found them the most rewarding with astonishingly beautiful views of untouched mountains as far as the eye could see. It would have been tempting to spend more time there but they had to press on and meet the polar plateau by 22 January.

The slopes were so steep that they were forced to relay the loads on the sledges, ascending with half-loaded sledges and then returning for the rest. At the top of one particularly steep slope, Monica suddenly found herself right on the edge of a huge crevasse. 'The cornices hung out in a big overhang and the blue hole merged into black at the bottom. I signalled to Jacob and turned sharply to my right. Larm followed close behind me, but all the time I looked anxiously back to be sure that the team and the sledges were managing safely. We stopped and Jacob shouted to warn Jan and Neil.'

They camped four times during the ascent of the glacier. Sometimes the tents were pitched at such acute angles that they slept whilst holding on to a rope to avoid sliding downhill. On one occasion when in radio contact with *Aurora* they got extracts of a telex from the Division of Polar Programs in Washington, pointing out that the South Pole closes on 14 February. Looking out over the glacier where an avalanche was cascading down the mountainside, Monica felt a message from faraway Washington seemed out of place among mountains halfway up from the Ross Ice Shelf. 'Closed,' she said. 'Can you close the South Pole?'

At one time, attempting to climb a 45-degree slope with the sun burning their faces, Monica became so exhausted that she nearly gave up. Frost sores were stinging her lips and cheeks. Time after time she stopped to get her breath. The exertion of hauling themselves and the sledges up the slope made it unbearably hot, and when they eventually reached the top they immediately returned with the empty sledge to reload and start up again. 'Larm pulled past me all the time and Jacob had to stop the sledge continually. Restarting each time was an excessive burden for both him and the dogs. In the end Jacob drove past and left me. OK, I said to myself, it's the only thing for him to do, but I felt abandoned all the same and tears ran down my cheeks. Damn Jacob for not waiting for me! But it was more important for him to get the sledge up than keep me company. And what was a woman doing in a place like this anyway … I looked up at the last steep climb to the top … I swung round on my skis and took on the final challenge. Eventually I crept into camp more dead than alive.' But the work of gathering the dog harnesses, unpacking the dog food, feeding the dogs, tidying and roping the sledge, all needed to be done before there was any question of sleep. The next day they reached the polar plateau. 'I was gripped by a feeling of awe. We were the first people since Amundsen to have climbed up this route from the Ross Ice Shelf and be able to stand and look out over the plateau as he did. Behind us the fog smothered all the details of the landscape. The Axel Heiberg Glacier had concealed herself behind a veil. "That doesn't matter," I said to myself. "We know you now."'

The way to the South Pole was open and the greatest obstacles lay behind. It was only a two-day journey to Depot Four. There they had to take the decision whether to go on to the Pole – they had promised each other not to discuss the question until then. Amundsen had swung due south across the edge of the plateau and had pitched a camp at a place he later named the Butcher's Shop because there he killed twenty-four of his dogs. Resuming his direct route to the South Pole, he crossed ice formations which he called

Hell's Gate, Devil's Glacier and Devil's Ballroom. Monica could see why. 'Here in this thin air so close to the sky . . . it was the forces of evil that came to mind.' Her team were taking a slightly different route, swinging in a gentle arc along the high ground towards the interior of the plateau – '90 degrees South'. That night Monica lay awake in her sleeping bag going over figures and calculations. In the morning her lungs were aching, her throat felt raw and her cheeks were burning. As she skied beside the sledge over the flat surface she felt as if she were skiing up a steep hill. Having covered twenty-five miles they decided to pitch camp. Monica cooked dinner for the others, but she couldn't eat anything herself. When Jacob told them later he'd found the fourth depot nearby, she took two aspirins and fell into a deep dreamless sleep. Her throat infection improved the next day and the fever subsided.

The final decision, however, could no longer be put off. Their late departure from the Bay of Whales had put them over a month behind schedule, but they had caught up several weeks. They reckoned that it would only take a further ten days to reach the Pole, and that their return trip could be done in seven-tenths of the time. They would therefore be back at the Bay at the end of the first week of March, but this left *Aurora* and her crew in a difficult situation. The Captain had worked out that 28 February should be the final departure date. They contacted the ship by radio and in spite of the poor reception and the use of Morse code, they discovered that messages of advice had been converging from all parts of the world.

'Several sources,' Neil wrote, 'raised the possibility of continuing to the South Pole and of requesting to be flown out by one of the US Hercules which would be servicing the base until the 14th of February. We also heard that we might be flown out but that our dogs would not . . . . Much of the advice was informative and reassuring.' When they asked the Captain if it was possible to postpone the departure date by a few days it became clear that this was not acceptable. They discussed a series of alternatives. Monica suggested splitting up the teams with one continuing to the South Pole while the other returned to the ship. Neil was enthusiastic, insisting that Monica, as leader, should be the one to continue. Jan and Jacob were at first worried about the dogs but in the end they found the proposal 'a possibility'. They managed to make contact with the National Science Foundation at McMurdo to ask if they would fly out one team with dogs from the Pole with the proviso that all costs would be covered by the expedition. The NSF replied that there was no question of any transport being offered.

'The thought had been in all our minds,' Monica wrote, 'but the disappointment was hard to bear . . . the expedition was our pride and joy. We'd been so pleased with our two splendidly co-ordinated dog teams and that our equipment had worked so well. We had been the first since Amundsen to climb the Axel Heiberg Glacier . . . but that day we were to part company with Amundsen. He carried on to the Pole, while we turned and went back . . . at that moment we said farewell to our great dream.' Jacob stayed with the others, knowing Monica needed to be alone. With the glow of the primus flames reddening the frosty walls of the tent, Monica had nightmares and imagined she heard voices shouting, 'Couldn't you have foreseen this? Couldn't you have forced the expedition on harder? Who are you to challenge Amundsen? Why didn't you drive the dogs harder? Would it have mattered so much if you'd lost a dog or two? This isn't a game for sentimental sissies.' Very early on 31 January they turned their back on the Pole and set off north over the white wastes. Later Monica recalled her feelings. 'The shock was deep – both emotionally and intellectually – a continuous pain. I felt myself tugged in the opposite direction like a magnet. In fact I kept thinking that we were going south because there were so few disturbances throughout the day – just a white sheet of ice and a white sky – three other people and the dogs and that's all. There was time to think and daydream – as if one were half alseep. It took a long time to face the truth of what was happening and of all the people we would disappoint.'

During the four days of painful decision-taking at Depot Four, speculation on their safety was mounting in the headlines. *Trouble Looms for Polar Expedition – A Big Question Mark Now Hangs Over Exactly How Dr Kristensen Will Get Out of Antarctica – South Pole Team Races Against the Clock – Winter at Pole Looks Likely.* Some of the reporting was decidedly alarmist – 'Tension is beginning to mount among Antarctic observers . . . as the four-person party . . . faces the onslaught of the polar winter and perhaps death if nature beats them.'

In fact Neil and Monica had a few days more than they reckoned for their journey and were busy completing some scientific work. On 30 January, after raising their national flags, they set off north for the mountains. The return journey proved almost as eventful as the outward one and sometimes even more dangerous. As they approached the head of the Axel Heiberg Glacier they were engulfed in low cloud and were forced to descend the upper half of the glacier in 'whiteout'. They strayed off course and came into an area of very steep cross-slopes and heavy crevassing, but had gone too far to turn around. Both sledges overturned on the same steep slope only a few metres uphill from some yawning crevasses. 'A shiver went down my spine. We were on our way down the place I had named the Witches' Cauldron. As I skied along, it seemed as if I could see the shadow of a man on skis in front of Jan. Up here on the glacier . . . we all felt Amundsen's presence. I had an inescapable feeling that he had recently gone before us.' Monica remembered Wally Herbert's words in a letter he had written to them. 'You will pass over historic ground . . . it can sometimes happen that you feel the "presence" of those who have gone before you . . . keep it in your hearts, and you will come back wiser than all those who missed out on such a chance in life.'

They had driven down the whole of the Axel Heiberg Glacier in one and a half days and they camped at Mount Betty on 3 February where they visited the stone cairn built by Amundsen and left a memorial bronze plaque to identify his achievement. With Depot Three still two days' drive away, Monica was to experience the most frightening moment of her life. They were driving down the bottom part of a glacier, which they had blundered into unexpectedly and where there were huge crevasses which they tried to cross at right angles. Jacob was in front and Monica was having difficulty in holding the sledge straight. 'Suddenly the sledge slipped sideways as we were accelerating towards a crevasse and I caught sight of the holes between the snow bridges. I braked with my skis, but they slipped beneath me. I fell and lost hold of the brake. For a brief moment I could see a dark blue hole gaping under me. I caught sight of a wall that disappeared down as far as the eye could see. The wall came at me and hit me hard. The rope slipped a few inches, but I held on to it for dear life. Then we were past the crevasse. I was dragged several feet after the sledge, but I managed to grab the brake and jam down my skis. We plunged on over the crevasse and ice, and at last, miraculously we were through . . . . My knees didn't stop shaking for several hours. For the first time I noticed the smell of my own sweat, that special smell which occurs when you are very frightened.'

Their zig-zag path through the crevasses had put out their navigation and once again Depot Three proved elusive. But this time they decided to cut their losses and continue north. This meant they were on very short rations. Monica normally managed on about three thousand calories a day while the men needed five or six thousand. Now they were existing on not much more than dried fruit, nuts and tea. Monica had endured some drastic slimming cures in her life and had built up a psychological tolerance to hunger, but for the men it was more difficult.

However, these hardships only built up the solidarity which had grown between them. They had worked together for a long time and had achieved a harmony which overcame the tribulations of cold and hunger. Nothing gave Monica a greater joy. They reached Depot One on 23 February and contacted *Aurora* to say that they would be at the Bay of Whales on the 27th. The temperature had been dropping steadily and was now between −30 and −40 degrees C, and for the first time in several months they saw the sun touching the horizon. Setting out on the last stage to Base Camp (Amundsheimen), they crossed more than eight hundred miles in three days. 'It's strange to think that Scott died only thirteen miles from a depot,' said Neil. 'Maybe we can learn something from that,' Monica answered. 'In the Antarctic you must never take anything for granted. We mustn't be too confident even now.' They reached *Aurora* a day and a half early, and, as the sea was beginning to freeze fast they hurried on board with the dogs and equipment. Within a few hours they were heading for the open water of the Ross Sea, arriving in New Zealand on 12 March. Monica was reunited with her fiancé; the dogs and team members flew to Europe, while most of the equipment and the crew returned with *Aurora*, arriving in Oslo via the Panama Canal on 16 May 1987.

The expedition was generally considered the most scientifically successful privately funded polar expedition of the modern era.

Three years later Monica put it differently. 'I know in some ways it was extremely worthwhile, and some successful scientific studies were carried out, but I know it will always be something that I didn't achieve. I want to keep the knowledge of that grief as a proper loss. In that respect I want it to be a failure, although people say we achieved so much. We tried the best we could and we couldn't do it.'

This Calvinistic approach to life seems to be the key to Monica's character. She describes herself as a very religious person. 'My religion transcends everything I do and when I have to make a choice – if there is a moral relevance – my decision is dictated by the moral argument. As I learn more about right and wrong, I find it more and more difficult to make these choices. It takes a lot of intellectual effort to explain to myself what is really important. Although I lead a very complicated life in terms of logistics with many responsibilities and ambitious projects, I have to tell myself, "This may be important to me – it's not important to God – it's nothing to do with the soul." Maybe this keeps me on an even keel and from being too superficial and clever at managing my life, my family's life, my husband's life. I take stock and say, "I know nothing."' Monica has been drawn to Catholicism and Buddhism, and she has studied many other religions. Yet she always returns to the teaching of Calvin – 'By Their Works, Ye Shall Know Them'.

When Monica got back to Vangen, she and Neil had to go through the painful process of parting with the twenty-two huskies. Some were going back to their old owners and some to new homes. As scientists, there was no way they could keep them. She remembered one particular day on the expedition. 'We'd just driven down the "ski jump" – a particularly steep part of the Axel Heiberg. Behind us the glacier reared up like a runaway horse. The hood of my anorak was full of snow thrown up by the sledge brakes. My cheeks were burning red with excitement. We'd crossed over snow bridges right beside yawning gulfs, we'd raced downhill at a speed which took our breath away. Then we were down, and I laughed with joy.' Later she wrote, 'As I looked at the dog teams lying side by side in the snow, I knew that nothing had given me such joy as making the journey through Antarctica. There was no greater honour than that the dogs had regarded me as their driver. Every day was full of experiences that we had shared together.' As the last husky was driven away Monica wept 'as though her heart would break'.

But a few months later, in January 1988, she and Arne were to be married. This was a major media event in Norway. Since the expedition she had become a national celebrity which she admitted she quite enjoyed. She stage-managed the wedding with all the efficiency of a major expedition (which in a sense it was) and this time everything went without a hitch. She and her husband live near her parents in a small house in Kongsvinger where desolate polar scenes decorate the walls. But she never stays in one place for long and her fertile mind is endlessly planning more projects – scientific, geophysical and archaeological. With new infra-red probing equipment, she plans to check out the existence of buried sites, particularly at Cambridge, where the archaeologist T. C. Lethbridge claimed to have discovered three giant chalk figures under the turf of the Gogmagog Hills. Monica is both a realist and a bit of a mystic. If there was a route to Utopia, she would plan the logistics down to the last detail, but she would be philosophical if she failed to arrive.

Christina Dodwell

Now I seemed to be steering upwards, riding high,
riding free, scooping up life's ecstasy and terror in
handfuls, throwing it in the air and catching it
again.

Christina Dodwell,
Travels with Fortune

'I'm no feminist – I'm an individual and I believe in independence.'
Christina Dodwell was chatting in her house in Shepherd's Bush in
a room full of books and curios which she had collected on her
travels. In her thirties with a willowy figure and long sun-bleached
hair, the only clue that she is someone quite exceptional lies in her
enquiring blue eyes which seem always to be focused on far
horizons. In fourteen years she has made six remarkable voyages
travelling mostly alone, often through uncharted territory, and has
used every conceivable means of transport, from horse, camel and
zebroid to canoe and microlight.

Christina was born in Nigeria, in the deep bush; the nearest white
people lived on a Catholic mission about thirty miles away. Her
grandparents had lived in China from 1919 at the time of the
warlords and her grandmother, Doris, had been an unconventional
lady and had done a lot of travelling as a special correspondent for
various newspapers. Christina became fascinated by the stories of
old China and the faded photographs in the family albums. She felt
certain that one day she, too, would travel to distant countries. Her
father was in the colonial administration and when she was six the
whole family left Nigeria and came back to England. The children
spent six years at different schools around Camberley and Oxford
and then their parents returned to Nigeria.

At boarding school Christina felt different from the other girls. 'I was sometimes ridiculed but I wasn't unhappy, and there are advantages and disadvantages in having your parents abroad – no one to come to sports days or to take you out, but at least everyone feels sorry for you and you get away with murder. My sister was older and my brother younger which has always made me feel free. Eventually my sister married and produced the grandchildren and my brother went away to work, so I could do my own thing; and now that I'm established in what I do people don't expect me to be conventional. It's a great relief.'

When she left school at eighteen she moved to London and took a series of different jobs. Her first was with *Queen* magazine, originally in the art department and then for Betty Kenward on 'Jennifer's Diary'. 'She was writing about the social scene and girls I'd been to school with, and when it was "charming so-and-so wearing a delightful blue taffeta dress", and it was somebody I'd loathed and thought a boring old cow, I'd cross out the compliments. It wasn't the best of partnerships although she did say she thought I had potential.' Christina left the magazine after four years and did some work as an interior designer, then was advertising manager for an engineering firm, and subsequently became the manager of the Mayfair branch of a car-hire company. During these six years she was actually engaged to be married. 'He was a lovely man but very radical and while I was envisaging a life of domestic bliss, he was never very keen on marriage and became very jittery and we drifted apart.' After another romance went wrong, Christina felt it was time to get away and cut loose completely. For years she had longed to travel and now events pushed her into it. She says of herself at the time that she was home-loving, materialistic, possessive and insecure. The next phase of her life was to bring out opposite characteristics.

In 1975, at the age of twenty-four, she set out with Lesley, a nurse from New Zealand four years older than her, and two boys contacted through a travel magazine. They planned to spend a year driving through Africa in a Land Rover. 'When I told my mother, she said, "How wonderful!" A lot of mothers would have said, "Oh my God, you'll be killed!" But my parents felt that having been brought up in a foreign country, I'd know how to behave. Their confidence in me gave me confidence in myself. If your mother doesn't believe in you, then how can you believe in yourself?'

They bought a Land Rover, equipped it with everything they could possibly need and travelled across Europe, through Spain and over to Morocco, then journeyed across the Sahara. Occasionally they would spot the brown tents of the Tuaregs, nomadic tribes known as 'the blue men'.

'Conversation consisted of them exclaiming and touching our clothes, and while Lesley attended to everyone who was sick or injured, I either helped her or sat and sketched my surroundings.'

One day one of the tribe, Moktar, came galloping over on his camel and invited them to the *fête de Mohammed*. After a meal of couscous and camel meat, the dancing started. In a wide empty space lit by flaming torches, men in white robes fired gunpowder-packed rifles into the sand, moving to the noise of the drums. The villagers were chanting and singing. 'Their lovely soft sighing chant was backed by a stirring hand-clapped rhythm, and as they clapped the women danced with their hands and arms with synchronised flow, while a girl from Mali sang a solo harmony above it all. The sky overflowed with stars, the night grew cold and the ground shook with the stamping circle of flickering men. Then there was a thud as one of the men fell flat on the ground. "Ah," said Moktar, "he has drunk too much music." One by one they slowly crashed down in an exhausted stupor. The dance had come to an end.'

Setting off on the last half of the Sahara crossing, they headed out of Algeria, through Niger and towards Nigeria, still nine hundred miles away. The desert was devoid of features, and Christina remembered Moktar's words: 'This is the land of thirst and mirages which is called Emptiness.' Finally, only a month after leaving England, they reached Kano in Nigeria and it was there that their expedition came abruptly to an end. They had parked the Land Rover in a camping park and had unpacked their gear, when suddenly the boys jumped into the Land Rover and drove off. Two days later they had still not reappeared. After a desperate search, Christina and Lesley found them sitting at a table in the town bar. It was a bitter meeting. The boys calmly admitted that they had sold the Land Rover – at a ridiculously low price – but eventually agreed to pay them half the money, which was a thin wad of naira notes worth about £400. The Land Rover and equipment had cost them at least £3,000. 'I really don't know why they did it,' Christina said years later. 'They really had no interest in exploring the countryside or chatting to the tribes. We sent a cable to my mother telling her we'd been deserted by the boys, and she cabled back suggesting we take a plane to nice safe East Africa and travel there. Lesley and I looked at each other and said, "Well, let's think that cable didn't reach us and what about you and I looking a little bit further?" I'm very drawn to the next horizon – just a little bit further – just another day. I can go on for years just a little bit furthering.'

Their 'little bit further' saw them hitch-hiking around northern and central Nigeria in an amazing assortment of vehicles: Chinese water-tankers, an old jalopy driven by Scottish Quakers, a van full of students on their way to a dig in the Central African Republic, an air-conditioned Cadillac and clapped-out Land Rovers. 'Lesley and I had no schedule. We made plans according to our mood of the day. We never argued. Some days she'd lead and I'd follow – another day I'd lead and she'd follow. Our destination seemed irrelevant. It was the journey now which was an experience in itself.' Eventually they acquired two horses at an Italian road construction camp and, in search of grass, they decided to make for the mountains of south-west Cameroun. Guided by the sun, carrying only sleeping-bags and water-bottles, they followed tracks and paths which led through tiny, scattered villages; as they approached the villagers would run away in fear. They were in the territory of a primitive tribe known as the Pagans. Losing their way frequently and besieged by flies, they came to a village where the women's heads were bald and their bodies covered in rows of raised circular scars. This, they explained by sign language, was juju to prevent them being killed by spears. 'The African's mentality about juju or witchcraft seemed to me to be pre-logical. They accept its power as part of their cultural heritage. In contrast to Europeans, who tend to laugh at juju, the Africans laughed because they believe it works.'

The next day the sky turned yellow and the sun disappeared behind a dusty fog which became so dense that they were unable to see more than a few paces ahead. It was the *harmattan*, a dry wind which coated their hair and faces with dust and made their eyes stream with tears. They were unprepared for it as it usually blew in the dry season; this was mid-May, which should have been the beginning of the rainy season. The villages became scarcer and they drank the last of their water. Soon there were no villages or people, and for a week which seemed an eternity, they found nothing to eat. They could think of nothing but their thirst and hunger. At night they dreamed of feasts and banquets. 'Strangely I didn't hate this mile after mile of sun-punished wilderness – colourless, immense and godforsaken. To me it was beautiful even though our throats were parched and our stomachs ached. Suddenly, one sultry hot and heavy day, some clouds yellow with dust and rain loomed up and one came our way. When it reached us, we stripped off our clothes and danced. However, we didn't have any salt and our horses craved it so badly they would lick the sweat from our arms. Our own extreme lethargy was induced in part by our own need of salt.' By the time they eventually reached a village they were so hungry, exhausted and sunburnt they only felt a vague fuzzy sense of relief. This was the leanest time of the year for the villagers who could only offer them yoghurt made from milk, fresh blood and urine, a few groundnuts, some spinach-like leaves and two cakes of maize. 'It was one of the most delicious meals I have ever eaten.'

They were directed to a town called Mubi where they were given shelter by a young English teacher until they had regained their strength. Continuing their journey across semi-desert towards Cameroon, they came across the nomadic tribes called the Fulani; the women had delicate Hamitic features and wore nose rings and loops of cowrie shells threaded through their ears. In one village an old man, who spoke a little English, took them to his home and taught them some words of Fulani. He had three wives and lived with whichever wife was not pregnant at the time.

As the horses' backs had become sore and their feet too tender to carry them further, Christina and Lesley decided to sell them when they reached Cameroon. The horses were bought by the brother of a local chief, for £20. The girls then hitched to Bamenda and walked around the highlands. Stopping one day in a village they were suddenly encircled by a ring of dancing and chanting men carrying six-foot long spears, which they flung into the ground only inches from the girls' feet. As the exercise was repeated with increasing jubilation, Lesley's fixed smile fell from her face. 'I wish we hadn't got into this,' she muttered. 'But isn't it wonderful music? It makes me want to dance,' Christina replied. 'Christina, if you want to dance, then you go ahead and dance.' Which is what she did. Her dance bore no comparison to the men's spectacular performances but it brought them to a halt. Faces broke into smiles. They shook everybody's hand and left rather hurriedly.

Later Christina said, 'I have had great fun with my tested exits. You must try to defuse the tension away from anger – away from violence. When I've offended or caused anger, I leap in with smiles and handshakes and praise of their village and their country. Even when they don't understand, they are usually disarmed – I know it's a bit of a con trick, but it mainly works.'

Noticing that their Cameroon visas were due to expire in five days, they decided to make for Kenya. They arrived at Bangui with two ideas in mind: to collect mail and eat a huge meal. But acquiring visas to cross southern Sudan and then to enter Kenya proved impossible – they were told that it was now the height of the wet season, that all routes would be impassable and it would take many months to hitch-hike to Kenya. Shocked by the sudden end to their plans, they decided to look at a map of Africa for inspiration. 'As we were now almost in the centre, we found the decision impossible. I pulled out my tobacco pouch to fill my pipe. As I lit it I noticed there were seven matches left. That's the answer, I thought. We marked each match in biro with the name of a different country, choosing at random: Chad, Egypt, Ghana, Senegal, Gabon, Angola and Botswana. Lesley picked a match – it said Gabon. We looked at the map – it was a thousand miles to the south-west on the coast just below the bulge. 'There don't seem to be many roads,' Lesley said.

But Christina was looking at a tributary which flowed past Bangui towards the south, joined the Congo and continued south-west past Brazzaville and on to the sea. If they could get downriver to Brazzaville, then Gabon would only be a few hundred miles north. They decided to buy a dugout from some fishermen. It looked like a hollowed-out tree, long and thin with warped gnarled sides. 'I was convinced that our voyage was a perfectly normal undertaking and had no idea what the thousand mile journey held in store.' She also had no idea that she would be following the route taken by

Stanley in the 1870s. 'I wrote to my parents telling them not to expect to hear from me for several months, as we were going by boat to Brazzaville and it was very slow.' Taking only some coffee, a jar of jam and five loaves of bread, they set off, slightly alarmed by the warnings of the locals: 'It's a dangerous journey, you'll be killed or get lost, there'll be hurricanes and fog.' But no one mentioned the whirlpools.

In her book, *Travels with Fortune*, Christina gives a harrowing account of her first river journey. She describes how they gradually mastered the dugout (which they called *La Piroque*), paddling through the strong current and treacherous clumps of water hyacinths which wound round the rudder, making steering virtually impossible. One night, they set up camp by the river bank, rigging up their mosquito nets over poles in the central section of the dugout, which was long enough for them to lie down comfortably. Suddenly there was the loud whining of mosquitoes inside their nets: the insects were so small that, by folding back their wings, they had penetrated the netting. 'It was a hot equatorial night and I became slimy with sweat. I wrapped a towel around my head, leaving only a tiny slit for breathing, but the mosquitoes crept through it and stung my nose, lips, tongue and all round the inside of my mouth. The high-pitched howling made me feel twisted with loathing, my stomach felt knotted, and I wanted to scream and scream and scream.'

When dawn came at last, they found their Nivaquine pills and decided to increase their daily dose to two a day. The river alternated between glassy calm and raging roughness. The days were extremes of paradise or hell, exhilaration and fear. Once, floating downriver, they heard a series of grunts. A hippopotamus surfaced; then a second and a third. One hippo opened his massive jaws, displaying his tusk-like teeth, and went for them. Desperately padalling in reverse, they managed to reach the nearest shore just as a storm broke overhead and the hippos disappeared.

The river folk all held different opinions about the opposite side of the river. The Congolese would point at Zaire and say in hushed tones, 'Don't go over there. Over there they eat people!' The Zairois would point at the Congo and say, 'Beware, those men are cannibals!' Among these people, human sacrifice and cannibalism (known as *bouiti*) is not considered murder, but simply the traditional and established method of reversing bad luck or appeasing the anger of the spirits. The victims of *bouiti* are chosen by the tribal witch-doctor, who is in charge of the physical and spiritual welfare of the people. Although there are variations from tribe to tribe, the ritual usually takes place after the accidental death of someone important: then a child is sacrificed to pacify the ancestral spirits.

Christina and Lesley met a group of young men whose teeth were sharpened to V-points. 'Don't worry,' they said 'We don't eat white people.' One man, who was called Heko, showed them how to catch crocodiles and how to extract a waxy resin from a tree, which was dried and mixed with oily fibres and then burned as a torch for twenty-four hours. Heko spoke a little French and was very frank and open. He explained that his tribe sharpened their teeth because they ate monkeys instead of human flesh and the meat tended to cling to the bones.

One night, some men tried to take their dugout. Christina shouted at the top of her voice, shaking her fists at them until they disappeared into the darkness. 'With a sudden shock I remembered that I was afraid of the dark, but now wasn't the time to dwell on that. It occurred to me that I was constantly having to deny all my inbred reactions to situations; they were no longer appropriate. Every shred of my old character was being re-evaluated, not by myself but by the circumstances which now governed me. My lifelong craving for security was turning into a love of the unpredictable. I didn't question the changes.'

When they reached the River Congo the current picked up speed and they raced along in the roughest waves they had yet encountered. The dugout rose up the crests and slid down into the troughs. The river broadened to about ten miles in width, a labyrinth of channels and lagoons among galaxies of swaying papyrus reeds and hundreds of flat, sandy, uninhabited islands, covered in grass and ferns and flowers. Around this time Lesley's movements became unco-ordinated and she began shivering and groaning. Suddenly she sat bolt upright and announced lucidly that she had malaria and discussed the correct dosage of Nivaquine. She then lapsed into delirium and alternated between hot and cold sweats. The illness lasted for four days during which Christina nursed her as best she could. But their food supplies were running out. When Lesley partly recovered, they made for Mongolo, where they were surrounded by hordes of people who had come to check the truth of the rumour that two white women were paddling down the Congo. They were presented with smoked fish and turtles and dried monkey and antelope. Back on the river they ran into a seething mass of whirlpools and rocks. *La Piroque* smashed into a rock, and when they got her to the shore and rolled her on her side, they found four deep gashes. But Brazzaville was only a few miles away. They had been seven weeks on the river, and when they arrived on the shore of the city, their arms were shaking like jelly, but they felt quiet and sad that the journey was over.

At Brazzaville they were immediately arrested and accused of being spies. In Third World countries the word 'spy' includes anyone who is in the wrong place at the wrong time. The police did not believe that they had come by dugout down the river, insisting it was impossible. However after seeing the dugout they were released, but without their passports. News of the arrival of the two white girls spread quickly round the city and they were surrounded by people wanting to shake them by the hand. Congolese television made a film about them. They were heralded in the newspapers and journals of the Congo as intrepid explorers who had completed an extraordinary odyssey. Ambassadors gave parties in their honour; they were entertained by government ministers; their passports were returned.

After two weeks, they began to find the social whirl more of an ordeal than the whirlpools of the river so they sold *La Piroque* to a fisherman for two pounds, put on their rucksacks and walked out of Brazzaville into the depths of the forest. There they spent the next three months roaming at random through the jungles of the Congo and Gabon and over forested hillsides which were scored by eroded canyons of red laterite. For fifty miles they hitch-hiked in a rail buggy used for collecting railway workers from their villages. The railway led through lines of immense trees with vast tangled roots, ferns growing ten feet tall, vines and creepers covered with blossoming jasmine, purple convolvulus and turquoise butterflies. Arriving at a village they dined on crocodile stew, with meat the texture of lobster. Once they flagged down an aeroplane passing overhead. By the end of October they had crossed the border into Gabon and, on their way to Port Gentil, they stopped at Lambarene, where Doctor Schweitzer had founded his hospital. He had always refused to allow the hospital to be modernised; there had been no running water, even in the operating theatre. Things had hardly changed in 1976: a place was still set for the dead man at every meal.

They never reached Port Gentil, but they did stay in a pygmy village, where the huts were made of pieces of bark. The tallest among the pygmies was no more than four and a half feet. Christina and Lesley were treated to a celebration of dancing and singing and feasted on antelope. The pygmy girls' faces were dramatically painted, one half blue and the other dotted with large white spots; as they danced, they whirled their hips in swift circular thrusting movements and sang a high-pitched warbling song.

Christmas was approaching. They had been travelling for ten months and their money was running out. They decided to make for South Africa to look for jobs. One day they found a dilapidated cargo boat bound for Pointe-Noire, and from there, they were told, it would be easy to find a connection to Cape Town. The captain was a tall, lanky Frenchman, shy and courteous, and they celebrated Christmas dinner with lobster and shark steaks, and sang carols in French and English.

On arriving at Point-Noire, the captain found a boat going to Cape Town and handed over his female passengers. The captain of *L'Augure* was also French, thickset and swarthy with a heavy jowled face showing the ravages of many fights and too much alcohol. Three days later they were still anchored at Pointe-Noire. Lesley and Christina were put in separate cabins and every time they left them they were followed by the captain or a member of the crew, making it impossible to go ashore. The captain took a fancy to Christina, pinching and pawing her with his large hairy hands. The first night she locked the door of her cabin, but he kicked the door down and tried to pull off the bed covers which she was clutching to her neck. After a row, he left and she barricaded the door with a table. 'The Captain was a constant visitor to my cabin and he harassed me until I thought I was going insane. I tried feigning illness, and he gave me aspirin; when he forced me to lie on the bunk, I faked such a terrible coughing fit that he brought me a glass of water. I don't know why he didn't simply rape me and have done with it, but something held him back.'

The boat was still anchored in the harbour four days later and the captain confessed that in fact he wasn't going to Cape Town but north to Libreville in Gabon. He threatened that if they tried to escape, he would hand them over to the Congolese authorities as spies. They had no choice but to bide their time. One day after a heavy lunch, the captain leant back into his chair with his arms behind his back. The rope with which he had beaten her the night before when she had repelled his advances was lying by his side. Christina, without really knowing what she was doing, tied his hands behind him. With Lesley's help she then gagged him with his handkerchief and poured a bottle of tomato sauce over his head to look like blood. She then grabbed an iron bar which lay on the floor and, as one of the African crew approached, she brandished it in the air. She found the crewman at the wheel and shouted, 'Turn the boat. Set a course for Cape Town.' He hesitated for a moment and then started turning the wheel. 'Suddenly a thought at the back of my mind told me what we could have been letting ourselves in for. The sentence for piracy was ten years' imprisonment.' She decided to pretend it had all been a joke. They released the captain and they all started laughing. Although the captain had laughed as heartily as the rest, his attitude towards her changed and he treated her with an air bordering on politeness. He now walked beside her quoting poetry and love songs while she munched cloves of garlic as though they were peanuts. But it did not deter him from asking her to marry him. When they at last arrived in Libreville harbour the pilot of the tug boat came on board. Although Christina was locked in her cabin, Lesley had packed their bags, determined they would find a chance to escape. Soon the boat was moving and the cabin door was unlocked. The pilot handed *L'Augure* back to the captain and climbed back into his tug; the girls grabbed their bags and leapt on to the open deck behind him. The pilot never said a word, but dropped them at a wooden jetty and went on to the next ship. Freedom at last.

After a period of recovery in Libreville they flew to South Africa and then on to Rhodesia where they found jobs sixty miles apart, Christina as a manager of some dog kennels at Hunter's Moon, fifteen miles from town, and Lesley in a hospital in Bindura. Christina's life in the bush could have been uneventful, but she filled it by learning to train dogs, teaching French to the children of a neighbouring farmer and taking a course in reading dynamics. On 1 February 1976 it was her twenty-fifth birthday and Lesley joined her for the day. She had decided to fly home to New Zealand to marry her boyfriend, and that evening was the last time Christina saw her, but she knew that she could never replace her. She valued Lesley's friendship more highly than she had valued that of any other girl. Although there was nothing physical in their relationship, it had reached an ultimate in partnership that Christina had never dreamt could exist, the true meaning of sharing, the closeness that was possible between two people. Now she was alone. 'I was aware of this empty space beside me. I felt I should find someone else to travel with and then I thought: why? If I can travel on my own, there's nowhere in the world I can't go, when, where, and how I want to without waiting around, so I thought, well, let's just do this as a test.'

She yearned to leave civilised life and return to the bush, choosing the eastern region of Rhodesia because it was mountainous and wild. Wearing sandals, a long skirt, two sweaters and carrying a light rucksack, she spent a month touring the eastern highlands, once getting lost for three days in the Chimanimani mountains. 'One night I gathered armfuls of dry grass and made a bed inside a cave, then built a fire as the night was cold. Then it crossed my mind that this was terrorist country, so I killed the flames, but ensured that the embers smouldered hot and red. A second thought came to me: I was alone, lost in wild mountains at night, and I was still scared of the dark. I had two options: either I could huddle in my cave and sink into terror, or I could disregard my nervousness and sleep soundly in my cosy grass bed. At that moment, the full moon rose slowly above the jagged skyline. I curled up and watched the moonshadows. I had become part of the night, it had become part of me. I slept a deep, untroubled sleep.'

She spent some time with the rangers and game wardens and learned bushcraft and survival strategies: how to skin animals and cure the hides, how to follow game by the spoor and to identify edible varieties of plants. Remembering the hunger she and Lesley had suffered in Nigeria, she became a good pupil. Ten years later, she was to write *An Explorer's Handbook*. 'I wrote it originally as a send-up of everything I did – it's the book I had the most fun writing.' In fact, Chris Bonington described it as the most practical guide to adventurous travelling. She lists essential items to take and survival techniques. When Robert Byron set out on his road to Oxiana, he was convinced that one should consume three new books a week and a bottle of wine a day. Christina herself takes the bare minimum. Usually a book, sleeping-bag, sheet inner, nylon hammock, mosquito net, a lighter, rope, hunting knife, catapult, fishing line and hooks, adhesive tape, needle, thread and pins, plastic bags, water bottle, water purifying tablets, map and compass, billycan for cooking and a first aid kit. Finding salt the only really essential food, she will add nuts, raisins and dried meat. She wears canvas rather than leather boots, a long skirt that can turn into instant pantaloons, and takes a sarong and an extra crease-resistant long skirt for festivities, and a sun hat.

When Darwin sailed in the *Beagle* to Tierra del Fuego he took bonnets to soothe the savage breasts of the Alacaluf Indians. She takes along tiny presents such as flick-lighters, pens and pocket mirrors and nail clippers, photographs of home and family. Pictures of the Royal Family have proved very successful. A chapter in the book on unusual eatables includes how to cook tortoise, armadillo, crocodile and snake. From extracts from the diaries of early explorers such as Thomas Baines she gives a recipe of how to cook elephant's foot: 'Dig a hole, make a fire in it until the sides and surrounds are well-heated, then rake out the fire. Cut off the front foot of the elephant at the knee joint, place it in the hole. Cover with embers and hot earth. Make a new fire on top, light it, and let it burn all night. In the morning the meat is ready. Best eaten warm.'

But in Rhodesia, the 25-year-old Christina was still learning survival techniques. A game warden lent her a small brown mare and she wandered the countryside on horseback over plains of tall, dry grass and rocky hills called kopjes. Eland scattered at her approach and she saw zebras, kudu, impala and troupes of monkeys. 'One day while searching for bushmen paintings on a kopje, I met a leopard. He had been lazing in the sun and leapt up startled when I landed within a few yards of him. We both froze and stared at each other. I waited for him to run away. He was probably waiting for me to run, too, and he began to flick his long tail from side to side. I turned slowly and stomped off angrily (I knew better than to run away from a leopard which would give chase just for sport).'

Once, when she was returning from the acropolis of the ancient ruined city of Great Zimbabwe, she was attacked by a large black-backed jackal. As she struck out her hand to ward off its jaws, it latched on to her right wrist. She smashed her left wrist down on its neck, then grabbed for its throat. Quick as a flash, the jackal dropped her right hand and bit into her left. They fought ferociously until all she knew was the jackal's yellow snapping teeth and gurgling snarl. When it hit the ground she aimed a kick at its head: it sank its teeth into her foot. She stamped downwards and kicked it with her other foot. Suddenly it turned and slunk off into the bush. With blood dripping from her hands and foot she limped painfully to the nearest road. Eventually a passing car picked her up and took her to the doctor who stitched her up and administered a course of anti-rabies injections. She had thirteen tooth-holes in her arms and had to live for weeks without the use of her hands.

The civil war in the country was escalating and when she recovered Christina decided that she must be on the move. She planned to ride around southern Africa, and she applied for permits to take a horse across the borders of South Africa, Swaziland, Lesotho and the Transkei. Friends asked her what she was searching for, what goal or purpose. 'It was a question for which I had no answer. Purpose sounded too single-minded for me. I preferred to be flexible. Also I rejected the concept of goals and ambitions. They implied success or failure. I wasn't interested in measuring myself against others or in competing with them.'

In Johannesburg, finding a horse was more difficult than she had imagined – either nobody wanted to sell or the prices were much too high. Someone suggested that she contact the municipal abattoir, which auctioned horses for slaughter. They were pitiful creatures with emaciated bodies. All she knew about horses was that black feet were good because white feet were softer and tended to go lame. The first horse she bid for had four black feet, but a man standing next to her tugged her arm and pointed out it had a broken leg. After about forty horses had been sold, each more battered than the last, she began to despair. Then a thin but rakish bay gelding plunged into the ring. Her neighbour seemed to think it looked all right and with only one bid against her, in no time at all the auctioneer yelled that the horse was hers. She decided to call it Xoza.

She wanted to go to the Eastern Transvaal and simply drew a straight line on a map from the top of the eastern Transvaal, through Swaziland to Empangeni on the Zululand coast. She felt that by going in a straight line she would stand less chance of getting lost, and from the sea she would turn right and follow the coast to Cape Town. It was the beginning of a journey of three thousand miles, which would last seven months and take her over the soaring jagged range of the Drakensberg Mountains. She zig-zagged interminably upwards and finally emerged on top of a bleak, windswept and barren plateau. Sometimes leading Xoza down the steep mountain paths had been almost impossible, and once she feared she would have to abandon him when he slipped and fell off a cliff into the rocky depths below. She thought the only way of extricating him would be by airlift. But unbelievably, imitating a mountain goat and picking his way from one boulder to another and testing every foothold, he managed to slither down to a lower path. Later, Christina rode through the dense Tsitsikama forest, where she met a herd of elephants and one vast solitary male with long pale tusks. 'The Knysna elephants are reputed to be the largest in the world and as they don't like horses, I had no wish to argue with one. Emergency stop. I hauled on the reins, Xoza stopped dead, spun round and galloped in the opposite direction.'

From Cape Town she could have gone anywhere, but in fact she made her way north through South-West Africa (Namibia), Bot-swana, Zambia, Malawi and Tanzania to Kenya. From there she intended to hitch-hike across the middle of the continent, returning to West Africa and then continuing up the western Sahara by camel. The journey would probably have taken two years. But a letter from her parents changed her plans – her brother was getting married in seven months' time. She wrote and said she would be home for the wedding. She had found a good home for Xoza in South Africa with friends she could trust to look after him. 'I don't regard my horse as a companion – he's a horse – he's my transport and requires the best. If I'm demanding a lot out of him I've got to put a lot back. I'm not sentimental or soppy about animals.'

Christina's journeys were never made for the sake of getting somewhere else. Destinations were irrelevant. She found pure travel like dancing – moving in time with the land and the sky. 'That is why I decided not to recross Africa. I hadn't finished being in East Africa. Here was the Rift Valley, the cradle of mankind.' Her new plan was to ride north from Nairobi up the Rift Valley, over the Cherangani Mountains, and down into the desert of the Northern Frontier District, and then continue north across Ethiopia, down the Blue Nile into the Sudan. Ideally she would need a companion, and she found one. Toni was an American girl, a primatologist doing research into the behaviour of monkeys and baboons. They were warned about the many dangers ahead of them, from lions to snakes and hunting spiders. 'I never take much notice of warnings. Other people always seem to know better than me – they mostly pretend. Take endurance riding: it's very different from normal riding, there's no magic answer. For instance, someone told me a horse ought to stand with its feet in water for half an hour a day. Absolute nonsense: they'd get very soft and crack in the heat. People always offer advice about things they know nothing about.'

By December 1977 they were 10,000 feet high in the Cherangani Mountains, Christina riding Zen, a full-blooded Somali pony, and Toni a big dun gelding called Toroka. They also led a pack pony carrying their provisions. It was wild, remote country – to the east the sharp escarpment falling to the desert, and to the west Mount Elgon and Uganda. They caused great excitement when riding through villages because horses had hardly ever been seen in the region. Until now the safari had been going well, but then a series of disasters struck. The pack pony went lame, and they had to leave her and the bulk of their provisions with a local chief. After crossing the boundary from Kalenjen into Pokot, they descended sharply into the blazing hot desert where at a temperature reaching 50 degrees C (120 degrees F) the water in their canteens seemed almost boiling. When they crossed into Turkana territory they found the Turkana people just as primitive as the Pokot, but much friendlier. The horses were managing remarkably well in the desert – without a bucket to drink from, they learned to drink from a plastic bag – and both looked in peak condition. But then one night camping about thirty miles from Lodwar, the girls were woken by a noise of terrible screaming and stampeding horses. The camp was being attacked. Christina charged towards the centre of the commotion brandishing a long knife and howling her battle cry in full throat and in varying tones to sound like a man. The attackers ran away. The girls found Zen and, eventually, Toroka. The horse was still alive but he had been slashed open and his front legs severed. He could never have survived. Shocked and too miserable for tears, they knew there was no alternative but to have him shot.

After resting up for a few days in Lodwar they bought a camel to replace Toroka. To control it they learned some words of Turkana: 'TU TU TU' accompanied by violent hissing meant 'sit down', 'HA' meant 'stand up', and 'go forward' was 'HA HA' or burring like an alarm clock. Gradually Zen and the camel got used to each other and soon were inseparable. But the journey was ill-fated. Either the camel or Zen would keep wandering off, and it would take hours to track them down; the lack of water was telling on the girls' nerves and they were not working as a team. It seemed they brought out the worst in each other.

Continuing northwards along the west bank of Lake Turkana or the Jade Sea, after a week they reached North Island and were greeted by a sandstorm with flashes of lightning. Heading for a Catholic mission, they found that the priests' Christianity extended only as far as the natives. One said, 'We are not here to help people like you.' That evening walking away from their campfire, Christina felt a sharp stab of pain in her foot. There was a trickle of blood from a mark which hurt like fire. Knowing the Catholic fathers would not come to help her, she tried to reach the nurses' bungalow before the poison overtook her. A nurse laid her on a bed and sent for antihistamines. 'The poison moved slowly up my leg and when it reached the glands at the top, the agony was almost unbearable.' As the poison progressed, she grew numb and felt paralysed. At last, the nurse gave her the injection and sent her away. As she couldn't walk, someone carried her and dumped her near their camp. Within a couple of hours, she was completely paralysed and unable to speak. Her throat closed up, she was gasping for breath and choking on her saliva. Toni managed to haul her clothes off, for she was drenched with sweat, covered her with dry clothes and lay close to her for warmth. 'It was without doubt the longest, most terrible night of my life,' Christina said later, 'and worse than any danger I've been through since. Mosquitoes swarmed round my face, but I couldn't feel my hands to brush them away. No amount of covering stopped me from feeling I was freezing to death.' In the morning Toni persuaded the reluctant nurse to give her a bed in the infirmary, where for two days she was unable to move. The nurses gave her no painkillers, nor a kind word, thinking she was making a fuss over a scorpion sting. In fact she had been bitten by a hunting spider, the African equivalent to the tarantula. Eventually she managed to sip a little thin porridge and stand up; her feet 'felt like raw stumps of flesh on a carpet of nails'.

Christina travelled on crutches for a week and a Turkana boy accompanied them as far as Lokitaung to help them on their journey. In Lokitaung they received an official letter from Lodwar confirming that they would be allowed to cross the border into Ethiopia. This was just as well as their visas were out of date, which they rectified with a pen and matching ink. They felt their troubles were over as they began the easy climb over the mountains and rocks, many of which were lined with crystals of quartz and amethyst. Occasionally they met nomadic Turkanas herding their goats. They were completely naked, but they stowed the tobacco the girls gave them in their lip-plugs, or in their earrings, which were jars of cow-horn. At the Ethiopian border the guards seemed impressed by the letter from the embassy, but when they looked at their visas they said, 'There appears to be something wrong with the date.' Christina's heart sank. Her attempt at forgery must have been discovered. But in fact it was not so – the Ethiopian calendar was different from the English one and seven years behind. It was now only 1971 in Ethiopia. After a while they were allowed to proceed along the banks of the Omo River. Unfortunately this border area was closed to foreigners, and they were soon afterwards arrested as imperialist spies. They were told they had to return to Kenya – all their official letters had been worthless. Back in Nairobi, the house where they were staying was burgled and Christina, standing amongst her few remaining possessions, felt as if she was back at the beginning, in the camping park at Kano with Lesley. The film had rewound, and in April 1978 she flew home. She had been away over three years.

In England, reunited with her family but in poor health, Christina found herself restless and short of money. The obvious answer was to write a book, which she did, describing her African journey. She does not allow herself the luxury of self-analysis, but after her three years in Africa where she had experienced pain and terror and exhilaration, she was a changed character. Recalling her African adventure she said: 'There had been the realisation that you're on your own – not knowing where you're going to camp or where your next meal is coming from. That empty uncertainty had niggled me at first until I realised that, after the sadness of leaving good friends, the emptiness ahead was wonderful – days waiting to be filled.' She had conquered her fear of the dark and had recognised that security was something she carried within herself; she was living the life which she had always wanted and loved wholeheartedly. 'When I thought about the future I was scared. A voice in my mind told me that I was doing what I had chosen to do. I realised I had never been happier. What I made of my life was my responsibility, though chance had much to do with it. The life of an explorer was not one I would have chosen for myself, but it had happened and it felt right. These facts cancelled out any idea of settling down, and I began planning my next trip.'

Looking at the world atlas between Indonesia and the north coast of Australia, Christina started studying the island of New Guinea – the second largest island in the world. The eastern half, Papua New Guinea, is also called 'the Last Unknown', being one of the least explored places. 'Doing some research, I learned that it also had the wildest landscape, more impenetrable jungle than any other tropical region including the Amazon and Africa. The prospect of travelling there excited me.'

The story of Christina's two-year expedition through the highlands, jungles and along the Sepik River, which she describes in her book *In Papua New Guinea*, reveals her at her most adventurous and courageous. Yet she herself would not admit necessarily to seeking any perilous or risky situations in her quest for travel. 'I don't see my journeys as dangerous and I don't believe in challenges, they're both neither to be courted nor avoided. I learned early on that fear seemed to be irrelevant: you just have to deal with potentially dangerous situations as best you can, fear has no part in that – in fact it would make the wrong thing happen. Wits sharpen with experience.'

Christina was twenty-nine when she entered Papua New Guinea in an outrigger canoe. She had taken eight arduous months to reach her destination, the last of which was spent in a cargo boat sailing from Java to Jayapura, sleeping in a hammock surrounded by cattle, goats and oil drums. In Yanimo she stayed with an American missionary family where she picked up some neo-Melanesian (the national language of the country, known as 'pidgin'). A stranger was 'man bilong long-wei ples', a language was 'tok-ples' and a home was 'arse-ples'. Looking at a map of the sparsely populated country she made her usual random decision for her voyage. 'I took hold of a pencil then reaching out I let it drop to touch the map.' It landed on the highlands at the remotest end of the mountain cordillera – the least explored area. As there were no roads out of Yanimo, she managed to hitch a lift in a small plane to Oksapmon from where she planned to walk to Lake Kopiago. Setting out amongst the locals to look for two guides to accompany her (she had been told they insisted on being two, as one would be afraid to return alone), she found neolithic-type bowmen, with spikes on the tips of their noses made of beetles' antennae. Several men wore penis-guards (long curly bean gourds attached at the top with bush-string) while the women wore double-layered grass skirts, were bare-breasted and carried 'bilums' (net bags slung from a hoop across the forehead) full of firewood. Eventually two men with wild pigs' tusks through their noses stepped forward saying, 'Yu-mi go long wokabout.'

The two-week-long walk was a salutary introduction to the journey ahead. Christina was unaccustomed to the altitude and found her lungs straining with lack of oxygen. She abandoned her sandals, which had turned slimy with wet clay and found that, bare-foot, it was easier to clamber over the trees which bridged the numerous ravines. They spent three nights at the occasional huts along their route where the local tribespeople, after overcoming their amazement and disbelief at the sight of a lone woman traveller, were hospitable and shared their evening meal of *kaukau* – a type of sweet potato. At Sisimin the river was in full flood and everyone tried to dissuade her from making the crossing. Her guides were ready to return home, but two Hewa men appeared who said they also wanted to swim across. Their appearance was somewhat startling – their earlobes were stretched around bamboo hoops and their nostrils were pierced at the side with crossed feathers inserted as nose quills. But they found Christina's appearance equally strange and soon she was surrounded by a curious crowd. 'Their attention didn't worry me. It seemed that the deeper I travelled into the wilds, the greater was the people's honour and integrity. Also it occurred to me that perhaps their "primitive" moral values were more civilised than in so-called "civilisation".' The first Hewa to attempt the crossing, holding a log float in both hands and kicking with his legs, launched himself into the churning current and to their horror was swept downstream as his float broke apart. Finally he managed to catch a log and made it to the shore. As Christina slipped her wrists through the loops of vine attached to her float, two men held it steady, pointing it at a slight angle upstream. 'Cold, calm terror gripped my stomach, far colder than the icy mountain water around my legs. . . . I kicked my way with desperate determination but was being swept mercilessly downstream . . . nearing the centre of the river, my terror began to turn into a sense of wild exhilaration. Waves were washing over me and I was dragged into heaving rapids. The opposite bank loomed slowly larger. Briefly it flashed through my mind that the gorges must be close and I swam with every last ounce of strength. Closing in on the bank the current was less turbulent, and I dragged myself to the shore. I sat and trembled with fatigue, too tired to feel elated by success.'

With two new guides and her back-pack which had survived the crossing, Christina found herself once more travelling through cannibal country, in the borderlands between three tribal groups: the Hewa, Min and Duna. 'I didn't feel threatened. Partly I think that my safety lay in the fact that I can't imagine why anyone would want to harm me: being a woman is more of a novelty, while a man can be seen as a threat. A woman traveller has advantages over a man. As a woman in the tribes that I've visited, I'm often treated as an honorary man and given the privileges of a man, but the women take me to their huts and teach me cooking. Although I don't have brute physical strength I do have tremendous inner strength, endurance and the ability to withstand hardship without suffering.'

She decided to do the next part of her journey by horse. She managed to acquire a pure-bred Arab stallion from some ranchers who were moving home, and set off to visit a highland clan called the Huli Wigmen who lived in the Tani Basin about 150 miles north-west. The stallion had no name, so she simply called him Horse. Leaving the Ialibu Basin grassland, she rode towards the mountains. One day she stopped at a hamlet where a woman was tattooing a girl's face, using needle and charcoal. The women clustering round all had dots tattooed on their foreheads and noses in the shapes of suns and stars, and parallel lines drawn under their cheekbones and across their faces.

Christina and Horse reached the Tari Basin and she decided to explore the Enga Province, a turbulent region known for the roughness of its mountains and the warring instinct of the Enga clans. She camped at night, trying to make the camp as invisible as possible in order not to attract attention, although even the local hunters were said to be afraid of the dark. One night, with Horse tethered near her and the noise of a waterfall close by, she sat and watched the sun go down. 'Shortly after the sun had set, a full moon had risen. At that altitude the clarity of air made moonlight bright enough to read by. The night was cold but my sleeping bag was warm. At dawn I was woken by some wild dogs. They stopped and stared at us but after several minutes turned and ran away. Soon after, we moved on. I enjoyed being on the Gap, partly because of its desolate atmosphere and bleak sweeping slopes, and partly because there were no people or sign of habitation to show that humans existed. It gave me a tremendous sense of freedom to know that I didn't have to identify myself as a person or justify myself to anyone. I was free to be just part of the land and sky.' Stories about Horse and 'Horse Lady' had spread far and wide and they were always greeted with excitement by the single word '*tua*', meaning 'she comes', by the Enga tribe. Their travels were to become a legend; particularly after the Rodeo.

Christina had heard from one of the missions where she was

resting that a Rodeo was shortly to take place at Mendi. She decided that Horse had become fit in their two months together and might be as fast and sure-footed as the best. She found the other competitors a mixed lot – ranchers, Catholic missionaries, cowboys and American members of the Peace Corps. Christina was the only female participant and entered for the cross country race and the bronco-bucking events. The course ran up and down hills, through bogs and streams and over deep ditches. As the horses surged forward, mud splattered everywhere. Approaching a slippery, angled bank, the leading horse fell and, somersaulting awkwardly, broke its neck. As Christina galloped up the next hill, down a slope with treacherous pot-holes and hurtled towards a muddy stream, she saw four horses floundering shoulder-deep in the muddy track. Another missed its footing and fell into the mud, too. 'I don't think that more than a handful of horses finished the race; we were fourth or fifth. There was no jubilation at the finishing line, just a worried crowd of people pressing for news of fallers. The sadness of the news of the dead horse was shared by everyone.'

Meanwhile a group of wild horses was being herded with some difficulty into the buck-chutes. The bronco-bucking was about to begin. The qualifying time was eight seconds, and as Christina's name was near the bottom of the list, she had time to study the tactics of her competitors. It was forbidden to hold onto the saddle; one hand held the halter rope, leaving the other free. Eventually her name was called. 'I felt composed as I climbed over the chute rails and held myself poised above the stallion's back while someone tightened the cinch. I noticed how every muscle in his back was tense with anger. Lowering myself gently I settled deep into the saddle, my feet seeking the stirrups and taking care not to touch his sides lest he leap into action too soon. The chute-gate rattled open, the stallion hesitated for a second, then sprang out into the arena. Suddenly it was real, he was bucking like crazy, the jerking jack-knife of his movements jarring and wrenching my body in every direction at once. A sharp twisting thrust nearly dislodged me, and I doubled the grip of my knees. In the whirling confusion of my mind I noticed that I hadn't yet fallen off and felt strangely relaxed. Only a few seconds could have passed; mud was spraying up from his plunging hooves, and through it the crowd was a vague roaring blur. Then inevitably I lost my balance and, knowing I was about to fall, kicked my feet out of the stirrups and let go. I felt a flying sensation, and landed unhurt in the mud. People said I was laughing as I staggered from the arena.' As she went up to receive third prize, the crowd cheered wildly.

Christina enjoyed her temporary celebrity, but soon became restless: once again, it was time to move on and the fact that no foreigner (let alone a woman) had ever tried to paddle down the Sepik River whetted her appetite for a new adventure. Looking down from the small plane which was taking her to Ama near the frontier of West Irian on the upper Sepik River, she could see the flat, wide river valley running east to west between the coastal hills and New Guinea's mountainous back. In her rucksack she carried provisions: salt, corned beef, rice, sugar, coffee and tea, plastic bags, flashlight batteries, gifts, and a fishing line and hooks.

On the ground the heat was oppressive. A government canoe took her to a village on the May River where the headman arranged for her to buy from one of his wives a small sturdy canoe, hollowed from a tree trunk. The price was 15 kina (£11). 'I put my backpack in the middle and sat at the back. It was just wide enough for me to fit comfortably. Villagers gathered on the banks to see if I could manage it, so I said my goodbyes and set out downriver at a slick pace. Soon my arms were aching but I didn't want to slow down until I was sure I wasn't being followed. When eventually I felt safe, I relaxed and looked around.'

She had planned to go downriver to where the May joined the Sepik, but the canoe got caught in a back-spinning current and she found herself being pushed upriver instead. Years later she said, 'I'm not a fatalist, but I'm spontaneous without being impulsive – life's a game of chance. I don't stick to my general plan one iota.' Not sticking to her plan took her through swamp forests into an ox-bow lake, and virtually into the arms of a team of crocodile hunters. 'The men moved slowly and silently. I watched and waited. Then suddenly one man ducked underwater and came up holding a wildly thrashing creature. He put it in their canoe and another man raised a bush knife to kill it.' Christina was full of curiosity but, rather than approach them directly, decided to make a fire on the bank and brew tea. When they noticed the smoke they approached and accepted her offer of tea. This was the start of a four-day stay with the hunters. She hung her hammock near to their bush shelter in a lakeside clearing. Every night they went out to 'call' crocodiles, using a flashlight to spot their prey and a long harpoon to catch them, and finally an axe to kill them by hitting the most vulnerable spot just behind the skull. Every morning they skinned the crocodiles. Christina learned this somewhat gruesome art with interest. 'I am no expert at skinning reptiles and it was slow, meticulous work, but I didn't mind dissecting them; it gave me a chance to study them in detail . . . . They roasted steaks from the tails which tasted superb.'

Later in her journey she witnessed the skin-cutting ceremony dedicated to crocodiles. The boys who were awaiting their initiation, or skin-cutting, were kept segregated for seven months in a *haus tamboran* (spirit house), where they learned about the role of men in the tribe, underwent tests and prepared their minds to achieve the trance-like state necessary to endure the ordeal ahead. It was taboo for the young teenagers to be seen by women during their waiting time, but because Christina was treated as an honorary man, they were brought to meet her inside the palm-fronted enclosure which hid their living quarters from the village. Skin-cutting was not compulsory; the decision had been made by each boy's father and uncles. When the day came for the ceremony the boys were led in single file through the village, winding between the huts.

'The atmosphere was charged. The initiates sat on the floor, leaning back onto the chests of their uncles. The first cuts of the razor drew the mark of the crocodile on their stomachs and continued up their chests, shoulders and arms in a wide series of short dashes, representing crocodile scales. Circles were sliced around their nipples like eyes. Blood poured down their bodies and one boy screamed with pain. I felt weak and stunned. After that their backs were cut, the men deftly pinching and slicing the skin in lines from shoulder to thighs, with embellishments mid-back. It was a weird ritual that I watched through a mist of blood. When the cutting was finished their wounds were packed with red mud (reputedly high in sulphur) to ensure that the cuts remained open and that they formed the right scars. Then their skin was anointed with thick, honey-coloured plant oil which was brushed gently onto their skin with white feathers. Exhausted of emotion, they lay quite still with their eyes closed.'

Christina was then asked if she was ready to be marked. She felt unable to refuse. They started by cutting the crocodile's star mark on her shoulder. Blood trickled down her arm and sweat poured down her face. 'I didn't want to disgrace myself by fainting. The crocodile was biting; the women were chanting; the flutes were rejoicing. At the end I felt dizzy but knew it would be a scar I would bear with pride for the rest of my life.'

Back in England, Christina never tried to hide the scars she had received from the Crocodile tribe. Once more she had learned how to deal with pain and fear and had acquired an inner confidence unrelated to the outside world. She felt enriched inside by the accumulation of her experiences among the people of Papua New Guinea. In 1983, Christina returned to the wilderness there with a team to make the first descent of one of the wildest rivers in the world, the Wahgi, or Eater of Men. This was filmed by BBC television for their river journey series which won several international awards.

Like Mary Kingsley before her, Christina was justly proud of her expertise with a dugout and when her unquenchable curiosity took her to China the following year, she once again used her skill when she found herself canoeing on the Yangtse and facing formidable currents and rapids. She was returning to the country where her mother had been born. Later in her house in London, sipping a glass of red wine, she expounded on her reasons for wanting to go to China. 'My grandmother had a restless spirit and loved travel for its own sake as I do now. She used to take my mother on weekend jaunts riding on horseback along the coast of the Yellow Sea. My mother remembers occasionally meeting smugglers coming ashore from the sampans carrying bundles and baskets. Grandma Doris left China on the Trans-Siberian railway just before the outbreak of the Second World War. She died when I was nine – I only remember her in a wheelchair crippled with arthritis. I wanted to follow in her footsteps and rediscover the temples and monasteries she had described in her journals. In fact, I was unsuccessful for, according to the peasants I asked, most of them had been destroyed. But although I lost the trail I didn't consider this a failure. To be there in the country where she had travelled and remembering all the stories told to me by my grandfather brought the past to life. But now I wanted to blaze my own trail.'

Her trail was to take her to the fabled city of Kashgar and along Marco Polo's route to Beijing, past the ruined cities of the old Silk Road (which once linked China to Europe) and on to Xinjiang where she camped with the migrating Kazakhs. She stayed at a famous lamasery and visited the oldest surviving frescoes in China. But her most precious moments were off the tourist track, camping alone on the edge of an ice-bound lake, climbing a remote sacred mountain in Yunnan Province, its monasteries desecrated during the Cultural Revolution, or paddling her small craft cautiously into the mighty Yangtse.

She had no romantic expectations of Urumchi, the state capital of Tartary where she started her journey. Peter Fleming, who was there in 1935, wrote about banquets where the guests were beheaded one by one, and in 1930 the missionary travellers wrote: 'No one enjoys Urumchi ... it is full of people who are only there because they cannot get permission to leave.' But Christina wanted to explore the newly opened city of Kashgar, where the crossroads of Asia met. The basic Mandarin she had learnt before leaving England proved invaluable in spite of the fact that she found that many of the people didn't speak Chinese.

On the bus she was the only European. The other passengers were Han tribesmen in their drab costume, Turkis and Uighurs. After four days they arrived at Kashgar. Approaching the town over the Samir Mountains, Marco Polo had described 'a fifty-day march along elevated peaks and summits which seemed to be the highest in the world.' A road leads up into the Pamirs, linking China with Pakistan. It is not usually open to foreigners but, together with a Danish boy called Peter, Christina managed to obtain a permit and hitched a lift in a truck which was going to the Pakistan border. As they rode up, round the base of Mount Kongur, the cold became intense. 'It felt like being on top of the world; its lunar scenery was bare and barren, sharks' teeth mountains stretched in long ridges, capped with snow and ice.' Christina parted from the truck and Peter, as she wanted to try her inflatable canoe (which she had been carrying in her backpack) on Lake Karakol, the blue lake created by thick glaciers melting off Mustagh Ata. Sven Hedin had paddled across it, surveying the area in 1884, and had nearly drowned: she hoped to fare better. 'The altitude was probably about 11,800 foot, the wind gusted, the lake became choppy and despite wearing every piece of clothing I'd got, I became bitterly cold.'

She found a river outlet, which followed the base of the vast Kongur mountain and then descended down through an area of silvery white sand mountains. 'The beauty was something special. Perhaps it was enhanced by being so little known and untraversed. At this point the river was not fast and although there were some long, semi-turbulent stretches, they looked rougher than they really were. At one of the quieter pools I stopped to have a short rest and munch on some dried food. It was rather idyllic. I doubted that the river had ever been run before, since for most of the year it's swollen and totally unnavigable. But being the first wasn't important, I wasn't trying to achieve anything. I just wanted to try out my canoe.' It was a short voyage but it was to be a memorable one. An innocent-looking ledge jettisoned the canoe into a barrage of rocks, and it reared up against one which was partly submerged. To Christina's horror the canoe overturned and she floundered towards the bank, swimming a rapid in the process, and was washed up on the shore. She could see the canoe jammed against some rocks ahead. Forgetting her numbness, she ran along the bank and managed to grab its rope and pull it ashore. 'I wanted to stop my canoe journey then and there, but felt I should paddle on until I reached a place to climb out of the gorge and rejoin the road. Despite my wet clothes and miserable state my spirits picked up as I continued downriver. It would be hard to stay depressed in such magnificent landscape.'

After managing to obtain an extension to her visa, Christina explored the Desert Cities and the famous beauty spot in northern Gobi, known as Heaven Lake. Canoeing and trekking further north, she was befriended by some migrating Kazakhs setting up their summer camp. Once part of the Mongol Golden Horde until they became an independent nomadic group in the sixteenth century, their territory was taken away by Russia in the nineteenth century. Now about a million live in China and seven million in Russia.

Famous for the horses they breed and renowned as riders, they call their horses their 'wings' and often value them above their wives. Their shelters were *yurts* – small areas of land with domed felt tents secured by ropes over a round wooden trellis framework with walls made of felt from sheep's wool. Splitting into family groups, they laid claim to hillocks and unpacked their laden oxen and cattle. Christina entertained the children while their parents erected their tents. 'There was something in *yurt* life which appealed to me. Perhaps it was the warm hospitality of the old metal stoves with a kettle keeping hot on the hearth to replenish your tea, or the attraction of a life which flows with the seasons. Perhaps the nomads' success in living their insecure existence comes from not clutching at the illusion of stability. Their *yurt* homes show what we house-dwellers may have forgotten, that security is a state of mind.'

At Dunhwang, a city in Gansu Province, the north and south arms of the Silk Road meet, and roads converge from Lhasa, Mongolia, India and Siberia. Christina travelled there by train in a six-berth sleeping compartment which she shared with a family of White Russians. When she entered the region of the Black Gobi, she hired a camel and rode amongst the sand dunes surrounding a crescent-shaped lake; but her main aim was to explore the Magao Caves which date from the fourth century and shelter the oldest surviving frescoes in China. When Aurel Stein was there in 1907, he bought some scrolls and manuscripts which he sent to the British Museum. One block-printed roll dating from AD 868 was recognised as being the world's earliest example of a printed book. In *A Traveller in China* Christina describes her visit to the caves together with a young nurse whom she had met in her hotel dormitory. They were so carried away by exploring the caves that they missed the last bus back to town and had to hitch a lift with a busload of Chinese factory workers. Later that week they visited Nan-Hu, an oasis sixty miles from Dunhwang which was once called the 'Barrier of the Sun'. A ruined watchtower marked the barrier on the pass between the Lob Desert and the Tsaidam Basin, an important site in 100 BC, guarding the entrance to the southern arm of the Silk Road. 'It is a beautiful spot ... the vast plain beyond the barrier had been the site of Sachu city, though nothing now remains. What excited me was knowing that beyond the horizon and on and on lies only desert, to stand gazing at its unconfined immensity brought a feeling of elation.'

After visiting the Great Wall at its furthest point inland and travelling further east along the Silk Road through Ningxia, Christina reached Beijing and tried to track down her mother's old home. It proved to be extremely difficult. She had the address: 57 Sui An Pou Hutang, which was near the Old Tartar Wall, but when she came to No. 57 it turned out to be a modern concrete bungalow. An old woman told her all the numbers had been changed and took her to a three-storey house which fitted the description her mother had given her. The resident of the house said that she had been told that foreigners had indeed lived there and had kept many pets, including dogs, a donkey and four or five racing ponies. As the Chinese are not fond of animals, this had stuck in their minds more than the human inhabitants. Christina was glad to have tracked down her grandmother Doris's last home in China, but now it was time for her to continue on her own trail and to search out some lesser-known territory.

Her search was to take her to a remote province bordering Tibet called Quinghai Autonomous Region, also known as 'Inner Tibet' – the most sparsely populated province in China. After obtaining a special permit to be in the Xining area, she hitch-hiked towards Lake Qinghai – the largest lake in China. The driver of the truck said he was going to Lhasa – why didn't she come? 'Of course I longed to go to Tibet but I had no permit. It seemed unnecessary to look for trouble and possible deportation.' She hit on a compromise. Her permit prohibited her from stopping in any towns which were not listed on it, but didn't state that she couldn't be in the surrounding areas. She asked to be dropped at a Tibetan nomad camp anywhere in the mountains before reaching Lhasa. They drove for three-and-a-half days, sometimes sleeping in the truck, sometimes at truckers' inns. 'It was a relief to feel I could travel as an individual without sex hassles. Chinese men don't look at you with that sort of eye.' The driver reluctantly let her off about halfway across Tibet, in an area dotted with tents, but he said he would be back in three days' time and would pick her up.

As she wandered across the valley, the camp seemed deserted and fierce Tibetan dogs were chained to the tents, but towards evening people started to appear and one family offered her shelter. Her days at the camp were spent helping to round up yaks and take them to greener pastures, milking them and ear-tagging the family's sheep. Braving the fierce dogs and armed with a pocketful of stones, she would go on long walks in spite of the intense cold. 'My walks were the only opportunities I got for washing – a custom my hosts didn't seem to use. Some believe that not washing saves them from being turned into fishes after their death, or that spring water contains evil spirits because it comes from inside the earth where the female principle rules. The water only becomes good if exposed to sun and air, part of the male upper world.'

Christina had read ancient accounts of a lamasery called Kumbum, which had ranked third among Tibet's most sacred monasteries and once housed more than 3,000 monks. Once again, names had changed and people shook their heads at the name. After showing them her photocopies of old maps, she discovered it was still a functional monastery now called Taer'si. 'In the centre stands the Grand Hall of the Golden Roof, whose gold-plated bronze roof is supported by marble walls. I didn't try to find a way into the Hall, being content to listen and watch the rays of sun stealing over the tiled roof. Mist was rising slowly from the valley below, the drums were beating, growing faster and more rhythmical and I could smell fresh bread being baked somewhere nearby. When the first rays of sun touched the temple doorsill, the formal meditation period ends.' The following day she ate the evening meal with the *sannyasis* (novice monks). 'It was a glittering scene: the red and gold prayer wheels surrounding the temples, green and gold roofs, carved pillars, marble and incense. There were about two hundred and fifty monks in residence. The chanting of the monks and the pilgrims joined together in a pulsating chorus, as they were led into their evening meditation period.'

Still following Marco Polo's route, Christina travelled by train to Kunming and Yunnan, searching out the many different minority groups which ranged from the Wa head-hunters, whose village lanes used to be edged with human skulls on posts, to the tribes who, until the 1950s, kept slaves and had feudal systems. Marco Polo wrote of animists and nature-worshippers, people who excelled in magic and the search for the secrets of immortality. Indeed one of his reasons for visiting Yunnan was to look for the elixir of life. Christina had come to look for a strange beauty spot: the stone forest of Shilin. She chose the smaller, unmapped paths through mossy dungeons and water dripping into pools. Climbing upwards led her into a different world. 'Soaring pinnacles made shapes like cathedral arches. Fir trees in high crevices were stark outlines against the sky. I didn't see anyone until finally I emerged onto a sharp ridge overlooking the mass of the stone forest.'

The bus journey from Kunming to Dali along the Burmese road built during the Second World War takes only a day. When Marco Polo travelled by mule along the same route it took him nearly two weeks. In Dali, Christina met a couple of people who told her of a sacred mountain – Ju Jie Shan – which was two bus rides and a pony-cart ride away. The next day they all set off but after two bus journeys they still had forty miles to go. Christina would have looked for a horse but as her companions were not used to riding they decided on a pony cart. They knew there had been 350 monasteries on the mountain in times past, and around 5,000 monks, but they had no idea what, if anything, still existed. The driver of the cart said that no foreigner had ever come that way before. They spent the night at an inn near the foot of the mountain. The people were friendly, but the rooms rat-infested. Early the next morning they took a rocky, slippery path up towards the lower slope. The mist obscured the summit. But after about four hours they saw the impressive gates of a monastery. 'According to one of the monks its heyday was in the Ching Dynasty in the twelfth century. Now it has only nineteen monks and eleven nuns. One I talked to was seventy years old – she wore a black woollen beret and blue tunic and trousers. Her role was the daily cleaning of the temples, which left her one-and-a-half hours for prayer and meditation.'

Before they departed, the monks showed them a map, marking all the old monasteries on the mountain, but they said that apart from a couple of temples and a monastery on the summit, they had all been destroyed during the Cultural Revolution. As the travellers continue their upward climb they passed many ruined temples with old beams and timber charred black. The forest had begun to obliterate the remains. As twilight faded into night they reached the summit monastery. An old monk seemed delighted to see them, prepared tea and showed them straw pallets where they could sleep. He told them he had lived there for fifty years and had hidden there during the Cultural Revolution, and that he had once had fourteen novices. He now had one, a Kunming boy. He told them that most of the pilgrims came from southern Tibet and some of the inscriptions were written in Tibetan script. 'Finally, exhausted, we retreated to the damp straw pallets with wet covers and a copious number of rats. Somewhere along the line I had also picked up fleas. The itching awoke me soon after dawn and without hope of further rest I went out to look at the mountaintop – its rounded summit with cliffs dropping sheer from one side and on the topmost point on the edge of the cliff stands a tall pagoda. With the dawn light and swirling mists it was almost ethereal.'

But the climax of Christina's Chinese adventures was to see her once more paddling her tiny canoe, this time on the mighty Yangtse. She had left most of her luggage in Dali and was intending to spend a few days gently moving downriver. Paddling lazily, she could see beyond the river banks the fertile plains cultivated with emerald green rice. Women bent over the paddies, thinning out the shoots. After a few miles the stream flowed into a gorge and as she approached the foaming water ahead and gathered speed, rocks poked out of the water, making minor rapids.

'For a moment, when a strong eddy pushed me broadside against two rocks and the current roughed up against us things got serious but, digging my paddle fiercely backwards and throwing my weight onto the canoe's high side, I managed to free the prow and slid safely between the rocks. The moment made me cross with myself; a professional would never have let it happen.' She camped at night on the banks of the river and by day paddled through the turbulent waters. The gorge grew deeper and craggier and in one fast patch a broad but invisible rock caused a trough which held her in its eddy.

'I was in what canoeists call a hole. Equally abruptly we were free, racing downriver into some rocky turbulence and chutes. Running them gave me a tremendous thrill and sense of exhilaration which is timeless. The gathering speed of the current made me hope that I hadn't taken on more than a sensible person would do. It's not necessary to kill oneself; neither to be so cautious that risk is nil.'

When the rapids became really dangerous she took to the bank, carrying her canoe under one arm and her rucksack under the other. Around a bend, she saw that the river converged with another, even larger river. Looking at her map she realised they had now joined the Upper Yangtse. Back in the water, she was instantly swept right out into the middle. 'On the far horizon I noticed a long bridge road but it came no closer; my canoe was going in a parallel direction. I wished we were nearer the shore.' When she did reach the shore she got a lift in a truck towards Lijiang, so avoiding the roughest part of the river where it plunges into a narrow gorge and becomes stupefying in its power. But at the next bend, she left the surprised truck driver and once again put her canoe into the water. 'The largest chute was still ahead, far larger than anything this canoe had tried before. . . . It raced down the chute and plunged into the chaos below. Water came pouring in from both sides, but I told myself that inflatable boats cannot sink. We were virtually under water but I was still sitting there, thrilled to have made it through in one piece.' It was her last adventure before her return to England.

Christina Dodwell has never embarked on a journey with a prior commitment to publish a book. She feels this would inhibit her sense of freedom of movement and that the journey must make the book. Being thrifty and abstemious she has never felt the need of the security which comes from possessions. A capable craftswoman, she could make her own saddles and tack and could improvise in most situations. This self-sufficiency enabled her to live on a tiny income. But on her return she wrote *A Traveller in China*, describing her journey by land, lake and river in a country which is constantly changing and redefining its internal philosophy and political values, but never ceases to fascinate. The book was an immediate success and she was described as coming from the same mould as the great inveterate woman traveller – Dame Freya Stark. She has also been described as a natural nomad with an insatiable wanderlust. 'I don't want to follow in other people's footsteps – although that's not my criterion. Not really making plans ahead, I find the route gets built in the doing. It could be easy to travel to the exclusion of everything else but I want to live fully, too.' She comes from a very close family and relishes the reunion and being able to spend time with them again – 'Real time, not just the odd day.' But aged thirty-six she decided to leave England once again, this time to explore Eastern Turkey and then move further east over the border into Iran.

It was 1986 and the early stages of her adventures in Turkey and Iran were idyllic. Once again people tried to dissuade her from travelling alone, saying that it was too dangerous and she might be killed. Her instinct told her this was unlikely, yet when she arrived at the Iranian border, near Maku, she found the atmosphere decidedly surly. All the local women were wearing *chadoors*, leaving only their eyes and nose showing. Christina was dressed in trousers, a long-sleeved shirt and a headscarf which she swathed round her face. Taking a bus along the historic traffic route from Tehran to Gonbad-el-Kauus, she visited the famous tomb-tower there, which Robert Byron had described as one of the four most beautiful structures in Iran. But the tomb's brickwork had been pockmarked by bullets during the revolution. As she was hitching a lift outside Gonbad, a van with its sirens wailing screeched to a halt across the road. 'Bearded men grabbed hold of my arms, pushed me into the van, threw my backpack in after me and with sirens still wailing drove to the headquarters of the Revolutionary Guard.

'We parked in a prisoners' exercise yard and I was hauled over towards the cells. My protests and resistance met with rough treatment; the guards shoved me over to a cell door and unlocked it.

'Inside was dimly lit through a barred window; it was a tiny cell with four dirty bunk beds, already occupied by three women who cowered back in fear. Every fibre in my body screamed NO, but things were happening so fast that I hardly knew how to react. Whatever the penalty, I wasn't going into that cell, suspecting that once you're locked inside it's easy for people to forget you're there.

'"Take off your shoes." The guard indicated I must leave my shoes outside the door.

'"First tell me what I've done wrong," I requested.

'"No, take off your shoes," he snapped back. So I bent down and unbuckled one sandal, then stood up and asked to speak to the boss. "No," he yelled, "take off your shoes." After slipping one sandal off I tried a fresh protest which met with some expletives in Farsi. So I put one sandal back on and took the other one off, trying a new argument between each move. I was playing for time, hoping that someone might see us from an office window and intervene.

'Eight times I managed to take off one shoe and put on the other! Then just as the guard lost his temper an officer appeared, and he beckoned us back into the exercise yard. There he searched my handbag and confiscated my passport and the dictionary of Farsi words that I had been trying to build up. (It had been impossible to buy a Farsi dictionary written in western alphabet, so I had begun making one in a notebook.) "That's not incriminating," I said. "Look, these words are mother, father, house, village." But the officer couldn't read my alphabet and he seemed to think I was lying. He couldn't speak English, none of them knew more than "No" and "Take off your shoes", and without my dictionary I couldn't speak any Farsi. They locked me in a solitary cubicle which adjoined a row of cells, and left me for four hours.

'My mind was in turmoil, going from bewilderment to anger and down to despair. There was one brief interruption when a guard came in but he wouldn't tell me why I was being held, and he refused my request to telephone my ambassador. Although the British no longer have an embassy in Iran I knew that British problems are handled by the Swedish Embassy. It seemed I had no rights at all.

'Later another guard came in carrying a prison dress, which he told me to put on, but I refused politely saying that I'd not come to stay. He left me again, clanging the door and locking it behind him.

'This time I was more active, and by talking through the grille of one of the adjoining cells I located a male prisoner who could speak some English. I explained that when an opportunity arose he must ask on my behalf why I was under arrest. Outside the daylight faded into night.

'Mosquitoes arose in clouds. Supper time came: bread and soup. I refused to eat but the men in the next cell asked if I would mind giving them my share, so I slid the bowl in under their grille.

'And such was my welcome to Iran.

'At exercise time all the male prisoners were released into the yard. Some uniformed men were standing to one side, and I called to my English-speaking ally, "Please ask now."

'This led to me being taken out for interrogation, with my ally as translator, and finally the problem became clear. When I had entered Iran the frontier police had stamped an extra piece of paper with my entry details, and these Revolutionary Guards had noticed the police stamp and assumed that I'd been in trouble with the police.

'The officer waved the paper at me, I explained it was a frontier formality, and suddenly they all began to laugh. My arrest had been a mistake. They apologised and asked me not to think badly of Iran. Would I like some tea and sweet pastries?'

This was by no means the only time she was to get into trouble with the authorities. She was returning in a pick-up truck with a Kurdish friend, Ardeshir, from the Valleys of the Assassins, when they were arrested outside Mahabad at a road block and driven to the local Revolutionary Guard headquarters.

The guards searched through her baggage, throwing the contents in the dirt. Ardeshir was taken for interrogation and she was left on her own to worry for several hours. 'I closed my eyes but was sharply reprimanded: sleep was not permitted. At one point my guard was a boy of about thirteen years old, fingering his machine gun restlessly and refusing my requests for him to fetch his seniors or someone who could speak English. The only successful request was for the loo. On the way back I saw a flashy jeep enter the yard and persisted in my argument to see the boss; this attracted their attention and I reached an officer. The next five hours followed an almost familiar pattern, similar to my first arrest in Gonbad but with the addition of continual searches. However, in the searches they ignored my diaries, and were mainly interested in the pictures on my old tourist map of Quetta and my photographs of home. At times I felt angry and so helpless but kept my temper, even when I was blindfolded and locked up. All my luggage and papers were confiscated, Ardeshir's car was confiscated .... It was a twenty-one-hour ordeal.'

The root of the problem was that they were apparently in a war zone and the guards had no specific work to do, apart from terrorising the Kurds. Eventually Christina was released but she refused to leave until Ardeshir and their car were also freed. 'Not a popular idea; from the *pastares*' expressions it looked likely I would be re-arrested. But perseverance and dignity were the keys, and by 2 p.m. Ardeshir and I were speeding out of town .... When the time came to take leave of him in Tabriz, we looked at each other and burst out laughing. We had shared a slice of life together and had developed the bond of those who share adversity. We shook hands and said farewell.'

By now it was July and Christina was about to fulfil the original purpose of her journey, which was to travel on horseback around the remoter regions of Turkey. Crossing the border, the atmosphere at the immigration post was as if the clouds cleared and the sun shone through. 'You may take off your *mantau* and your scarf. Your permit is valid for three months. Welcome to Turkey.'

At Erzurum she visited the bazaar and bought a fine grey stallion for 300,000 Turkish lira (£300) which included his tack; the bridle had beautifully beaded straps and the browband had a small round mirror inset in beadwork and four beaded tassels. His name was Keyif, meaning 'high spirited'. 'As to where Keyif and I should travel, I flipped a coin. This decided we would go first to Lake Van, about 145 miles to the south-east; we could then loop around the lake and head north via Ararat and up into the north-east. It would take at least two months to ride that far.'

Christina tells the story of her journey in *A Traveller on Horseback*. She rode through hamlets and villages where no foreigners had been seen before. Women would reach up to touch her breasts, not believing that a solitary woman on horseback would be travelling in such remote areas, particularly as she dressed as a man with her long hair caught up in a man's hat. However, she was always given shelter and food. As the peasants were too proud to accept any payment she would give presents of lighters to the men and scarves and earrings to the women. At one village named Gumuslu, she and Keyif entered a scene of festivity. A family was celebrating a *sunnet* or circumcision ceremony. Two boys aged four and six had just been circumcised and the family proudly showed their bandaged cuts. Relatives had travelled long distances to attend the event, and there was singing and dancing to the accompaniment of guitars. All feasted on beef and stuffed peppers with sheep's yoghurt served on a big round tray in the middle of the floor. Later,

Christina was offered a bath: she was taken into a dark smoky room and put in a shallow tin tub, where the women poured jugs of hot water over her and scrubbed her all over.

The following day she headed off towards a snow-capped mountain range. She had been warned that she would be crossing bandit country and was told not to stop in the Hinis region. 'When we reached the summit we seemed to be higher than the snowy range ahead . . . it was like being part of the sky more than the land.'

In spite of the warning she was determined to pass through. Although she got completely lost on several occasions, attacks by bandits were the least of her worries. On one occasion, she and Keyif met two wild horses who turned out to be stallions. Christina was all too aware that stallions often fight other stallions invading their territory, and she tried to make her escape – but she was too late. 'I saw the larger horse rear up above me and begin striking out with his forelegs. Fortunately I had the long end of Keyif's halter rope in my hand, so I swung it in rapid circles. The knotted end caught him on the nose, he snorted and wheeled away, kicking savagely out with his hind hooves. I kept whirling the rope until we were able to escape.' A few days later they were surrounded by a swarm of bees and only got rid of them by riding through a herd of goats. They crossed a mountain divide making for Lake Ercek and then rode north across a flat plain. The road led close to the Iranian border and she was twice stopped at army outposts. 'At the second outpost the soldiers who checked my passport relayed the news that here was a girl, and when I explained that I'd ridden from Erzurum via Van they all began to applaud.' She took a short cut over the mountains to Dogubayazit along a dry riverbed which steepened into a ravine. 'Then slowly I saw the summit of Mount Ararat appearing above my ridge. A shepherd was playing his flute to his sheep. Its notes were reedy and zingy and its song carried in the breeze over the hills. Some young shepherd boys sauntered over to say hello and respectfully called me *Agha*, a man's title.' Having been stoned by shepherd boys earlier, Christina thought about the line between distrust and caution. 'I prefer to trust people than to expect the worst, believing that in general one has a choice over whether one brings out the good or the bad in people.'

Continuing her ride to Digor and Ani her philosophy let her

down. Ani, the capital city of the Armenians' greatest dynasty, now straddles the Russian border and a special military pass is required by visitors. Christina was hoping to acquire one on her arrival, but was prematurely arrested by the police and taken to their head-quarters at Kars. They bombarded her with questions: '"Why was I avoiding the road?" "Why was I travelling so near the Russian border?" "Was I particularly interested in Kurds?" My letter from the Royal Geographical Society which states that I am non-political and merely studying village customs and rural life cut not a lot of ice, but by a stroke of luck a film I made for the BBC had been shown that very week on Turkish television.' It helped . . . but her interrogators still made an itemised search of her saddle-bags and put her into prison accusing her of being without a permit. At one stage she was threatened with deportation. 'We played some little power games but the police treated me with courtesy and eventually a permit was produced and Keyif and I were released.'

Before Christina's Turkish journey came to an end, she was to be arrested again at Kars and interrogated at Erzurum, but nothing could detract from her extraordinary and unique experiences. The farthest north-easterly point she reached was Ardahan, where Turkey bulges into Georgian Russia. In Çeltik Kuzu she met a forest ranger who wanted to buy Keyif. Feeling unable to part with him, she at first refused. 'But it was time, we had now finished our journey and Keyif deserved a long fattening rest and he would be well cared for.' She accepted the ranger's offer and caught a bus to Erzurum. 'Through the window I kept catching glimpses of the mountains Keyif and I had crossed, things I'd seen from high above, distant villages we'd been to. Some people in the bus knew my story and were telling how far we had travelled and when someone asked if I'd had a good horse, the men replied yes, and a very beautiful one.'

Back in Shepherd's Bush, Christina said, 'I think it was the happiest time of my life – it was glorious – Keyif made it because all he wanted to do was to put his head up and canter over the hills. It was towards the end of my journey high up in the mountains where just every other mountain seemed lower than we were. I never wanted that trip to end.' A mist had prevented her from reaching the summit of Mount Ararat, but this had never been her objective. 'I didn't mind about not reaching the summit. One cannot fail unless one sets out to succeed. Goals are like destinations, they don't always matter. Our journey was enough in itself. When I return here what I most enjoy is having my own key to my own space.'

She takes pride in the narrow rambling three-storeyed house. Each room has its own identity and purpose and Christina, an excellent carpenter, has built some of the furniture herself, including a chest of drawers in the living room to house all her tools. Her latest pride is her roof-garden, spilling over with wild roses, clematis and sweet peas and reached by climbing a ship's ladder through the skylight. 'I should have used hard wood, but this will have to do.' Behind her bed she has painted an acacia tree which climbs across the ceiling. Her boyfriend is understanding and supportive about her chosen career. 'He still thinks I'll just go off one day and not come back – but he's wrong. Maybe we'll marry, but our marriage won't be of the conventional variety.'

After publishing *A Traveller on Horseback* Christina was eager to return to her first love – West Africa. In order to reach the more remote regions, she decided to acquire a new skill. 'Just when you know how to do something is the time to move on – otherwise you stagnate. I hate complacency.' She had just read Saint-Exupéry's *Wind, Sand and Stars* and was so inspired by his description of being 'no more than a mortal strayed between sand and stars . . . of seeing from the air what is invisible from the ground, enthralled by the sorcery of flying' that she was determined to learn to fly. Microlighting could have been invented for Christina's method of travel. 'You're not enclosed; you can land on a mere seventy-five yards; you can detach the wings and fold the whole thing into two parcels when you get tired of it.' Despite her preference for solo travel, she decided to acquire a Pegasus two-seater and a professional pilot who could teach her to fly *en route*. No one had ever attempted to cross West Africa by microlight before, and people tried to persuade her to fly down the eastern side. In fact one diplomat said, 'She doesn't have a snowball's chance of making it.' But Christina has always preferred the unknown.

David Young, a professional pilot who had only been abroad

once or twice, was enthusiastic when she suggested the job of accompanying her on a seven-thousand-mile flight starting from the equatorial rain-forests of Cameroon, flying north to Lake Chad, then through northern Nigeria across sahel and desert, into Agadez in Niger and the remote desert mountains of mid-Sahara. From Niger to Gao and Tombouctou in Mali, then Mauritania and down along the Atlantic beaches to Dakar in Senegal. 'Perhaps it was a bit ambitious but there was only one way to find out.' It was the reversal of everything she had previously stood for. This time she would have to get sponsors and pre-plan everything in detail. Mobil Oil agreed to stash fuel in jerrycans for them throughout the route – in the remote places, jerrycans would be left at military outposts or with the chiefs of the villages. In return Christina agreed to have the flying horse emblem on Pegasus' wings.

At first she didn't enjoy the sensation of flying their tiny craft. 'Sitting with the belt tied round me and feeling the ripples and turbulence in the air, I felt utterly unsafe. Put me on a crazy African stallion, I'm fine, but it was probably just as well I didn't realise beforehand the complications we'd encounter – the unpredictability of the wind, the endless engine failures, the bent propellers, running out of fuel.' But gradually as the journey went on she became more philosophical: 'Who cares if we do have to suddenly come down – I can always walk away or borrow an animal.'

In her book *Travels With Pegasus*, she tells how they nearly came to grief towards the end of their adventure, flying to Mauritania. They had been buffeted by thermals over massive rice paddies when their fuel became critically low, and with only about six minutes of flying time they decided to land on what looked like flat, smooth dry mud. But as they touched down they saw an irrigation ditch right across their path. David put on full power and they managed to hop over the ditch and landed at speed, only to find two further ditches ahead. Cleverly negotiating the ditches, David managed to stop just short of a fourth channel and Christina made some facetious comments about entering Pegasus for the next Grand National. But the delights of flying more than compensated for the disasters, and Christina particularly loved flying low over Mauritania. Pilots had told her they had seen nothing but desert, but flying at only a thousand feet, she got a totally different perspective.

'You can see camel trains, families on the move with their donkeys, the wonderful geometrical and geographical patterns of the canyons, the mushroom-shaped clumps of rocks, the tombs and burial grounds – sometimes we could see a distance of a hundred miles.'

Amelia Earhart had been exactly Christina's age when she took the same course across Africa in the 1930s, setting out to fly solo round the world. She was three-quarters of the way when she went missing while flying over Papua New Guinea, and no trace of her was ever found.

At one time, after taking off from Ngaoundere in Cameroon, Christina looked down from her flying horse and could see to the west the line of her horseback journey of 1975. 'It felt a world apart, yet, just here, crossing my tracks, life felt timeless.'

Even at the start of their journey the inexplicable engine failures began. The plane really ran better on rougher fuel and David had to calibrate the engine to get it running on high octane fuel. At every stop he would tinker with the machine and as the journey went on, he became more and more worried, his health deteriorated and he began to lose weight. Christina would leave him to try and sort out the problems while she took off by horse, camel, truck or canoe to journey into the unknown.

Once, returning from a peaceful camel ride through the Air Mountains in Niger, she found David very sick. 'He was still getting agonising bouts of stomach cramps and had all the symptoms of ghardia. . . . Often we had joked about the way I looked after him like I've looked after my travelling horses, trying to keep him fit and strong, watching and not pushing him too hard. This time I resorted to saying meanly, "If you were my travelling horse, I'd sell you." '

It was in Gall that Christina was to experience the most thrilling event of the journey. Leaving the depressed David to deal with repairs, she set out in a Land Rover to explore a region where someone on a recent hunting trip had reported seeing some unusual fragments of bones. She returned to the same spot and found some low mounds in the sand that were speckled with white. 'I saw that they were fragments of huge bones . . . skeletons . . . sticking out was an outsize thigh bone four foot long.' Later she found an even larger bone measuring over six foot. She had discovered a whole mass of dinosaur remains. 'Actually it was like magic to scoop back sand from the bones and reveal these skeletons and realise they hadn't been disturbed since they lay down to die and then I had to cover them up. It gave me the feeling that one sometimes gets as a traveller of a tremendous sense of privilege – something I'll have for the rest of my life.' On her return to England, the Natural History Museum identified the bones as having belonged to a four-legged camarasaur and the experts reckoned that, alive, Christina's specimen would have measured about sixty feet from snout to tail. The large leg bone is now displayed in the Museum.

Christina's first solo flight was along the coast of Mauritania. 'My main problem was that the accelerator was sticking so my first landing came in much too fast. I put in an extra flaring check, mistimed something, hit the ground and bounced back into the air. Then, remembering my pitch control, I brought her down more neatly.' On her second landing she missed the runway and landed on the verge and on the third the propeller was damaged again. But her big moment was at the journey's end, piloting Pegasus in to land at Dakar airport. 'Take number one runway,' came the command from the control tower. Christina didn't argue and made a perfect touchdown. 'I had perhaps earned the title of pilot.' In spite of a sorcerer's prediction in a Cameroon village that the journey would be completed without major injury, Christina had never believed they would reach the end in one piece.

Standing in her house in London in front of a photo of the dinosaur bone, she said, 'I had so much good luck and found more than I'd expected to. I don't believe anyway that you ever find what you set out to find – things don't happen that way. I just want to have a journey and in that context all sorts of other things will happen. But I suppose my favourite moments have been travelling alone. Loneliness is something I suffer from in a city or in a crowd of people. Travelling alone is not lonely; it's an extremely powerful feeling, very similar to love – it's that kind of strength. It's partly the joy of total aloneness – not loneliness – of being part of the land, as far as you can see and knowing there's nobody you need share it with. Once in Papua New Guinea I wrote in my diary, *Why does someone sit alone on a mountaintop, and hold counsel with the rocks and clouds rather than with people?* I believe that if there's any kind of relation between inside and out it is that you can't find what you're looking for while you're looking for it. I don't tend to look inside – I feel all this soul-searching people go in for is a bit self-indulgent. Travelling has taught me to look and to listen and to give thanks.'

Clare Francis

With my own hands I had done my trick at the
wheel and guided a hundred tons of wood and iron
through a few million tons of wind and waves . . .
when I have done some such thing I am exalted. I
glow all over. I am aware of a pride in myself that
is mine and mine alone. It is success.

Jack London

Somewhere in the middle of the Atlantic in 1976 a young woman
sailing her thirty-eight-foot sloop through waves roughly the same
height had just survived her second gale.

'The exhaustion I felt was total. My efforts had drained my
energy and the storm had emptied my mind. I lay on my bunk in a
heap, not bothering to remove my oilskins and too cold to have the
energy to get warm. After a short dream-filled sleep I knew exactly
what I must do. Before I did the navigation, changed another sail or
ate another soggy oatcake, I must wash my hair or, rather, my
"spikes". Standing up like prickles on a hedgehog, fashioned by the
wind and held in place by salt, they defied the hairbrush and itched
like crazy. Wedged against the sink, kettle of fresh water in hand
and shampoo close by, I washed my spikes until they became hair
again. The feeling of relief was immeasurable. I felt a new person.'

In an elegant five-storey house on a secluded tree-lined street in
Kensington, Clare Francis lives with her twelve-year-old son,
Thomas. The ground-floor drawing room, with its bay window
overlooking the garden, is spacious and decorated in pastel shades.
There are neatly arranged rows of silk cushions on the large pale-
grey sofas; a mottled antique mirror hangs over a grand piano and
books on contemporary art and photography lie on the low glass-
topped tables. The minimum of clutter gives an atmosphere of

serenity and order which, apart from a battered violin case, might be the setting for a pampered lady of leisure.

Clare herself looks casually chic, her slight five-feet-one-and-a-half-inch frame curled up in the corner of a sofa, her sleek blonde hair tied back, revealing her high forehead and large brown eyes. When she smiles, showing two deep dimples, she appears the essence of femininity and her direct approach contains a sense of nervous energy. It is August 1990, and she is talking about her next novel, *Requiem*, an environmental thriller. Her books now sell in millions, have been published in twenty-six countries and translated into thirteen languages including Japanese.

It is difficult to believe that this is the same person who was for nearly ten years the best-known woman sailor in the world, competing in the toughest races in a male-dominated profession. In 1976 she became the first British girl to take part in the *Observer* Royal Western Single-Handed Transatlantic Race, and she succeeded in beating the French-held woman's record by completing the course in twenty-nine days, despite the fact that, in terms of the weather conditions, this race was the hardest ever: people died on it for the first time, and one-third of the boats had to drop out. She survived the threat of icebergs, violent gales and a two-week fog. 'The fog was the single, most terrifying thing – fog hides everything – icebergs, ships, fishing fleets like the enormous Russian vessels, not looking at their radars, just concentrating on their fishing. But I don't think there was ever a moment when I thought I was never going to make it.'

Fighting talk – but then Clare has been fighting all her life. She was born in Thames Ditton, Surrey, in 1946, the second daughter of Joan and Owen Francis. Her father was a civil servant who later became chairman of the London Electricity Board and, on the face of it, she and her sister Anne had a happy middle-class upbringing. 'One of my earliest memories was when we were living at Thames Ditton in a part of a manor house, and there was a wonderful garden with a cedar tree and everything happened under the cedar tree. There were always a lot of children because the manor house was split up and it was like a sort of commune.'

She attended the local primary school. The family moved to Esher when she was eight and the sisters went as day girls to Claremont, the local boarding school. 'Looking back, it was a wonderful school because they did believe that girls should have careers and they had very good science.' She was there for four years, and it should have been an idyllic time. But both sisters were dogged by chronic ill-health. Their mother, whose first-born had died when he was only three months old from a hole in the heart, took them to see an eminent specialist. She was particularly concerned about Clare, but it proved to be Anne who was seriously ill and had to have a kidney removed.

From the age of eight, Clare had suffered from a mysterious illness akin to glandular fever, which affected her for four years. 'My digestion stopped dead and I developed severe food allergies. If your gut goes, it does have a profound effect and I didn't feel well for a lot of my teens. I'm sure it turned me inward. I felt pretty bad all the time. I never wanted to play games – I was a real wimp. I couldn't play tennis, I even found the racket too heavy – pathetic! I'd been put into hospital twice but decided hospitals were bad news.'

She began to take ballet lessons to make her tougher, and her teacher suggested she should audition for the Royal Ballet School. 'I didn't know what I wanted but everyone except my father seemed to think it was a good idea and I desperately wanted approval. I didn't seem to have any will of my own. But I did have a very unattractive streak of stubbornness and once I got the idea fixed, I decided to try. When I arrived there, aged twelve, I realised I was years behind the other girls and now I can't forgive myself for not saying immediately that I wanted to give up. But I was too proud to admit that I couldn't cope and there was this closed-up feeling that the world wasn't going to listen to me anyway – which was unfair of me because I'm sure my parents would have listened.'

While she spent hour after hour at the barre, forcing herself to fitness until she could make the graceful movements of a ballerina look easy, she was also studying for her O-levels. Being a year ahead academically, she sat them at fifteen. As she was not considered ready for the Senior School, she took a year off to be privately coached and then was auditioned and accepted. But it was not a happy time. She antagonised authority, marched to a different drum. 'I had one teacher every day for a year who never took any notice of me – never even spoke to me – she just didn't think I was worth bothering with. Most of the other girls would behave sycophantically and they were the ones that got the attention, but it wasn't my way. I put on a brave face but I'm an Aries – too honest for my own good. But ballet taught me that you achieve nothing without a lot of hard work, that you must push your body to its physical limits and then push some more because you know that the only person preventing you from doing it is you.'

Although she had made a dramatic improvement she realised she lacked the talent to become a professional ballet dancer and left the Royal Ballet School after a year. 'But I felt a failure. It's one thing to fail in adulthood, because somehow you get a sense of proportion. As a teenager it's very different. But I thought that if I persevered in purely academic subjects I could win through.' This resulted in four A-levels in two years and a degree in Economics at London University. 'In retrospect, I wish I'd done philosophy or English.'

Leaving university without the slightest idea about what she wanted to do with her life, she drifted into market research, working for Beecham's, and then to another job in marketing with Robertson's, the jam manufacturer. She had by now bought a flat in London. 'I've always had a need for security of that sort – somewhere to curl up and sleep and be alone.' But she was dissatisfied with her life and becoming rather restless. Below the surface was the urge to do something completely different – to prove to herself that she could succeed in her own right.

Since Clare was a child, her parents had been taking a holiday home on the Isle of Wight and they started messing about in boats. But it wasn't until she was twelve that she was really hit by the sailing bug. At seventeen she had her first dinghy. 'It was a wonderful feeling just to be alone with the waves and the wind.' This was the beginning of Clare's love-hate relationship with the sea. A few years later a legacy from a great-uncle enabled her to buy a thirty-two-foot long-keeled Bermuda sloop, *Gulliver G*, and in 1973, on an impulse, she decided to leave her job and take to sea. 'I really just wanted to get away by myself, to read and listen to music and to try and explore something just for *me* – a totally private adventure. I needed to come to grips with what I wanted in life – to give myself a short sharp shock, to take life by the throat and experience something intense – as people years ago would trek across the Himalayas before everyone else was doing it. I felt I had just been going through the motions of living – going to work every day – and I knew that was not for me – there must be something more.'

She had a boyfriend at the time. 'He was an Aries like me and although we had a very sparky and lively relationship, I felt it wasn't the answer and I still had a lot of finding out to do.' In fact the actual decision to cross the Atlantic alone was made when her boyfriend issued the challenge; it was in response to this bet that Clare tackled such a potentially dangerous voyage. With little preparation, apart from teaching herself the rudiments of astronavigation, she set sail from Plymouth to Newport, Rhode Island, completing the crossing in the creditable time of thirty-seven days. 'But I really scared myself, and when I arrived the other side I said, "Never again". It was the most frightening voyage I've done. I was inexperienced and there were lots of nasty moments.' Once she got her navigation slightly wrong and put herself too far north. 'I looked out and there was one of the Azores Islands with a volcano coming out of the sea and because the air was so clear, it looked much closer than it really was – what a shock. I had no radio and was totally out of touch and lonelier than I'd ever been. When you're in a race, although you may be on your own, you can contact people on the radio and also there's the psychological encouragement knowing that people – although miles away – are rooting for you. On this occasion I did see one ship and flew a flag saying, "Please report me to Lloyd's, London" – it seems pretty primitive now. The ship circled round me and they did report my position. My parents danced a jig when they heard.'

One of the worst things Clare suffered on that crossing was constant seasickness; another was the fear of ships running her down. 'Bad weather never really worried me. But in retrospect I suppose it was an extremely selfish thing to have done – I was giving my family enormous worries, which never figured in my decision. But I took good care of myself afloat, and life was so simple, with no complicated psychological decisions to make – only the practical ones and the day-to-day problems. For the first time in my life I could sleep when I felt tired, eat when I was hungry and read when I had the desire. The journey had been a symbol of what I wanted to achieve. I'd done some thinking, written a bit and listened to a lot of music – it gave me a sense of freedom in the knowledge that everything is possible. I realised I hadn't been running away from life but running towards it.'

Although she would probably never admit it, Clare must have been proud of herself. The sickly child, the failed ballerina, the younger sister of Anne (now a successful barrister) had proved that she could succeed in her own right, against all the odds. She no longer had to seek the approval of others.

After the crossing, two friends joined her and they spent some time exploring America's east coast and the Caribbean. By writing a few articles and taking Americans on day charters, she managed to spend the whole of the winter in the West Indies. While she was wondering what to do next, a solution unexpectedly presented itself. Early in 1974 she was encouraged to take part in that summer's two-handed *Observer* Round Britain Race and to be the first all-girl crew to do so. She persuaded Eve Bonham, a great friend, to join her. A sponsor was found, and within an amazingly short time *Gulliver G* found herself with a temporary new name, *Cherry Blossom*, after the well-known brand of shoe polish. 'There were the usual pre-race dramas – a lot of crews fell out with each other and there were the endless jokes about divorces among the married entrants.' Clare had known Eve all her life. 'I used to love staying with her in one or other of the beautiful houses she'd lived in. We were perfectly complementary. Eve would get a little nervous in bad weather and so then I'd do the work, but in calms she'd be great while I'd get totally restless and start muttering to myself. But we had a marvellous time.' She and Eve finished third on handicap, and received their share of acclaim.

This was Clare's introduction to long-distance racing, and she loved it. It was also her introduction to an attractive pipe-smoking Frenchman with blond hair, a dark tan and bright blue eyes. Jacques Redon was a world traveller at heart, but had taken a job as a teacher at a school in Tunisia as an alternative to National Service. He'd then joined an expedition across the Sahara, and in the following years, by working in and around boats in Australia and the Mediterranean, he had worked his passage to take part in the 1973–74 Round the World Race. That summer he'd jumped on a Round Britain boat as a substitute crew. He had no steady job and very little money but, undeterred, they decided to start living together that September.

For a while they lived in Devon, where Jacques found a job refitting a yacht and Clare began to replan her life. There was no doubt that at this time she had become addicted to the racing drug and was already a name in the sailing world. Later she said, 'I'm fairly dismissive of people applauding me on my sailing prowess. I see myself as someone who was fairly blind to the risk, and got away with it. Of course I exerted a lot of determination and had a natural ability to sail, but fame and renown is such a lottery – it rarely bears much relationship to the actual achievement. I think you have to judge yourself by your own standards. "Unto thine own self be true", my father used to say. You're really competing against yourself. Every day when you do your navigation and work out how many miles you've done you think, can I do better? If yesterday you did a hundred miles and today you did a hundred and ten, you get a real kick. I think you have to have a certain pride in yourself to really enjoy life.'

Some of Clare's sailing friends were contemplating taking part in the 1976 *Observer* Royal Western Single-Handed Transatlantic Race, and she got caught up in the excitement. It had begun in 1960 as a wager between Blondie Hasler and Sir Francis Chichester, and was open to all kinds of boats, not governed by the restrictive international racing regulations which required boats to be built 'to the rules'. In 1960 five boats had entered the race; in 1976 there would be a hundred and twenty. Although she kept reminding herself that she had no desire to sail the Atlantic single-handed again, Clare was seduced by the idea that *racing* across would be quite different. 'There would be the companionship of the other competitors, unseen but tangible – the greatest draw of all.'

But before they could start making plans they had to find a boat. Although *Gulliver G* was a tough sea boat, she was not fast. The race was three thousand miles from Plymouth to Newport, Rhode Island, and would take anything from three to five weeks. Clare would be the first British girl to enter and, although no feminist out to beat the men, she knew that there would be a lot of women who would be very disappointed if she dribbled in towards the end of the fleet. Luckily fate intervened when she was made the generous offer of an Ohlson 38 which had been built specially for the Azores and Transatlantic races with the idea of lending her to a worthy entrant. 'How they picked on me, I'm not sure,' Clare said.

The Ohlson was sleek, long and elegant, but after a few trial weekends of sailing, Clare and Jacques realised that with her present rig she would be much too difficult for Clare to handle comfortably, and it was clear that they would need a lot of financial help to pay for the necessary changes. After receiving about fifty negative letters to her requests for sponsorship, Clare became extremely despondent – until one day she happened to get in touch with an ex-colleague from Robertson's who was now the marketing director of the company. Fortunately, they were able to supply a small part of the money. It was an encouraging start. The Ohlson 38 was renamed *Golly*, and had a little golly painted on each bow.

By the New Year of 1975 Clare and Jacques had moved onto *Gulliver G* at Lymington and, with the new boat berthed next door, were able to start work in earnest. The *Yachting Monthly*'s Azores and Back Singlehanded Race was to take place in June as a warm-up and qualifying race for those wanting to enter the Transatlantic Race in the Jester class (for boats under thirty-eight feet in length). There was very little time, and every spare moment they spent sailing, trying to tune the boat to get the best out of her. They modified the rig from a cutter to a sloop, made countless alterations to simplify the sail changing, and exchanged the existing self-steering gear for the powerful and sensitive Gunning which Clare had become experienced with on *Gulliver G*.

As the Azores Race approached, Clare became worried that she had only just managed to clock up the minimum requirement of three hundred miles single-handed in the entry boat to qualify and had never even weathered a gale. As it happened, her fears were groundless: the race was remarkable for the steady following wind on the way down and almost total lack of wind on the way back. Clare finished tenth out of over fifty boats and was once again the darling of the press. On arrival back at Falmouth there was a bad outbreak of what to single-handers is known as 'Never Again' disease. Many of them reversed their decision to enter the Transatlantic Race, some denying they had even contemplated such a mad idea. It is certainly not a race to be undertaken lightly, described by various newspapers as 'the toughest race in the world', 'the last great struggle between one man and the sea' and 'an impossible race in improbable craft'. But to Clare it was simply a great adventure to pit her wits against the sea. The direct and shortest route between Plymouth and Newport, also known as the Great Circle, is 2,800 miles where the participant may encounter shipping, icebergs and thick fog, not to mention gales, storms and possibly hurricanes. Some people opt for the longer southern route of about four to five thousand miles but *Golly* was best suited to cope with medium to strong headwinds along the direct route.

'The work on the boat seemed endless, the number of jobs ever-multiplying, so many things to be fitted, repaired and maintained; electrics, engines, generators, pumps, spare instruments with their dials and repeaters, the compass and spare compass. In a sailing race the engine is not usually important, but I was going to use the Volvo Penta to generate power for all the electrics on board as well as the transmitter.' Marconi had generously lent her a radio telephone which meant she would be able to make calls to Jacques and her family, which was to be her greatest morale booster.

One of their main problems, apart from constant money worries, was finding a method for Clare to handle the large foresails. Everything on the *Golly* was so large and powerful that whereas Jacques might winch up a sail in seconds, it would take Clare much more time and effort. Once, when lifting up a heavy sail from the deck to push down the forehatch, she lost her balance and followed it head first down the sailbin. On a final try-out before the race, they had a chance to cruise across the Channel to Cherbourg, the Channel Islands and St Malo, and a salutary experience it proved to be. The small boat fought her way through a fierce gale and heavy seas, corkscrewing and digging her nose into a wave, then rising suddenly to throw it off. Although she lurched badly she soon responded to the helm, recovered and headed into the walls of sea once more. But water was finding its way into the boat, not only over the deck, but running off the cockpit seats and seeping below. Pumping hard and leaving the boat on self-steering, which was also giving trouble, the crew suddenly saw to their horror that the tiller had split in two. To make matters even worse the radio had ceased to work, becoming overheated because of the fluctuating power supply. 'A wet leaky boat, a tiller that came away in your hand, a radio that wasn't working and a steering gear that was trying to do itself in – not the best news just weeks before the race!'

But thankful that the disasters had happened before and not during the race, they set about putting things right. In spite of the setbacks, Clare felt more and more confident that she could handle the boat. The build-up to the race was beginning in earnest.

There was no size limit to the boats, and one monster, Alain Colas's *Club Méditerranée*, was 238 feet long, more than six times the length of *Golly*. The press began to descend in droves to interview the only British girl competitor, although two French girls and one Italian were also in the race. Sporting the Robertson's golly emblem on her sweater, Clare had to pose in various nautical positions, clutching the inevitable coil of rope while photographers suspended themselves from the masts to get the most spectacular shot.

The two weeks leading up to the race were hectic. Provisions to last the crossing had to be stowed, and like a woman who takes more than she can possibly wear on a holiday, Clare packed into the lockers three times what she needed. Having a passion for fruit she took endless tins of peaches, pears, plums and prunes, all of which had to have their labels removed and be marked with waterproof ink. All single-handers have strong ideas about which provisions give a healthy diet. Mike Richey, who was sailing the best-known junk-rigged boat of all, *Jester*, believed in baking his own bread on board and usually took a hunk of cellar-dried Norwegian reindeer, beans, spaghetti, rice and a liberal supply of red wine through which he would happily drink his way without rationing until it ran out – 'Usually about the halfway mark.' Bill King, who had achieved a remarkable record sail round the world, was an organic food fanatic and would grow his own cress and beansprouts on board and live on a diet mainly consisting of dried fruit and nuts. Clare took fifteen gallons of fresh water, enough for drinking and hairwashing, and plenty of fresh fruit and vegetables at different stages of ripeness. Failing to find in Plymouth any wholemeal bread – the only kind to stay fresh for weeks – she sent an SOS to London to her press agent who staggered off the train carrying sixteen loaves. All Bran was bought at the last minute and had to be wrapped in polythene bags before stowing. Clare's mother was worried that she wasn't taking enough food and suddenly arrived with tins of artichokes, asparagus, chestnuts, rich soups and other delicacies. 'Just a few essentials,' she said and then proceeded to give her a set of what she described as thermo-nuclear underwear and a mass of paper knickers. These were all carefully packed into polythene bags and stowed into side-lockers. At last Clare checked her list to make sure she hadn't forgotten anything. The sextant, spare sextant, navigation tables, charts, ship's papers, passport with visas, medical kit, tin-opener and many other items were all ticked off. At the end she had written: 'Buy small tin of face cream for panic bag.' 'There you are,' said Jacques, 'you're hardly prepared at all.'

Clare was fully occupied in the last two days dealing with the BBC technical team which had arrived with cameras, tape-recorders, remote controls and miles of leads. She had agreed to make a film for *The World About Us* series, as well as to send reports three times a week by radio to the *Daily Express*. The BBC had told her that the filming would be simple. 'A small camera with built-in automatic sound – all you have to do is press the switch and speak into the microphone.' Instead, she was faced with a mass of complicated equipment. After the BBC man had explained about loading the film, fixing the camera onto a bracket on the stern, working the microphone and the tape-recorder, he expounded on sound synchronisation. 'Now when you have everything running, if you could just say "Roll Three" and hold up three fingers and then clap your hands, careful to make sure the noise is picked up by the mike.' So I was to be a human clapperboard, thought Clare in despair. But there was no time for a change of heart. The send-off parties at the Royal Western Yacht Club were in full swing. Clare's mother arrived with last-minute gifts, pressing a small bottle of what was known in the family as 'Mother's All-Purpose Pills' into her hand and 'just a few little extras, darling'. More tins of asparagus and exotic soups had to be stored in the 'treats locker'.

After a final family supper Clare and Jacques slipped away for an early night at a hotel. 'From the hotel window I looked out towards Plymouth Sound where ships lay at anchor ... and tried to imagine being out there with three thousand miles of ocean ahead and no Jacques to help.' It must, indeed, have been a lonely moment and maybe she even questioned why she was embarking on such a dangerous race. It wasn't as if she was really competitive. As a very young and enthusiastic dinghy sailor she had wanted to win every race, but now she was more philosophical. More than anything she wanted to arrive safely even if it meant sacrificing speed. Although not usually superstitious she wore a St Christopher medallion round her neck from which she was never separated. Maybe it would bring her luck . . . .

Most sailors find the hours leading up to the start of the big race the worst part of all, and Clare was no exception. About a thousand spectator boats milled round the contestants. 'When the starting gun for the big boats sounded you could almost feel the relief run through the rest of the fleet.' Next came the intermediate class, led from the start by Mike McMullen in *Three Cheers*, whose wife had been tragically killed in an accident just before the race. At last it was the turn of the Jester class. There were still spectator boats swooping about and helicopters buzzing overhead but Clare was underway at last.

Due to a navigational error, she made a bad start and spent the first night tacking round the Lizard which was shrouded in fog and swirling mist. For the first forty-eight hours she only managed to snatch a few minutes' sleep at a time. The winds were light and so the self-steering would hardly work. But eventually a breeze got up and although she was still in the shipping lane she judged the visibility good enough to risk some slightly longer snatches of sleep. Clare had also been cheered to see the monster *Club Méditerranée* not far away. 'I was beginning to realise that these large boats were not as fast as they were cracked up to be. If I could stay ahead for even a short time, then other boats should do even better. It was going to be an interesting race.'

Indeed it proved to be even more dramatic than Clare could have envisaged. Of the one hundred and twenty boats that started, only seventy-three were officially to finish. Another five completed the race after the official time had elapsed, forty retired to various ports around the Atlantic and five people were rescued from sinking boats. There were two tragic losses of life. *The Canadian*, Mike Flanagan's boat, was found drifting with no one on board, and Mike McMullen's *Three Cheers* had completely disappeared. Months later, yellow wreckage was seen near Iceland. It was assumed that the boat must have hit an iceberg; any suggestion that Mike had taken drastic action because of his state of mind was totally dismissed by those who knew him.

During the race Clare managed to make radio calls to the *Daily Express* and to shoot a documentary film for the BBC. This was achieved only after various disastrous attempts at setting up the complicated equipment, forgetting to turn on the tape recorder, and getting tangled in a mass of wires, with the camera whirring on its own initiative and the microphone hanging upside down. Eventually she found herself facing the lens, yelling 'Roll One', holding up one finger and clapping her hands. 'Three and a half minutes (the length of the roll) turned out to be a surprisingly long time and I was a little perplexed to find out how soon I had run out of topics, leaving me staring vacantly at the camera . . . but I wound back the tape to listen to my dazzling observations. It was a sobering experience. For two and a half minutes I heard some strange woman talking in a highly embarrassed British voice on a variety of topics loosely connected with sailing and strung together by loud umms and aahs. I didn't need to count the non sequiturs or split infinitives to know that my career was not going to be in television.' In fact she completed what was to be an expert documentary of the race, even managing to record some of her most hair-raising experiences.

Clare received news on her radio about her own position compared to some of the other boats and of the various retirements – Mike Richey in the original *Jester* being one of them. He had sent a laconic message merely saying, '*Jester* retired from race in favour of Irish cruise. No damage or incident.' She heard that Dominique Berthren's boat had been sunk after a collision with a ship, but she had been safely picked up from her life raft. The other French girl, Aline Marchard, had initially done well, but later had to head back to the Azores under an emergency jury rig after having been dismasted. There was no news from the only other female competitor, the Italian Ida Castiglioni, but she did in fact finish the course and received a tumultuous welcome from a huge crowd of Italian Americans.

Clare's aim had been to average a hundred miles a day and to arrive by 4 July, twenty-nine days after leaving Plymouth, but tearing along under a spinnaker at a roaring seven or eight knots she found she was covering one hundred and forty-five miles a day. The boat had an enormous spinnaker – a frighteningly powerful sail for Clare to cope with on her own. The traditional method of lowering a spinnaker normally requires many hands, so some ingenious methods had to be devised for her to hoist the monster sail. Sometimes there were disastrous results. Once, as she was admiring the spinnaker in the moonlight, she saw it shoot from the masthead and propel itself to a point about fifty feet ahead of the boat, where it fell into the water. The *Golly*, still travelling at seven knots, ran over the sail, trawling it along underneath her. After the boat had shuddered to a halt Clare had the long and exhausting job of pulling the sodden, weighty sail aboard. But, undaunted, she soon sorted out the shambles, reset the spinnaker and went roaring off again, making the most of the south-westerly wind. The boat rolled and yawed from side to side as she thundered along. Sometimes the self-steering could not hold her, and then Clare would have to lower the spinnaker. Lowering a spinnaker in a strong breeze when alone at night must have been a frightening experience: one mistake, and it could tear and wrap itself round the forestay, making it impossible to raise a foresail again. But in spite of the difficulties, she wished she had a more steady south-easterly – it was always a marvellous change to have a downhill run after the variable westerlies.

Clare had learnt to handle the boat in almost any conditions. Although in this race she was facing a much more inhospitable piece of ocean than ever before, she realised she felt less nervous and was not going to allow her imagination to run away with her. She decided philosophically to take each day as it came. 'Being unnecessarily worried is very wearing and I was determined not to get frightened unless absolutely necessary.' It was lucky that she wasn't clairvoyant or she might have been tempted to turn back early on in the race. The constant sail changing, 'humping one large sail on deck and fighting the other down, then pulling the new sail up and hurrying back to winch it in,' was taking its toll on her health. She was expending an enormous amount of energy and getting very little sleep. The result was a violent attack of diarrhoea and loss of appetite which lasted for several days. After the slightest exertion she had to sit down and rest; she was feeling weaker by the minute and rapidly losing weight. But knowing she must force herself to eat, she managed to get down some bread and honey and even a little porridge.

In the middle of the attack of 'lurgy', Clare encountered her first gale. Seeing that the barometer had dropped and the wind was freshening all the time, she made sure that everything was securely stowed and fastened and settled down to doze as best she could. 'There cannot be many worse awakenings than I had that morning. As the gloomy half-light of dawn filtered into the cabin, I heard the wind shriek in the rigging and the thunderous crash of the bows sinking into large waves. Water poured over the decks and down the windows and there was the ominous sound of water slopping up from full bilges. The *Golly* was heeled well over and I could almost feel her struggling under the excess of sail. It was time for me to get up. People wonder how one can find the willpower to leave a warm sleeping bag and get up after only a short sleep, but when the weather is worsening it's no problem at all. After changing down to the storm jib and putting the third and last reef in the main I sat in the shelter of the cockpit's spray hood to watch over the boat. The wind was now blasting across the sea and the waves were grey with long white streaks blown from their crests. It was blowing a gale and from the west so that, much as she struggled, the *Golly* could hardly make any worthwhile progress. Her course was north-westerly but, allowing for considerable leeway, her track must have been almost northerly. It was not a direction in which I wanted to go.

'As the gale continued to blow, the seas built up and the *Golly* crashed and shuddered into the waves until the din was appalling. More and more water poured over the decks and soon everything was imbued with damp and dripping with moisture. Finally, when a particularly powerful gust blasted down on us I could bear it no longer and, crawling carefully along the deck, I lowered the jib and then the mainsail to provide some much-needed peace. The *Golly* was quite happy without any sail up and lay beam on to the seas, rising to each wave until the crest had passed noisily away beneath. Inside the boat, the contrast was marvellous. The worst of the din had ceased, and the motion was almost gentle. Of course we were being blown back the way we had come, but at that moment I didn't mind very much; I could only think how delightfully peaceful it was compared to pushing on into those seas. I might even be able to get some sleep.'

The next day she sat in a mesmerised state of misery, her clothes damp and clinging to her skin and the wind blowing through her oilskins. In the cockpit she did manage the occasional doze. Once she hallucinated that Jacques was by her side, saying, 'I'm here, love, don't worry,' only to awake to the knowledge that she was alone, damp and terribly miserable. Changing into some dry clothes helped her morale and after stripping off the sticky layers – the paper knickers had completely disintegrated – she fell into her sleeping bag and four hours of uninterrupted sleep.

Clare had weathered her first gale and although there were even fiercer ones to come, she managed to reach the quarter-way stage a day ahead of the target she had set herself, by sailing seven hundred miles in six days. She celebrated by eating a whole tin of plums and some custard – not everyone's idea of a gourmet meal, but people at sea develop odd passions.

Meals, such as they were, became infinitely flexible, jammed in between short snatches of sleep, sail changing, doing minor repairs, filming, navigating and keeping in touch on the radio both with other boats to exchange information on positions and with Jacques. The lockers became wet from bilge water, which flowed up the side of the boat as she jerked and gyrated over the waves. The tins of food rusted and the careful marking eventually disappeared, which led to some interesting mixtures. The store of bread had become damp early on, but after Clare cut away the grey-green mould, the inside was still edible, and one of her favourite meals was scrambled egg and cheese on toast. Her mother had provided boxes of fresh eggs from their local farmer, which Clare kept finding stowed in surprising places – next to the engine, under the sink or hidden behind the batteries. The fresh fruit and vegetables, bought by her mother in varying stages of ripeness, lasted throughout the crossing. Unfortunately the ripening system occasionally went wrong, and once Clare ate a whole bunch of bananas at one sitting 'like a rapacious baboon'. At another time she put a hand in the darker regions of the fresh food locker to find a 'horrible squelchy mass of overripe tomatoes and damp mouldy coils of spaghetti'. Once, while grabbing her usual makeshift meal, Clare gave a rueful thought to her table manners. 'I couldn't help wondering how it would be to be amongst people again. As I cooked my cheese, eggs and tomatoes on toast, I would eye it like a vulture, then grab it and stuff it into my mouth, leaving debris over my hands and around my chin, eating so fast I usually finished with a loud burp, after which I felt marvellous.'

However, marvellous moments were few and far between. She had no sooner recovered from her first gale than she had to face a second, even more appalling. 'Not only was I feeling unprepared for another blow so soon after the first, but I was already exhausted from the sail changing throughout the night. Beating hard to windward not only involved a lot of sail handling, it meant life had to be lived at a permanent angle of thirty degrees. When moving about the cabin I came to rely on my arms and, rather like a monkey, would swoop from handhold to handhold until I could fall into my bunk or wedge myself behind the chart table. For some reason the galley was always on the uphill side and cooking became an exercise in juggling and balancing.'

For three days after the first gale the wind had twisted and turned, blown and then moderated. Having just changed sails yet again, she found herself at three in the morning lying in the cockpit, totally exhausted. But she wasn't prepared for the sight that greeted her as she looked out an hour later. By this time the gale was well established and the boat overpowered yet again. She staggered up on deck to pull down the flapping jib and get another smaller jib into the forestay, receiving the usual shot of water down her neck. 'I noticed with interest that the anemometer read well over forty knots of wind. Another blast and I went on deck to lower every-thing. . . . The gale finally settled in from the south and it was possible to make slow progress west under storm jib and treble-reefed main. . . . The movements of the boat were severe. She would rush at a wave, leap off the top and then crash down into the other side, give a quick roll or flip, then rush at another. Sometimes she found nothing but air as she leapt off a crest and there would be a ghastly moment of silence before a terrible juddering crash as the bows hit water again. At times like that it was easy to imagine that the mast had just broken or the hull split in two, for it seemed impossible that a boat could take such a beating. But with the *Golly* it was all or nothing and I could not slow her down without stopping her altogether. So I left her as she was, water streaming over the decks (and into the lockers) and her motion as wild as a washing machine's. Like a dirty dishcloth I was spun, rinsed and tumbled about until I should have been whiter than white. I tried wedging myself in my bunk but nearly got thrown out, so I tied myself in and lay there in a state of mental paralysis. I heard a banging and crashing sound above the racket of the gale, but was too tired to go and investigate. Even if I had known that the loo had broken loose and was committing hara-kiri I wouldn't have minded much; my memories of it were not exactly pleasant.'

Clare had to contend with a third gale before she reached the halfway mark and, although it was a Storm Force 10 with waves later reported to have reached forty feet at the centre, oddly enough the seas were not as uncomfortable or dangerous as they were during the previous smaller gales. By this time Clare had an even more serious problem on her mind. The strain on the self-steering gear had finally proved too great and two of the struts had buckled. Without self-steering Clare would have to abandon the race and somehow something would have to be done. Incredibly she managed to reach Jacques on the radio who reminded her that she had only one spare strut on board, so she would have to repair the other as best she could. Tying herself securely on to the backstay, she leaned as far as possible over the rail and tried to remove the struts. 'The wind had moderated to Force 8 to 9 gale, although I would never have known the difference from my position over the stern. One moment the sea was far below me and the next it was rushing up towards me. I concentrated on holding on to the two spanners in my hand and about five nuts and bolts between my teeth.' Eventually she managed to remove both bent struts and after a short rest and a meal of oatcakes (her staple diet during the storms of the previous days) got down to work. 'Welding was not one of the arts they had taught me at the young ladies' establishment I attended, nor did they get round to metal forging or iron work. But I'll try anything once if I have to, and on this occasion I'd have tried anything fifty times.

'For the next four hours the boat reverberated to hammer strokes, grunts, wheezes and the sound of sizzling metal. I heated the strut, I hit it, I pulled on it, I wrenched it, I put it in a vice and sat on it. I wedged it between two pieces of wood and jumped on it. Sometimes I just looked and pleaded with it. . . . The strut was a lot less bent than before but it was not exactly straight.' After a few hours' sleep she was upside down over the stern again putting the parts carefully back into place with infinite care. This was a crucial exercise – if the struts held she could continue the race, if not it would mean a slow and painful return to England. She noticed there was a tiny hairline crack across the main casting, which worried her, but with luck and no more gales it might hold.

Under a storm jib the *Golly* rode out the rest of the gale while Clare, too exhausted to sleep or even change into dry clothes, hallucinated that 'iron workers were bending metal bars as if they were putty'. Despite everything she was maintaining her hundred miles average a day. She celebrated Halfway Day by re-reading a few pages of *War and Peace*, her favourite book, and preparing to enjoy a celebratory dinner of spaghetti and tomato sauce and her favourite sweet: candied chestnuts and cream. The 'treats locker' contained both, and her disappointment was out of all proportion when she discovered that the chestnuts were in fact unsweetened *purée*. 'This was a real blow. I had to console myself with plums and custard and a tape of Handel's Water Music.'

As Clare approached the Grand Banks in dense fog and cold, she became aware of a sense of 'terrible desolation and emptiness'. Loneliness was not something she normally suffered from at sea – the boat and the sea were old friends and she felt safe in their company – unlike the loneliness she experienced in big cities. 'Out here in the deathly quiet and dark fog, I suddenly wanted to be where I was sure everyone else must be: in the warm and sunny ocean to the south. For a moment I even imagined I had been sucked hundreds of miles to the north, and it was only by frequent looks at the compass and chart that I convinced myself I was indeed heading south of Newfoundland ... but I felt an eerie atmosphere that made me shiver.' She knew she was approaching iceberg territory, but she wasn't too worried as only about twenty had been reported. 'Ridiculous to worry about a few icebergs in thousands of miles of ocean.' In the fog there was no point in going on deck and she fell into a deep sleep. When she did emerge, the fog had cleared and in the bright light she looked around. 'At first my eyes didn't comprehend; there was so much dazzling whiteness, the craggy mountains were so brilliant in the morning light they seemed to be part of the sky. But white they were and craggy, too. Two large icebergs a mile astern. One probably a quarter of a mile long, flat and rectangular, the other very tall with a sharp point at one end. And then my eye caught a third, grey with a shadow and jagged, too. I whimpered slightly and sat down before my knees did it for me. The *Golly* was as steady as a rock in the light wind and, guided by the indefatigable self-steering, was holding a perfect course. ... Following the course of that straight line I could see exactly where we had been a few minutes before. And that was between the two large icebergs.'

Clare had never been a particularly religious person. 'I suppose you'd say I was a humanist – I believe in the intrinsic goodness of the human spirit. As a child, during family discussions, I would argue vociferously against the benefit of religion. But there are times when one doesn't make an issue of these things. And I said a heartfelt prayer to the effect that if there was Someone up there I was terribly grateful ... and although I didn't merit it and was absolutely the least deserving, would God mind awfully keeping an eye on me just a little bit longer?'

After such a traumatic experience, winching in large sails became positively uplifting. Clare celebrated her good fortune by drinking a small glass of Scotch, and in the evening breeze she put up the spinnaker and enjoyed reaching and running before the wind. But her euphoria was to be short-lived and three days later a drama occurred which was to test her qualities of courage and resourcefulness.

As she was about one hundred and forty miles south of Newfoundland and two hundred miles south-east of Nova Scotia, the self-steering became really seriously damaged. Clare blamed herself for an error of judgement that led to the disaster. In the middle of the night she had found the boat careering downhill in a gale-force wind, veering from side to side as the large waves caught her from behind. 'Then I did something extraordinary. I decided I must reef the main immediately. Perhaps it was the unnerving rocketing into darkness, more or less out of control. Anyway, whether it was tiredness or fear, I did it. I unlatched the gear and pushed the tiller hard over so the *Golly* would shoot up into the wind and allow me to reef. As the boat turned, the self-steering was thrust sideways. Then, as she fell back again, the gear was pushed the other way. Instinctively I looked back and my heart froze. All four of the metal struts were bent out of all recognition.' Worse still, she discovered that the main casting had sheered, split across the middle.

After five hours of sweat and toil she still felt it was an impossible task to put the gear back into serviceable condition. She had become incredibly tired after her exertions and found herself falling asleep for seconds at a time, 'my head on my chest until the boat slewed off course and the motion woke me'. She realised she would have to put into port for repairs. The rules of the race permitted competitors to stop at any port they wished and then continue. It was Jacques who saved her from total despair when she eventually reached him on the radio. 'You can't even get to Nova Scotia without some self-steering. Somehow you must find a way to repair the gear so that you can sleep.'

His insistence gave her a new resolve, and after hours of laborious work she managed to join the main casting by placing lashings at every conceivable angle, and then she straightened the metal struts by using the engine as a lever. With superhuman efforts, stopping for rest, she manoeuvred it back into place. She then had her first good night's sleep for ages and started heading for Canso, Nova Scotia under the repaired self-steering. She realised she would undoubtedly lose three days, getting the gear fixed, and longed to change course for Newport again. 'I didn't care about the race – I knew I must be miles behind anyone else after the delay, but I did care about seeing Jacques and my parents. There was no doubt in my mind as I turned the *Golly* round. There was not a moment to lose . . . it was Newport or bust!'

Clare was to give a detailed and fascinating account of the race in her book *Come Hell or High Water* which she would write in two months directly from her diaries to meet a deadline in time for the Boat Show the following January.

Before her eventual triumphal arrival, she was beset by seemingly endless calm and patches of fog, but she was distracted by catching glimpses of seals, dolphins, pilot whales and even an enormous black whale at least as long as the boat – probably about fifty feet. But with the end in sight she developed a gritty determination that had her hoisting and winching sails with a new resolution. She heard on the radio that the famous French yachtsman Eric Tabarly had won the Pen Duick Trophy in twenty-three days and twenty hours, having been becalmed off Newport for four days. He had lost his self-steering gear in the early gales and had continued in his indomitable fashion without it. As she approached the Nantucket Shoals, Clare saw her first sunset in twenty-six days. That night was fabulous with the wind free and fast so that the *Golly* sped along, leaving trails of phosphorescence in her wake. The self-steering behaved itself apart from a few creaks and groans. 'One can sail for years to find a night such as that – a warm breeze, a steady sea and a harbour just a day away.'

As she began to appreciate how near she was to land, Clare gave a thought to her appearance. She washed her hair and went below to find some dry clothes. The trousers immediately dropped to her ankles. She had lost so much weight that her bones were sticking out in odd directions. After her fifth change, she found some shorts which seemed to fit her new shape. She put up the big red spinnaker and sailed past the finishing line on 4 July, escorted by Jacques and her sister Anne in a large motor boat, another boat with her parents, *Golly*'s owner, Ron Green, Eve Bonham, her crew from the Round Britain Race, and the BBC team, with Frank Page of the *Observer* shouting that she was thirteenth overall and the first woman to finish the race. She had taken twenty-nine days and had beaten the woman's record by three days. She was also the first British monohull to finish. It was only after all the celebrations, the endless bottles of champagne, the continual press attention, the blissful long hours of sleep on a static mattress, that the race seemed finally to be over. 'Would I do it again?' Clare asked herself. 'Absolutely and unequivocally not.'

After the hardships and rigours of the Transatlantic Race the thirty-year-old Clare announced her retirement from single-handed racing. She had never looked upon sailing as a career, nor wanted it to continue for ever. She and Jacques harboured a secret vision of a rose-covered cottage where they would live quietly, only going sailing in fine weather on weekends and holidays. They were living at the time in an unconverted farmhouse in Berkshire which some friends had let them have at a peppercorn rent. While Jacques was teaching French nearby, Clare was working for IBM as a lecturer and travelling as far as Los Angeles and Hawaii giving presentations with slides projected behind her on a large screen. There was no reason why their peaceful existence should not continue indefinitely.

In fact, within two years she was to take on the most challenging and difficult race of all, both physically and mentally. The 1977–8 Whitbread Round the World Race would cover 27,000 miles round the three Capes and would last seven months, including three stopovers at Cape Town, Auckland and Rio de Janeiro. The yachts were limited to class one ocean racers, boats between about forty-five and eighty feet in length. They had to be raced with a full crew which meant that the racing would be hard, fast and very competitive. From the mixed conditions of the Atlantic they would sail into the famous, much-feared Southern Ocean, would have to weather the legendary Cape Horn, the Roaring Forties and the Screaming Fifties, renowned for their harsh weather, large seas and drifting icebergs. It would be very satisfying to complete the course in one piece, thought Clare.

Jacques had crewed in the original Whitbread Race in *Burton Cutter* but the hull had started to break up after Cape Town and they never completed the course. He was keen to compete again and when two young men, Robert Jackson and Robin Buchanan, had contacted Clare in the autumn of 1975 and suggested she should skipper a boat in the race (because a woman skipper would have the best chance of sponsorship) Jacques was full of enthusiasm. Clare's book *Come Hell or High Water* and the BBC film she had made of the Transatlantic Race had resulted in a blaze of publicity and proposals from sponsors who wanted to back her next enterprise. In spite of her reservations she began to feel the old urge for adventure, that strange desire to overcome difficulties and reach an objective. With sponsorship a possibility, they now decided to consider the matter seriously.

Golly's sponsors, Robertson's, were unable to meet the hundreds of thousands of pounds involved, but one day while Clare was signing copies of her book at the Boat Show, her publisher telephoned to say he had met a man on a train who knew a mystery man who might be willing. . . . It seemed too far-fetched to be true but the mystery man turned out to be Gerry Jones, the advertising and marketing adviser to BSR, the company which made turntables for record players, and the firm agreed to provide all the money that was needed. The boat would be called *ADC Accutrac* – *ADC* after the products launched under an American subsidiary and *Accutrac* after their first product in the new range.

From the moment that sponsorship was confirmed, the rush was on. First they had to find a boat. It was too late to build a new one, so they decided to go for a Swan 65, the type of boat which had won the first Round the World Race, was well tried and had great proven strength. They eventually found what they were looking for on the continent, bought her the next day and then had to arrange to bring her from Antibes to Lymington.

The next most important thing was to assemble a crew. Clare had a clear idea of her priorities. Compatibility came first, with sailing ability a close second. Enthusiasm, an easy-going nature and, above all, a sense of humour, were vital requirements to survive incarceration in a small space for seven months with eleven other people. No one would be paid. Luckily she picked well and, apart from the odd incident, they were to be a united and happy group, forging firm friendships over the months to come.

In the meantime Clare and Jacques had decided they had been living as free spirits for long enough and would get married in July, six weeks before the start of the race. To complicate their lives still further, they decided to look for a house so that they would have somewhere to return to, preferably in Lymington. They tried unsuccessfully to keep plans for the wedding totally secret. This was one time when they did not want any publicity whatsoever, but nevertheless the story leaked out and they were upset by the press headlines: 'Round the World Honeymoon', conjuring up images of champagne and romance on the afterdeck, and 'Clare will take her new husband along in the crew.' The ceremony was held in a tiny village church near her parents' house and, in spite of the pressmen, nothing could spoil the occasion nor the two-day honeymoon that followed. To Jacques she was now 'the missus' and to Clare he was, as always, 'Monsieur' or 'the frog'.

Before the wedding they had managed to assemble all ten crew members. One of the most important was the cook. Bumble Ogilvy-Wedderburn was an extrovert with an earthy sense of humour and loved sailing. In spite of suffering some bad bouts of seasickness during the race, she would never fail to produce three cooked meals a day.

Robert Jackson and Robin Buchanan, whose original idea it was to attempt the race, were fairly inexperienced sailors and happily accepted their allocated jobs. Robert, a part-time banker who enjoyed such social occasions as Henley, became entertainments officer and also agreed to learn the secrets of marine loo installation. The more introverted Robin, a chartered accountant, was the winch expert.

One of the mainstays of the crew was the Swiss, Beat Guttinger, a first-class sailor whom they had met on the 1974 Round Britain Race, and he and Tony Bertram would be the two bosuns in charge of all the deck gear.

To Clare's delight, her close friend and sailing partner Eve Bonham agreed to join her once again in spite of being full of self-doubt. As she said, 'I may not be a brilliant sailor but I'd never forgive myself if I was left behind.' She became an indefatigable sail-mender and deckcrew but was to find that the eternal discomfort and lack of sleep slowly wore her down.

Nick Milligan, a registrar soon to take his FRCS in anaesthetics, volunteered to be ship's doctor. He had a dry sense of humour, a love of fishing, and all too soon was to find himself extracting under local anaesthetic a large needle embedded in Eve's finger.

Fred Donovan, a skipper of one of the Ocean Youth Club's ketches, the *Francis Drake*, was their engineer. He also helped Clare and Jacques with the filming for the fifty-minute programme, *The World About Us*.

Perhaps the most controversial member of the crew was John Tanner, an expert navigator who had been skippering another Swan 65 in the West Indies. It was inevitable that he should have his own strong views on navigational matters, as to how many sails they should carry and concerning the various decisions to be taken on tactics. From the beginning it was to become apparent that he had some ideas about sailing that did not correspond to those of Clare and Jacques. They also discovered that one of his favourite hobbies in fine weather was wandering round the deck naked.

The final but invaluable crew member was Sam Badrick – beady, bearded and piratical. He had been an army cook and was keen to do the race, 'but not as a bleedin' cook – I've cooked enough bleedin' meals to feed a ruddy army', but he was more than willing to climb the main mast in the fiercest of seas.

Apart from skippering the boat, Clare was to be radio operator with the task of getting through to England every day, while Jacques with his special skills would be general fixer and solver of insoluble problems.

Sailing the boat from Antibes had shown up many deficiencies. Her sails, although only two years old, proved disappointing and were to be a source of endless problems later on. Much of the equipment had to be replaced or mended. The main boom had to be renewed with a stronger, shorter one, and new sails had to be ordered – a costly business at £2,000 a time. The boat had to be lightened and non-essentials stripped out.

As the summer rushed on, the boat gradually approached a state of readiness, although there were still many last-minute jobs cropping up. In late July they took part in three races to flex their muscles – the Cowes–Dinard, the Channel and the Fastnet. Although the conditions were too equable really to test their handling technique, they could at least see how they matched up to some of the other yachts entered for the Whitbread, and were encouraged to find themselves level with their twin, the other Swan 65 ketch, the Swiss entry *Disque d'Or*. Looking at some of the other sleek yachts sometimes made Clare's confidence waver. Among them was the Dutch yacht *Flyer*, custom-built at a cost of well over half a million pounds, then the smallest yacht of all, the fifty-five-foot *Traité de Rome*, representing the Common Market, and *King's Legend*, a sloop-rigged Swan 65 with a mainly professional crew. There was no doubt that all the yachts had one thing in common. They were going to be raced very hard indeed.

During all the preparations, Clare and Jacques had finally found a house, near the marina in Lymington, and on their last day there before sailing for Portsmouth, packing up their bags preparing to leave the home they had barely lived in, Clare felt deeply sad that it would be seven months' time before they returned to its warmth and comfort.

At Portsmouth the *ADC* was besieged by visiting friends, family and journalists, which made the stowing of food, clothing and equipment even more chaotic than usual. Bumble had worked out a list of provisions which Clare thought would be enough to feed a platoon for a year – there were 1,500 lbs of tinned fruit alone. 'Like everyone who organises an ocean passage, I was beginning to wish I had a crew who never ate.' In the end Bumble solved the storage problem by rigging up netting above the bunks and across the saloon roof, which she and Eve filled to bursting point with cabbages, fruit and personal gear, while six vast salamis were hung from the grab rails over the saloon table. Bumble was also responsible for a gift of four cases of Famous Grouse Scotch whisky, and Robert, as entertainments officer, was given the job of decanting it ignominiously into plastic sacks and barrels to save precious weight. However, they did keep a few bottles just in case disaster, such as a puncture, should occur – and just as well, because early on in the race they found that all the whisky in the sacks had become tainted.

Clare had previously taken all the crew's measurements and had ordered oilskins, boots, sweaters and polar wear, and of course her mother, arriving two days before the start, brought along the thermal underwear and forty pairs of paper knickers. Jacques, who had vowed to give up smoking, smuggled on board two hundred cigarettes and a dozen tins of pipe tobacco. Finally the BBC equipment for a documentary film had to be housed. This was put in the aft cabin which Jacques and Clare would share with Bumble.

Clare had also contracted to attempt to call Capital Radio every day – a task which was to prove much more demanding than she could have foreseen.

On 27 August, to the sound of shouts and cheers from the crowds, it was time to draw away from the dock and approach the starting line. Clare found it difficult to imagine what it would be like to return to this same wharf the following spring, after 27,000 miles and every kind of weather. The Solent was thick with spectator craft. Clare spotted her parents looking very wet and miserable in an open boat and they saw the *Golly* – on one bow was a banner which read 'Good Luck Jacques' and on the other 'Good Luck Clare' – her owners were giving them a memorable send-off. When the starting gun was finally fired, a subtle feeling of exhilaration came over the crew, a feeling of release after all the months of preparation.

Clare had expected the first leg of the race to take about six weeks because of the calms and head winds they were likely to meet – this meant averaging 158 miles a day. In fact they took 43 days, were seventh boat in and ninth on handicap. It is 5,800 miles from Portsmouth to Cape Town and they decided on the direct course past Ushant, across the Bay of Biscay to north-west Spain and then the Canary Islands. The windless stretch of sea known as the Doldrums would have to be crossed before the long windward beat against the south-east trades.

As the days turned into weeks, life on board fell into a routine of keeping watch, sleeping and eating. Occasionally they enjoyed sailing under near-perfect conditions. Then Nick and Bumble would trail fishing lines behind the boat, and sometimes shoals of flying fish appeared on deck and would be cooked for breakfast. Sailing down the coast of Portugal the sea came alive with dolphins, pilot whales and, once, large rorqual whales. In these conditions the crew were able to indulge in their various favourite pastimes. Off-watch letter writing became 100-page epistles, and diaries were kept. (Clare's was to become the basis for her book *Come Wind or Weather*, published in 1988). They played word games in the cockpit, and as they had a stereo cassette system which ran through the cabins and each bunk had its own headphones, they could listen whenever they chose. 'Chat Hour', on which Clare could listen to news from the other yachts, was always riveting and full of surprises. Every day she made her call to Capital Radio. 'Somehow or other there were always technical difficulties. Either I could not hear the disc jockeys' questions, or they could not hear me, or Russian voices would come drifting over the air. When reception was really bad I usually shouted a few general comments down the line, hoped they had heard me, and then signed off. At the end of each session I felt like a wet rag.' Jacques and Fred had come to terms with the BBC equipment and were to take some exciting footage.

As they neared the Doldrums they were level with *Disque d'Or* and had gained on *King's Legend* and *Flyer*. Since the belt of Doldrums could often move 200 miles north or south, it was possible that they might have picked up wind at the same time as the leading boat. 'Theoretically we were in the right place at the right time . . .' and if they were delayed so too would be *Disque d'Or* – or so they innocently believed.

In fact, they lay virtually becalmed for four days while their twin sailed ahead. By the fourth day the tension on board was unbearable. Their position had looked so promising, and now it was slipping away with the whims of the wind. 'Some of the crew covered their disappointment by talking and joking too loud, others went quiet, and I repaired to my bunk to read.' They heard that *Disque d'Or* was now two hundred and fifty miles ahead while *King's Legend* and *Flyer* had overtaken them by four hundred miles.

When they eventually felt the first breath of the south-east trade winds, and the boat started to heel and pitch, John, Jacques and Clare had to decide on the choice of route. Clare and Jacques pressed for the windward course to the east of the high. John disagreed but in the end accepted their decision. 'As a reminder that our problems, though disheartening, were relatively small, we heard that *Condor*, who had been in the lead, had lost her mast and was making for Monrovia to fit a new one. A crew on the French yacht *Japy-Hermès* was suffering badly from kidney stones and they, too, were making for port. Compared to this, losing about five places did not seem too bad.'

After the Doldrums, their Halfway-to-Cape-Town Party was not a jolly affair. The invitation reflected the atmosphere on board. 'Are You Feeling Half-Baked, Half-Hearted and Half-Witted? Come to a Halfway Party at Half-Six, Half-Dressed, Half-Cut.' They were now beating hard to windward and the bumpy motion was having its effect. Robin and Eve were seasick and Clare had lost her appetite and got diarrhoea, leaving her weak and tired.

On 20 September they crossed the Equator. Apart from Jacques, John and Eve, none of them had crossed the 'line' before, which meant there would be little the small band of initiates could do in the way of dunking, wetting and other ceremonials. However, when the moment arrived the crew were either mending the hydraulics, trying to fix the engine which had just broken down, or just feeling sick.

'The sailing itself was the key to the boat's happiness. As long as the sailing was enjoyable and challenging, everyone was cheerful and full of verve. We liked lots of sail-changing, tacking and trimming. Sitting on the same tack, bashing into a short head sea day after day was not particularly demanding and, since it was also extremely wet and uncomfortable, the crew's spirits were not at their highest.' With the relentless slog against the south-east trades, they pushed *ADC* day after day into the short wet seas, the boat always heeled well over and the deck covered in spray.

Years later Clare described her feelings at the time. 'I think, as a woman, I worried too much about creating harmony – trying to give a feeling of family. The lads didn't worry about the fact that I was a woman, but I felt I could have done a better job.'

These were difficult conditions and tempers became short. Table manners had deteriorated, partly because they had to hold their bowls beneath their chins to be sure of getting the food into their mouths, but also because they licked their plates clean after the main course so that they could be used again for pudding. Fresh water was strictly rationed and Bumble used as much salt water in cooking as possible, but she still had to use about two gallons of fresh water a day to make up milk from powder and to reconstitute dried meat to augment the frozen meats. Food itself remained one of the great joys, and when Bumble was in the galley preparing a meal inquisitive heads would peer over her shoulder to ask what was on the menu.

A week before reaching Cape Town they found themselves becalmed once more. Clare did the only possible thing: she threw a full bottle of brandy overboard for luck and repaired to her bunk for a sleep. A few hours later her prayers were answered by a westerly wind. The downwind sailing had a revitalising effect on everyone but it was not long before a frontal system came through and shortly after that had passed the starcut spinnaker ripped and fell down – an experience that was to become all too familiar. Otherwise they had a smooth, fast and uneventful run into Cape Town.

'The prospect of land brought a change to everyone's appearance. Scruffy beards disappeared, hair got washed and clean clothes were shaken out ready for arrival. After a long sea passage the first sight of land is always magical and none was more so than our first glimpse of Table Mountain, a small grey outline on the far, clear horizon.' To entertain the boats already in, they retrieved the remnants of the heavy spinnaker they had lost in the channel, wrote WATCH THIS SPACE across it and hoisted it as they were being towed into the yacht basin.

Their stay at Cape Town was two and a half weeks long and they needed every moment. After moving into a hotel and enjoying the longest, hottest and most enjoyable bath in the world, Clare and Jacques started to plan the work. There were repairs and welding to be done, the new fuel pump for the engine ordered from England to be fitted, and the sails to be overhauled.

Their hosts, the Royal Cape Yacht Club, were extremely hospitable and arranged for supplies of lavish food at a reasonable cost. Several club members gave barbecues, swimming parties and dinners until they all started to put on the weight they had lost. Jacques and Clare abandoned work for two days to do some sightseeing. They visited the Cape of Good Hope and as they looked out to sea, remembered its other name, the Cape of Storms, and hoped it would be kind to them when they left on the long leg to New Zealand.

John, Jacques and Clare settled down to finalise their tactics and Clare held a crew meeting to discuss the next leg. Everyone was aware that it would be tougher and more demanding than the first and no one needed reminding that falling overboard would be fatal. On the first Whitbread three men had lost their lives.

The second leg to Auckland was to prove their most traumatic. It took thirty-six days and tested their racing skills to the utmost. At the end of their first day Clare was exhilarated to find that they were in the lead, until the breeze strengthened and the larger boats overtook them. Towards the third night their position was still excellent and they decided to put up the new spinnaker for the first time. Clare was steering and finding the *ADC* was rolling from side to side, so she suggested flattening the sail. But John insisted on pulling the pole further back, saying it would provide the extra stability. In fact it did quite the reverse. At the same moment the wind started to freshen. As the crew rushed for the winches, a squall hit. With the spinnaker so badly trimmed, they hadn't a chance.

'First she started to roll badly. Terrified of broaching to leeward, I flung my whole weight on the wheel to stop her from continuing to turn that way. At last I felt her start to straighten. As the mast whipped upright the spinnaker . . . immediately swung round and pulled the boat hard over the other way. This time she went right over and nothing could stop her. She kept turning until she was beam-on to the seas and held over on her side by the spinnaker. There was chaos. People were clinging on to the deck, trying not to slide down into the water. The entire boat started to shiver and shake as if it were in the mouth of a mad dog. The off-watch crew tried to scramble up the companion-way but, the ladder being at an angle of 50 degrees or so, it was not easy. My first instinct was to get the boat upright again. Eve was nearby and together we pulled at the wheel for all we were worth. At first nothing happened and then, quite suddenly, the boat responded and started to right herself. With horror, I realised what must inevitably happen. With the spinnaker still too full, the boat swerved the other way and broached to leeward. This time she went so far that the water was running along the deck up to the level of the cockpit. The spinnaker pole was buried in the sea, under the most terrible strain (we were still doing a good speed, even on our side). Fortunately the foreguy broke and the pole emerged still in one piece. I fought to right the boat once more and this time was able to keep her there, for the spinnaker pole was now thrashing about in the air and the spinnaker flying somewhere around the masthead. Tony, as always the one who leapt into action, rushed forward and started pulling the pole down with the lazy sheet. We realised that the boat was now more or less in one piece.' However, they had lost their best headsail overboard, and the spinnaker pole was bent. With only one pole, the numerous gybes in the weeks ahead were to be long, time-consuming manoeuvres.

The downwind sailing continued to be tense. Every day some new damage or injury occurred. Robin's palms and fingers were badly burnt when a halyard suddenly slipped on the winch and ran through his hands. Sam was hoisted about fifteen feet up the mast while pulling another halyard in an attempt to get the sail to refill. However, 'Chat Hour' made their experiences pale in comparison to disasters experienced by some of the other boats.

The whole fleet was racing flat out. In spite of the fright the broach had given them all, they were finding the fast downwind sailing exciting and were enjoying themselves as never before.

They sailed past Marion Island where fourteen scientists were living among 650,000 penguins. And as they headed up towards the Tasman Sea beautiful, aloof birds were always with them, and they identified dramatic black-and-white porpoises, prions, sooty shear-waters, pigeons, and albatrosses 'gliding high above our wake, hardly moving their enormous wings as they searched and waited for some meal we never saw them catch'.

The weather alternated between freezing headwinds and light warm tailwinds. To their annoyance they heard that the boats that had taken the southerly route were finding steadier westerlies, and their own overall position was no longer so encouraging. *Disque d'Or* was now more than a clear day in front. It was becoming colder day by day, and although they wore their longjohns, sweaters and balaclavas, the piercing cold penetrated their boots and gloves on the long night watches, and they had to go below to rub the circulation back into their hands. Then one particularly clear night they saw the Southern Lights, the Aurora Australis, and every night for a week they were to see the dazzling display. 'One memorable night the whole sky was ablaze with glittering curtains which undulated and faded and glowed and glistened over our heads. Wave after wave of silver and blue icicle-like fingers reached down towards us, shimmering and gleaming. On the southern horizon there were whole areas of light in the sky, soft blurred circles of arctic blue or snow white.'

It was on their sixteenth day that they really felt the Roaring Forties, when they were nearly 49 degrees South and the wind finally blew hard enough for them to attain speeds of twelve knots and fifteen to twenty knots when surfing. Surfing was the most thrilling experience for the helmsman who had to line the boat up as the stern started to lift and then hold on tight as she shot down the slope at fantastic speed. Below decks, the off-watch crew would hold their breath as the stern rose.

At almost 50 degrees South they became aware of the special atmosphere of the Southern Ocean, its changeability, harshness and isolation. They started being more careful about clipping on their harnesses as they moved around the deck. The average wind strength during their voyage through the Southern Ocean was Force 6 or 7. They were escaping lightly, but they longed for gale-force winds. The knife-edge situation was a strain on all their nerves, and in the Roaring Forties they were to broach twice more. But despite the hair-rising nature of the incidents they were becoming more philosophical and confident about how to deal with them when they occurred. In fact, during this time of fast, demanding sailing, life on board was rarely better. The only difficulties between individuals occurred over sailing policy. As before, John's ideas on certain crucial matters differed from Jacques's and it had reached a point where the sails would be completely retrimmed at the change of watch and a different course sailed. 'It was Jacques who suggested that to improve continuity he would move to John's watch, leaving Tony to fill his place. These are diplomatic terms, of course, for a brief war at sea.'

The furthest south they reached was 51 degrees after three weeks at sea. The tactic of staying north had not paid to begin with, but now the tables seemed to be turning. 'With any luck,' Clare thought, 'we might pick up a couple of positions before reaching Auckland.' They were averaging two hundred and thirty miles a day and morale was high. As they passed Tasmania, one hundred and fifty miles to the north, the seas became larger and the water bluer and more sparkling. The skies cleared, and they gradually shed their thick sweaters. One day they were joined by two shag cormorants which tried to balance on the edge of the rolling mizzen boom, 'counterbalancing the motion by recoiling their long, scraggy necks, then ascending them again in rapid, jerky movements like two Turkish contortionists'.

They held a strong following wind and found that the boats to the south were slowing down while their own position was improving daily. *Disque d'Or* was still ahead but, like the other Swan 65s, *King's Legend* was leaking badly. The wind was as boisterous as ever and they experienced the usual excitement of fast spinnaker sailing. At one point Beat was nearly lost over the bow when he overbalanced while poised on the pulpit waiting to release the spinnaker pole. Luckily he was already clipped on by his safety harness and soon hauled himself on board.

The wind held until the last two days before Auckland. They sighted Cape Reinga on the north-west tip of New Zealand and sailed towards it in a gentle breeze which became gentler all the time until they were virtually becalmed. But as they sat idly two miles off the coast staring at the beautiful green rolling hills ahead of them, a firm breeze sprang up and suddenly they were speeding, close-hauled, past island after island until they saw the glow of the city lights. 'It was the most thrilling finish to a race because it was so unexpectedly fast . . . halfway round the world . . . and the stop we were most looking forward to. Now we would spend Christmas and have four weeks well earned holiday. After 13,000 miles sailing round the world we could think of nothing better than a long, restful time away from it all and away from the sea!'

As they crossed the 'line' they performed a Maori war dance (which they had been rehearsing for the previous two days) to resounding applause from an astonished audience. They had taken five weeks and one day, were now the sixth boat, and their position after the two legs was seventh – two places up on Cape Town. The local press arrived and Bumble was heard to say to one reporter, 'I thought I'd be terrified but I was only frightened,' which more or less summed up how they all felt.

Jacques and Clare took a delayed honeymoon and spent ten days wandering through New Zealand from Lake Taupo to Rotorua, bewitched by the wild, beautiful hill forests of Urewera National Park with its spectacular waterfalls. But with the restart fixed for Boxing Day, they had to have all the food loaded and the boat ready by Christmas Eve. The hot summer weather made their traditional English Christmas dinner a bit incongruous, and they began to look forward to the long journey home. Having stayed too far north on the last leg, they decided to head down to 60 degrees south on the 7,500-mile leg to Rio de Janeiro. They would meet icebergs on this southerly route, but with short summer nights the visibility should be good enough to avoid them.

After rounding East Cape, they had a gentle easterly in which they reached off towards the Chathams on the great circle course for the Horn. On 30 December they were due to cross the date line and New Year's Eve was celebrated on the radio between the boats, many toasts being drunk in many languages. By the next day the wind was blowing Force 7 from the south, and they ruefully regretted their over-indulgence as they battened down the hatches in readiness for a hard windward slog. With the wind increasing to Force 9 and the boat crashing into the waves, Clare decided to put up the previously unused storm jib. Half an hour later it ripped. Clare was furious. There was nothing they could do but sit out the gale. Their speed reduced drastically and the conditions worsened as the seas built up. Wearing goggles to protect themselves from the spray, which flew across the deck like thousands of sharp hailstones, only two of the crew would stay on deck at a time. Clare enjoyed those conditions. 'It was exhilarating to steer, letting the boat climb the waves then flicking her nose up into a crest to prevent her from being knocked sideways. Up and down, riding the great waves in the powerful machine, feeling the strength of the wind against the sails – I loved it, just as I have always loved bad weather. I was only sorry we couldn't go faster still.' It was in this kind of weather that Jacques and Clare had their only disagreement over the wearing of safety harnesses. Although they both had a deep terror of losing each other at sea, Clare felt totally safe on deck in most conditions and had to concede to Jacques when he insisted. The cabins were running with condensation and damp, and they slept in wet clothes in extreme discomfort. Finally the gale subsided and they opened the hatches and watched a watery sun come through the clouds.

As they headed further into the depths of the Southern Ocean, south-east out of the Forties and into the Fifties, they entered the most isolated stretch of ocean in the world: no islands or ships, only the icy sea encompassing the frozen Antarctic continent 1,000 miles away. 'The occasional albatross circled the boat and swooped across our wake. Sometimes we saw smaller seabirds, but often there would be nothing.' Suddenly there was a yell down the hatch:

'Icebergs!' Clare leapt up on deck to see two tall angular magnificent icebergs about two miles apart. Luckily the boat could pass clear of them without altering course. At nearly 60 degrees south in midsummer, the nights were almost non-existent and icebergs could be seen even at midnight.

They discovered that they were the most southerly of the boats and chose a course due east until the time came to head north-east from the Horn. After a period of suffering from lack of wind on the seventeenth day, it swung round to the south-east, and the next morning it had risen to fifty knots and was blowing Force 10 from the south. 'I watched the large, grey seas with their white, torn crests and listened to the wind howling in the rigging, and thought here at last was the real Southern Ocean. This was what we had come to find and sail through: this beautiful, powerful, magnificent ocean. As I watched I felt no fear, only simple admiration.'

Although the sailing was exhilarating and most of them were enjoying it, Eve and Robin were laid low with seasickness and there was a bad epidemic of cold sores and chilblains. John lost the feeling in the end of his toes and Clare developed numb fingertips – injuries which would take weeks to mend. The storm blew for eighteen hours as *ADC* rushed eastward in a flurry of snow and white sea. Never before had they been so cold. The wind cut through gaps in their clothing and froze their wrists and necks while their noses felt like blocks of ice. They heard that *Disque d'Or*, further north, was rushing for the Horn and thought they could hold her if they pushed hard. 'I often horrified the others by wanting to put up more sail. John was a great ally who was also keen to press hard, while Bumble, carried away by the excitement, cried her usual, "More sail, more sail!"' Some of the others made pleas for moderation. With their spinnaker trimming and handling down to a fine art, they no longer feared broaching. 'With so few miles to go to the Horn . . . we were reckless, maybe, but those days were incomparable for a feeling of excitement and achievement. . . . After so many months together, the twelve of us knew each other as well as any members of our own families. We knew each other's foibles and weaknesses, each pet irritation and dislike. And, as in most families, we tolerated them with good grace.'

They rounded Cape Horn on Sam's birthday, 18 January. Jacques and Clare hugged each other, too overcome to speak. 'When one place has been the subject of so many legends and myths it is difficult to believe you are looking at it with your own eyes.' Bumble appeared at the hatch with Sam's birthday cake and Robert with two bottles of champagne. The celebration lasted until the weather closed in and they had their last sight of the jagged crag in its lonely position at the tip of the world.

After passing the Falkland Islands on their voyage north they arrived at Rio in fifth place in the race so far, enormously pleased to have improved their position so dramatically. But their pleasure was tempered by a drama which had occurred just four days previously, when a crew member on *33 Export* nearly lost his life. He had been flung across the cockpit and broken his femur. In the confusion and misunderstandings and crossed messages that followed, no rescue boat had arrived, and on the fourth day a doctor from the nearby *Japy-Hermès* had swum over to the boat with a bag of drugs held between his teeth.

The *ADC* had arrived a week before the Carnival and everything was in chaos. With many repairs to do to the boat they found the Rio Yacht Club less than helpful. Clare realised that the Brazilians were not great sailing enthusiasts, but she was unprepared for the animosity she found. Sailing into one bay after another to find somewhere to scrub the boat's undersides they were fired at by soldiers. The Club did, however, give a farewell prize-giving party for them round the pool with samba music and gyrating dancers, but this ended in disaster when people started jumping into the pool and uniformed men appeared wielding batons, bringing the party to an abrupt end.

Never before had the thought of returning to *ADC* and the restart for their final leg back to the UK seemed so appealing. The heat was oppressive and both Clare and Beat were ill with feverish flu. They were all determined to keep their fifth place and as keen as ever to outwit their rivals. Their speed increased to nine knots as they raced towards the Equator. The heat was intense and they threw buckets of water over themselves and wandered around in sarongs.

Their second experience of the Doldrums was in marked contrast to the first. This time they made quite good progress at about a hundred miles a day. At the beginning of the race they had felt the despair of a hopeless situation. Now it had become so exciting that every day was a cliff-hanger. During the long windward slog through the trade winds to the Azores, they sometimes went for days without a sail change. 'For nine days we were hard on the wind. The sparkling sun and flying spray of the trades burned our already suntanned faces until they were red and sore. . . . We raced past turtles as they paddled slowly along. We were overtaken by dolphins swimming and leaping effortlessly beside the boat. At night phosphorescence lit our wake and the sky was dark velvet, pin-pricked with a multitude of stars. It was magically beautiful and made even more intoxicating by the nearness of home, now less than 2,000 miles away.'

They decided by a toss of a coin to get through the Azores high by skirting round their western edge and emerged from the islands in a strong position. The grey windswept North Atlantic evoked memories in Clare of her single-handed voyages in seas like these, larger than anything seen in the Southern Ocean. 'However, the circumstances had been somewhat different – I had gone from east to west, against the wind. Here on this big, well tried boat running fast downwind, with my large family aboard, it was another kind of sailing.'

As the end of the race approached, the crew made bets as to the precise hour of arrival. They listened to the BBC World Service and were amazed at how little of importance seemed to have occurred in their absence. In the Channel approaches they had a memorable last day. In a Force 9 gale they optimistically put up too much sail. The first disaster was when they lost their number three genoa. Next the mainsail ripped at the seams and had to be repaired by Eve, who remarked hopefully, 'Could it be the last time I repair a sail?' Thirdly Clare herself, while lowering the mizzen staysail, was concussed when it slammed her to the deck. And finally they tore the storm spinnaker. Luckily Clare had not been badly hurt and was able to share in the excitement of the final dash under spinnaker up the Solent in moonlight, and in the last-minute panic as they searched for the buoy which marked the end of the line.

They finished in fifth place. *Flyer* had won the Whitbread Trophy but they had the satisfaction of beating her on the last leg. *Traité de*

Rome was second, *King's Legend* third, while their twin, *Disque d'Or*, took fourth place, although they had often beaten her when racing side by side.

The essence of the Whitbread was sailing hard, up to the limit of safety. For Clare the race had been an unforgettable experience. 'The passage round the Horn, the wild rides down the Southern Ocean waves, the occasional excitement of being ahead – but there had been many other moments which passed slowly: times of boredom, discomfort and longing for home. Seven months was a long time to be away.'

Several years later, reminiscing on the race, she said, 'All the crew were extremely positive and terrific characters in their own right, but I think to be a leader is an impossible task. It's inevitable that in a group of people you're going to have differences and upsets – people falling out and making up – disagreements over routes and tactics and sometimes in appalling conditions. I think in retrospect I worried too much about it. I'm a very hard judge of myself and felt I wasn't leading them well enough from the front. I wish a lot of things had been different.

'Maybe I should have taken a course in how to manage people because I think management of any team is something that has to be learnt – some people have it in their blood but I'm not a natural leader. We had our troubles, particularly in the first leg which I worried over and those worries stayed with me. Maybe if I'd had an all-girl crew like Tracey Edwards in the last Whitbread race it would possibly have been easier. As she said, men are so much more competitive and are always having to prove themselves. But in our case it wouldn't have been physically possible – we'd have needed a smaller, lighter boat – all the gear now is both stronger and lighter at the same time.

'We certainly had our terrifying moments – going downhill with too much sail up as if you're on a sleigh ride out of control. I always thought something terrible might happen – that something would break. If the mast had broken in the Southern Ocean and holed the hull. . . . But there were the compensations. On the night watches, with everyone else down below, except perhaps one other person – the beauty of the nights at sea could be staggering – and you're guiding this big animal to the sound of the sea and the swishing of the waves – it was extraordinarily seductive, almost soporific. I can't think of any other experience to equal it – you're close to the reality of whatever life is – it's something you don't experience again – even listening to music – a sort of ecstasy.'

Clare became pregnant almost immediately at the end of the race. She and Jacques were living in their house in Lymington at the time and it was one of the busiest periods of her life. Soon after Tom's birth in 1978 she started filming her television series *The Commanding Sea* which dealt with all aspects of man's relationship with the oceans. In the course of the series she was constantly travelling. When the 400th anniversary of Sir Francis Drake's voyage round the world was celebrated the following year, Clare sailed in a replica of the *Golden Hind* on part of her voyage through the South China Sea to Singapore. The contrast with her own experience of round-the-world sailing could not have been greater. She next joined the merchant ships the *Chaibosse* and *Monet* and followed a consignment of tea from the remote farm plantations in northern India to Rotterdam, eleven thousand miles away. The captain compared life on board to being in a golden jail – 'golden because we are so well looked after and jail because we are separated from our families and the world'. Collision with other ships, reefs and icebergs was the main fear of these ships, as it had been for Clare sailing single-handed. She then spent some time on the American aircraft carrier *Saratoga* in the Mediterranean and was allowed to accompany HMS *Blake*, the helicopter carrier, when she was taking part in an exercise to test the effectiveness of NATO procedure and tactics that would come into play in time of tension or war. In July 1979 she visited the Murchison oilfield, the most northerly to be exploited in the North Sea at the time, and the Shetland fishing community fighting for its fair share of the catch. But her final voyage in the submarine *Alvin* showed her that there is always more to explore, greater depths to visit in nature. 'Really,' her biologist friend told her, 'we don't know much about the sea at all.'

Clare felt ambivalent about her life at this time – 'I would be away filming for three months at a stretch and felt guilty about leaving Tom, and it wasn't doing my relationship with Jacques any good. We'd been kept together by our work and now our interests were so different.' It couldn't have been easy for Jacques to be sometimes thought of as Clare Francis's husband. The television series was produced as a book in 1981 and Clare was encouraged by its success and launched herself on her new career as a novelist. She used her knowledge of the sea as a background to some of the most dramatic episodes in her first book. *Night Sky*, published in 1983, is a wartime adventure story about a young Plymouth woman and her small son exiled in north Brittany; they become involved in the French Resistance and help to smuggle Allied servicemen out of occupied France. The sea chase across the Channel is a *tour de force*. Although the book was immediately acclaimed by the public, published in fourteen languages and sold one and a half million copies, the critics tended to sneer. Always sensitive to criticism, Clare said, 'I soon learnt that people don't like you to succeed twice – people love to knock someone who has switched careers, it's a British trait.'

For the second novel, always a test, she looked to 1968, the year of the student revolution – what socialist Klaus Mehnert has called 'the twilight of the young'. *Red Crystal*, a taut political thriller, saw her established as a leading writer of adventure fiction and finally welcomed by the critics who reached for superlatives: as the *New York Times* declared, 'The classically structured spy thriller has rarely been better done.' The fame she had achieved in the sailing world had given Clare the confidence to become a writer and she admits to enjoying a certain celebrity status. 'I'd hate to be well known like pop stars – that would be ghastly – but I have to admit I sometimes find it quite useful, like finding a plumber on a Sunday. But in this country I'll always be known just as a sailor. Maybe in ten or fifteen years I'll have earned the right to be known as a writer as well.'

At the same time as her literary career soared, sadly her marriage finally fell apart. Jacques continued to live in Lymington while Clare moved to London with Tom. 'I didn't feel I was depriving Tom of a father – they've always had an excellent relationship.' But Clare's health suffered. The allergy problems she had had from the age of eight became worse and, instead of giving in, she fought – going for early morning runs and sustaining herself by drinking endless cups of tea. She was lonely and missed the countryside. 'I was offered a cottage in the country but hate the idea of being totally cut off. And I love my impossible London house with its five floors and crumbling plasterwork. I'm always muttering about moving, but now I never will unless I have to. . . . Although I don't go around looking for the perfect man to come along – they seem few and far between. I do need my friends and love what London has to offer – particularly the theatre and opera. Opera gives me the only other sensation of ecstasy I experienced at certain moment while sailing. At times, listening to *Othello* or *Turandot* or *Carmen* that magical thing happens and you become transported. I've never felt it with another human being.'

Since turning to fiction Clare has produced a book every two years and finds writing a full-time, nine-to-five job. She never goes out to lunch and only goes shopping under duress. Once she gets a firm idea for the subject, she spends six months on research and working out the plot, then a year writing the manuscript, followed by six months of final editing and helping to promote the book. 'It's hard work and always a challenge. I know I push myself too hard but I indulge myself, too. My favourite relaxation is reading and the other is to lie in a hot bath watching television, just aimlessly flicking from channel to channel on the remote control like an idiot. But I'm a terrible worrier – particularly over Tom who was quite sickly for the first two years of his life. I don't ever seem to have had a worry-free time.'

Clare was in Norway researching her third novel, *Wolf Winter*, set at the height of the Cold War, when she contracted the chronic disease Myalgic Encephalomyelitis (ME). Within the space of a week she changed from a healthy woman to a confused creature with an aching body and throbbing head who could only just stumble across her bedroom. 'I suppose my health had been going downhill for some time and I was getting more tired, but suddenly the disease struck. My face puffed up and my eyes were streaming. I could hardly walk, I lost my concentration and short-term memory. Back in London I kept going to my doctor and he said, "Just pull yourself together." But it was terrible. I slept all the time, felt totally lethargic and sometimes my legs just wouldn't function. One day David Puttnam came up to me at a party and said, "I know what you're going through, I've had it too." The most frightening thing is when your brain stops functioning properly.'

It is only in the last few years that ME has been taken seriously by the medical profession with a Bill in Parliament resulting in GPs being allowed for the first time to write a sick note classifying a patient's illness as ME. Previously known as mono-nucleosis or Royal Free Disease, it was dismissed by doctors as psychosomatic, stress-related or a post-virus syndrome. Clare is President of the ME Action Campaign, a body which supports both orthodox and alternative treatments. 'We believe in self-help and our members feel free to speak out. Whenever I'm invited to speak to a group of psychiatrists or medicos I accept and jump straight into the lion's den. There is no magic cure – like a drug – it's just your immune system not working, but we're learning all the time. In the early days when I first went public there was an avalanche of letters. It was emotionally overwhelming reading of some of the really ghastly problems people suffer from.'

Clare has learned to live with the disease by resting and putting herself on a strict diet. She still admits to feeling only seventy per cent well even on a good day, but she refuses to be crushed. Instead, in spite of continuing bad health, she says she has never felt more fulfilled in her life, bringing up her son Tom, writing her complex thrillers and fighting on behalf of other victims. This mysterious illness for which doctors have no cure has taken her on a different journey which could yet prove to be her most intrepid.

Elaine Brook

'Whatever you can do, or dream you can,
begin it . . .

Goethe

'Shambhala is the living Tibetan legend which inspired the story of
Shangri-La. To reach this mystical paradise of culture and learning,
one must make a long and difficult journey through mountains and
wilderness. Having arrived at the correct geographical location,
only those who have prepared themselves mentally and spiritually
can perceive Shambhala for what it really is. To me, the journey to
Shambhala is a metaphor for the journey through life.' This was no
Buddhist lama addressing his novices, but one of our leading
mountaineers digressing for a moment as she talked about her latest
trek, when she led a blind friend up Everest.

Elaine Brook, far from being the stereotype of a hefty mountain
climber, is a slender girl of 5 foot 5 inches with straight fringed
blonde hair framing a friendly and vulnerable face. But then not
many of the early or contemporary famous climbers were or are
Amazons. It is said that the agility and balance of a ballerina more
than compensates for the lack of brawn.

Many of the early women climbers initially visited the mountains
for health reasons, only later becoming mountaineers. In 1872
Isabella Bird Bishop, a Victorian invalid, was so helped by the
mountain air that she later managed the ascent of the 13,650-foot
Mauna Loa, the world's largest volcano. In 1838, Mlle Henriette
d'Angeville, after consulting her doctor, and fortified by a diet
which included lemonade, blancmange and prunes, became the first
woman to reach the summit of Mont Blanc despite suffering acute
mountain sickness. She beat the previous record of the little maid-
servant of eighteen, Marie Pardis, who was dragged in 1808 up to

the top by determined guides as she gasped out, 'Go on, throw me down there and go on by yourselves.' Another Victorian visitor to the mountains for her health was Elizabeth le Blond, but in 1882 'Lizzie' was to become one of the best-known climbers of all time, managing to climb the main peaks in the Alps and founding the first women's climbing club in Britain.

In those days convention dictated that women had always to be accompanied by male guides, but in 1885 two English sisters, Anna and Ellen Pigeon, published their diary account which described ten years of climbing in the Alps, once crossing the Sesia Joch from Zermatt to Alagna, first done by a Mr G. Moore and said to be unrepeatable. The Alpine Club, suspicious that two unassuming English ladies had stolen their best climbers' limelight, investigated the climb thoroughly, but finally had to accept that their account was true.

The American climber, Miriam Underhill, inherited the feminist mantle of her predecessors when in 1929 she set out with Alice Dumesne to achieve the first manless traverse of the Grepon. In her autobiography, *Give Me the Hills*, she recorded one man's reaction to their achievement: 'The Grepon has disappeared as a climb, it no longer exists. Now that it has been done by two women alone, no self-respecting man can undertake it. A pity, too, because it used to be a very good climb.'

When Elaine Brook started mountaineering there were not many good women climbers around. She, too, experienced a certain antagonism amongst men, and difficulty in finding climbing partners, although not necessarily for the old reasons. Climbers' wives were unhappy with the idea of attractive young girls accompanying their husbands on the remote mountains. 'It was like a minefield picking your way through the established ideas that women were only good for one thing, and in England it was very difficult to get together enough women to form an expedition. In Canada and the States it was very different: women were finding ways to tackle rock and ice on their own terms and discovering where technique and co-operation could be finely tuned to compensate for lack of muscles.' But there were some men in England who were prepared to break with tradition and climb with a woman on equal terms. Elaine pays particular tribute to the opportunities offered by Doug

Scott, a well-established mountaineer who invited her on expeditions, providing valuable experience which later enabled her to organise her own climbs. This was a great bonus at the time.

Some climbers say that one of the joys of climbing lies in the variety of skills it requires and the unique way in which each climb draws upon those skills. The top-level climber must exhibit physical and psychological control through movement and keep calm under pressure. Because each climb is different, demanding varying degrees of strength and technical skill, there can be no single key to top performance. This keeps climbing interesting since failure or success on one climb is no guarantee of similar results on the next. Although women are often hampered by lack of reach, they tend to have smaller hands and fingers – a definite advantage on cracks or small face holds – and are generally considered to have better balance and flexibility than men. But many women are held back in their climbing by an inability to push past the point where all is reversible and risk the consequences, while men seem to thrive on trying climbs sometimes barely within the realm of their physical ability, willing to be bold risk-takers. But now, as women climbers continue to strive for higher goals and begin to understand their true potential, the margin separating the best male and female climbers is already narrowing.

Elaine was born in London in 1949, the only daughter of Alec and Isabel Turner. Her father was an experimental engineer and the following year her family was uprooted and moved to the Cotswolds, where her younger brother was born. Her mother, who had all but given up her music and photography to raise a family, remained an avid reader of travel books, and her father encouraged Elaine's adventurous spirit, which as a child took her up trees, down caves and over walls to places where her younger brother was reluctant to follow. Attending the local day school left her plenty of time to wander across the countryside on her own. Her first ambition was to explore the Amazon jungle, and she read everything she could find on the subject. In her early teens she became an expert in judo, fencing, sailing, ski-ing, kayaking and karate, but when she went to college to study art, it was pot-holing that filled most of her spare time. This passion was short-lived, however, because as she was always the smallest she was the one who inevitably got sent up the newest and often the wettest tunnel. So she took the decision to climb to the exclusion of everything else. 'At fifteen I was rock-climbing in Wales with a gang of boys and a very old rope and from then on my life became a series of crazy expeditions and trips all over the world.' An understatement: Elaine has traversed ranges and scaled mountains where no woman has set foot before. She was the first British woman to tackle and conquer some of the more difficult climbs in the Yosemite district in the United States. Joining Doug Scott's British Baffin Island Arctic Expedition, she became the first woman to take part in that type of tough exploratory climbing. She then went on to make first ascents of various peaks in the Bolivian Andes.

'Each mountain is a challenge, there's danger, discomfort, hard work – it's a huge effort to achieve something which is just an abstract idea in your head. After all, getting to the summit is of no practical use to anyone. There are no prizes or points – you just get a tremendous high being up in impossible places. Every time you get unfit and feel your body can't cope, you have to break through the fear barrier again. But eventually you get to the point where you're perched on a wall hundreds of feet up, you look up and know what you've got to do next. The next thing you know, you're doing it. For me it's an extending experience, almost travelling through the power of thought. You're aware that your body is acting in complete harmony with your mind, an intuitive synthesis that draws on inner reserves of balance and strength. It's pushing you to the limit, and when you lay yourself on the line like that, you do get to know yourself very well indeed. The satisfaction of achieving something you've set yourself really is enormous.'

To finance her passion Elaine had a series of jobs, working as an art teacher, a graphic designer, a photo-journalist and on ecological research projects. When she could take time off she went rock-climbing all over Britian, and in the early 1970s she became one of the foremost of the small groups of women rock-climbers in the country.

'One Whitsun I remember going to Eskdale in the Lake District with Kate Webb, a climbing friend. We bivvied at Esk Buttress in black bin-bags because we didn't have a tent. The weather was glorious and we swam and climbed every day – we didn't want to leave and kept eking out our food to stay another and another day longer. We were literally sharing out the last crust when a party of Venture Scouts came climbing over the hill and sat down to eat their lunch by our 'swimming pool' at Cam Spout. They took one look at our crust and shared their lunch with us before we said a word.'

Sometimes she would find herself following male climbers up some of the hardest climbs in the United Kingdom. 'As most of the men were large and heavy and I a mere shrimp of seven stone, I think they may have been justifiably concerned by the lack of ballast to stop a fall.' It would have been impossible for her to lead these climbs herself, and the experiences broadened her horizons both literally and metaphorically.

But Elaine's career has not been one long uninterrupted series of successes. One day while rock-climbing in Derbyshire, her male partner was not holding the rope and she fell to the ground, breaking her back. 'It was very difficult to learn to trust again – subconsciously something deep inside me didn't feel safe any more in that situation. If I'd stayed rock-climbing I might have got over it, but because I moved on to do other things I've never really got over it. Now Lhakpa does all the leading if we go rock-climbing – he's very good.' She looks across at Lhakpa, who smiles and makes a deprecating gesture with his hands. He is the Sherpa guide she met in the Himalayas in 1984 and married soon afterwards.

In 1975 she moved to the United States and became friendly with some of the leading American women climbers. She loved the informality of the American way of life and found it easier to earn her living there, working on magazines as a lay-out artist, selling her photographs and marketing her skills and experience by taking groups on guided trips in the mountains. With an English climber, Jill Lawrence, she made a fast ascent on the East Buttress of Middle Cathedral Rock in Yosemite National Park, and with Cathy Culli-nane she led several short climbs including Catchy, Cramming, and 'free-climbing pitches' of the Nose on El Cap. 'I can remember every move on one hard climb and how incredibly pleased I was having done it without scrabbles or near misses, but I can't remember when it was or what it was called. The wonderful smell of pine resin and bay leaves and the funny slang the Californian climbers used – that's what climbing was about for me – friendly people and adventures in magnificent places.'

The following year Doug Scott asked her to join his Arctic Expedition to Baffin Island and she accepted with alacrity though she was aware of the dangers involved, which included the threat of avalanches, the worst fear of climbers. Elaine had already lost some good friends who were very experienced climbers. But avalanches are unpredictable. They were in fact caught in an avalanche as they were climbing Mount Ulu. 'There was this rumbling sound and the sky went dark. I huddled into the rock face, thinking, "That's it, we're dead." There was no fear or panic, just a feeling of inevitability. Fortunately, it was a light avalanche of wet snow and it didn't bring down any rock with it, so I just got drenched as it swept past! Falls aren't too dangerous as long as you're roped together, which is why I'd never go solo on a mountain – if you fell in a crevasse, that would be it. I don't feel the need to take that kind of risk.' The climb was successful in swinging leads on a new route on Mount Ulu which entailed eighteen consecutive hours of climbing.

Elaine became a Canadian citizen in 1979 and worked as a lay-out artist for *Oil Week Magazine* in Calgary. During this time she married, but the marriage didn't last. Even now she finds it impossible to tell whether her passion for climbing was an escape from the breakdown of her marriage or the cause of it. She spent as much time as possible climbing in the Canadian Rockies with her great friend, Judy Sterner, a Californian with an exuberant personality. 'There was one time when Judy and I skied through the Rockies for a few days and lived in snow caves – supposed to be the ultimate in snow survival. Probably the coldest place I've ever lived – you put something down and it froze to the ground, touched it again and your fingers stuck to it. Another time we decided to ski into a mountain hut for Christmas, but halfway there a chinook [warm wind] blew in and turned the snow to six-feet-deep porridge. We spent Christmas in a wet snowdrift and didn't make the hut till Boxing Day. I think that must have been my worst Christmas ever.'

But Elaine's most satisfying climb was when she and Judy set themselves the task of making the first ascent of a 19,000-foot mountain, Nevada Millachuma, in the Bolivian Andes. After travelling by train through Peru they camped by Lake Titicaca, walked to Copacabana and hitch-hiked through Bolivia to Millachuma, one of the highest tin-mining villages in the Andes. From the village a dirt road led up to the mines on the mountainside. Although life was hard in the village and food and water extremely scarce, they were invited to supper and beer and given a warm send-off when they prepared for their climb to the peak. They were praised for their courage and toughness and the phrase *muy macha* constantly repeated.

Their progress up the glacier was slower than they had expected, and the snow was sugary and unstable which meant there was nowhere firm to dig in their axes if they slipped. They spent the first night bivouacking on icy rocks and cooked a supper for which they had little appetite. Night brought headaches and very little sleep and morning a feeling of lethargy. 'Casting unappreciative eyes on the scenery about us, we laboriously packed our gear and put on our frozen crampons. Then we plodded up the glacier hampered by our packs, ropes, prusiks, harness, ice axes and all the other paraphernalia designed to protect us from frostbite, starvation, falling into crevasses and any other perils.' They reached the base of the final climb by mid-afternoon and lazed in the sun for a few hours before getting into their sleeping bags. 'No headaches this time and we were able to appreciate the silent beauty of the moonlit peaks around us.' They were well aware of the danger of altitude sickness and they laboriously melted pot after pot of snow which they drank as soup, tea and hot chocolate.

The next morning, leaving their sleeping bags to dry in the sun, they set off up the face. Roped together they climbed carefully and slowly as the angle steepened from 65 to 70 degrees. They took it in turns to lead and as they neared the summit found a giant crevasse barring their way. 'Fortunately the ice wall was solid and took the first ice screw.' As Elaine reached the razor-edged peak she hacked out a small platform for them to sit on. 'Hope you don't mind me removing the actual summit,' I said to Judy. 'The sight that met us was spectacular, with the range laid out before us, gleaming gold and white in the afternoon sun. We felt marvellous. It was the first time I'd climbed an uncharted mountain with another woman. It really boosted our confidence in our methods and values.' Getting down was more difficult than the ascent and, as movement was severely restricted, after gasping for breath and taking a few pictures they started back almost immediately. 'There is never really enough time to savour the satisfaction of a successful ascent,' wrote Elaine. 'It has to be stored up and relived later when the dangers of the mountain are far behind.' It was getting dark before they completed the descent and they could see the lights of the village far below.

Two hours later, tired and dazed, they were surrounded by smiling faces, food, beer, laughter and endless questions.

After climbing La Monja Grande, Elaine and Judy then spent several seasons guiding trekking parties through Peru. Because the treks usually began at around 10,000 feet and involved several nights at elevations above 14,000 feet, proper acclimatisation to the high altitude was an important factor, although their burden was eased by the heavy equipment and food being carried by *burros*. The days were hot, but at night the temperature dropped below freezing. All the arrangements involved dealing with the local Quechua Indians, so a fluent command of Spanish was essential. A classic trek was from Santa Cruz to Llanganoco – a five-day 40-mile trip, all above 10,000 feet, circling such mountains as Huascaran, Huandoy and Alpamayo, some of the most dramatic in the Cordillera Blanca.

A few months later Judy met a British archaeologist whom she later married, and their tiny flat became overcrowded. 'I was happy for her, but I moved out, struggling to overcome a sense of loss and the discovery that attachment to a person can throw one out of balance as much as attachment to ambition or even materialism.' She and Judy had formed a strong personal bond and a unique climbing relationship. They were about the same size as each other which made climbing logistics easier, and they shared the same philosophy about exploring unknown areas and finding their way up a mountain. Their methods were unconventional – they didn't believe in being loaded down with equipment like most other climbers at the time. They had shared many experiences in organising their own expedition to the Arctic and South America and had found ways finely to tune their techniques of co-operation to compensate for lack of weight. Elaine was to find the break more difficult than she had imagined and spent some time getting over it by travelling in South America on her own. They lost contact with each other and later Elaine said, 'I've no idea where she is – I hope one day she gets in touch.'

But soon she was to find another climbing partner. Through Judy, Elaine had met Sharon Wood, the first North American woman to climb Mount Everest. Together Sharon and Elaine did a lot of ice climbing on frozen waterfalls in the Canadian Rockies. 'It was beautiful and terrifying – the ice was so hard that it splintered when you hit it.' Their most adventurous climb was up Massey's Gully and, with Sharon leading, they set off on skis between the railway tracks, then followed the stream up to the base of the falls. Massey had only one steep pitch, but much of it was vertical and on this cold day the ice was brittle and splintered, causing difficulties in making their placements. Leaving their skis they began their climb, chipping experimentally and averting their faces from the resulting spray of sharp slivers of ice. Elaine paid out the rope while Sharon fiddled with ice screws and karabiners. This was the longest vertical pitch she had ever led. 'She worked out in advance how many protection placements she would need before the space beneath her persuaded her that she needed more.' Eventually Elaine became aware of the sunlight gradually shifting position on the different peaks. She recollects, 'It would never reach in here, a north-facing gully. My feet were numb and occasionally a large lump of splintered ice would crash down a few feet to my right and I began to wonder if I wanted to be a good waterfall climber after all. Then there was a quiet 'OK' from above, the rope went in and it was my turn. I still felt unwilling to trust those delicate tips – only the placements the brittle ice demanded and I used up plenty of energy pounding away until they felt solid. 'Good lead,' I muttered as I grabbed the gear and led the easy pitch to the top.' They skied down into the deepening twilight as the Vancouver train lumbered slowly down the pass behind them. Then they planned other ice climbs. 'Ever done Silk Tassel?' Sharon asked.

But as usual fate intervened when Dr Peter Hackett asked Elaine to join his team of doctors and field assistants working on research into frostbite and acute mountain sickness – AMS – still one of the major causes of death among high-altitude climbers. The research was to be carried out on Alaska's Mount McKinley, the highest mountain in North America, and the main purpose of the trip was to examine the logistics of maintaining a field hospital at 14,000 feet and to find out how many climbers passing that way would show altitude effects. As human guinea pigs they had to undergo certain tests to measure their mental alertness and hand–eye co-ordination to see how their faculties diminished at increasingly higher altitudes. Altogether they made seven camps at varying altitudes, the final one at 17,200 feet where they experienced twenty-four hours of gale-force winds, typical of the Alaska range. When the wind finally dropped, they set off for the summit. As Mount McKinley is so near the Arctic Circle there are twenty-four hours of daylight in mid-summer with temperatures even colder than usual when the sun is not high in the sky. At 19,000 feet one of the climbers began to show signs of ataxia (loss of balance), but quickly recovered on the descent. The climb had taken them two weeks in temperatures 35 degrees below zero. It took them only two days for their return ski down the mountain.

But Elaine was beginning to develop a new passion which had nothing to do with mountains. She had made many friends amongst the Tibetan community living in Canada and had started studying the Tibetan and Nepali languages. She was particularly inspired by reading Heinrich Harrer's *Seven Years in Tibet* and *The Way of the White Clouds* by Anagarika Govinda. And in 1981 she visited Nepal to reconnoitre for a women's climbing expedition to the Khumbu region. But she soon became disillusioned with the amount of red tape, formalities and permissions necessary to organise an expedition. She also felt that most climbers in the district were no more than high-altitude tourists. 'They were employing all the Sherpas who'd been up the climbs many times before to carry all the heavy equipment – the whole thing seemed pre-packaged, phoney and hypocritical.' It crystallised for her what she herself really enjoyed in climbing. So instead she wandered off the beaten track amongst the Sherpa people who had settled down after crossing from Tibet five centuries before. She spent some time in a little monastery in the hills where there was an English translator. It was there she met the High Lama who became her teacher, and it is there she returns every year. Her love affair with Buddhism was deepening.

So when her friend Doug Scott invited her to join an expedition to Tibet, she hardly hesitated. Tibet was the source of Himalayan Buddhism. However, Doug was asking her to replace a climber who had dropped out suddenly from his expedition to Shishapangma, which was due to leave the following week. The cost of £1,500 would devastate her savings and put an end to her dream of buying a cottage in Colorado and settling down to do some writing. The previous year she had trekked with Doug and his family through the foothills of the Nepal Himalayas to Makalu Base Camp. They were accompanied by Reinhold Messner shortly after his solo ascent of Everest from Tibet. It had not been a happy journey. 'Before long Doug was accusing me of every sort of negativity. I knew well enough from the past how Doug's open enthusiasm and his gentleness had a way of swinging unpredictably into outbursts of blazing rage.' So instead she sought the company of Messner who would read her passages from the book he was writing on his Everest North Face ascent. His stories of adventures in Tibet had stirred her own drive to go there.

On this occasion she was nervous about the exact role she was expected to play. The plan was for the four most experienced climbers to tackle the unclimbed South-West Face of the 26,291-foot summit of Shishapangma. She knew this was beyond her ability and also beyond her ambition. Doug was persuasive. 'Well, Nick Prescott, the bloke who's organised the trip, will be taking an easier route. You could either climb with Nick or go and look round Tibet.' The thought of tagging along with such highly-accomplished climbers and possibly tackling a 21,000-foot peak with an unknown partner filled her with alarm, but romantic images of Tibet crowded back. The eleventh-century poet Milarepa had spent years meditating in caves in the mountains around Shishapangma. 'Maybe even in these days of Chinese occupation, I could find the caves and traces of the legend.' Five days later she was back in England involved in the last-minute chaos of preparation for the expedition, and within forty-eight hours she was boarding a flight to Peking.

Both Elaine and Doug wrote books describing their traumatic Tibetan journeys. They are very different. *The Shishapangma Expedition* written by Doug Scott together with Alex MacIntyre, two of the world's most influential Himalayan mountaineers, provides a unique commentary on climbing the South-West Face of the formidable mountain, which is over a mile high and twice as broad and one of the ten highest in the world, 'an unclimbed, unvisited Alpine playground'. To Alex, it was an ambition, but 'not just to climb it. We had to make the ascent with style, as light, as fast, as uncluttered as we dared, free from the traditional trappings of a Himalayan climb, free from umbilical cords and logistics. The wall was the ambition, the style became the obsession.' Elaine's book, *Land of the Snow Lion*, gives a vivid account of how she and her five male companions approached Chinese inscrutability, also of how she eventually made her escape to wander without permission, chased by the Communist authorities who were unable to restrain her movements or stop her from mixing with the people. She describes with humour and sensitivity an ancient and mystical way of life and a journey of self-discovery.

The idea was for Elaine to travel with the others to Base Camp near the village of Nyalam and then for her and Nick Prescott to join them on some of the short acclimatisation ascents. Elaine could then make her independent way back through the Tibetan villages. But even before it had left Peking, the group, all highly individualistic and strong characters, had several brushes with the Chinese Mountaineering Association. The male climbers found the officialdom and general nannying more than they could stand and began to display total disregard for the Chinese way of conducting affairs. Elaine found it a salutary experience to be looked upon as an inferior race, but she suggesed it might be more productive to conform to the local customs.

Eventually a *modus vivendi* for the expedition was reached, and they flew to Lhasa accompanied by Mr Wu Ming, their young interpreter, a small shy man with horn-rimmed spectacles, and an immaculate crisp Mao suit. Instead of being able to absorb the calm and other-worldliness of Lhasa and its famous monasteries, they found themselves in combat with the authorities. The Liaison Officer, Mr Pemba, was determined they should go to Base Camp by minibus, a form of transport way beyond their means. They felt an old army truck would suffice. Mr Pemba was adamant. It was forbidden for tourists to ride in trucks. If they wouldn't go by minibus, they would have to go home. Elaine used all of her Tibetan vocabulary and powers of persuasion to argue their case. Suddenly all was reversed and everyone was smiling. Yes, they could go in the truck. The expedition equipment was delivered from the airport with remarkable efficiency and they were on their way.

On their four-day journey along the Nepal Highway to Nyalam their efforts to stop and see the interesting sights were continually frustrated. At Shigatze, however, they managed to escape the tyrannical Mr Pemba and explored the Tashi Lhunpo Monastery, built by the first Dalai Lama. Elaine found herself overcome by the hospitality the Tibetan people showed to complete strangers, even greater than the Sherpas of Nepal. She practised her Tibetan on a humorous old monk who offered them a drink from his cup – the top of a human skull, an unorthodox use for a ritual object formerly kept by monks as reminders of the impermanence of all things, including human life. 'In the main temple about seventy monks were gathered, sitting cross-legged on low cushions, chanting in unison. We stood listening, the whole group silent for once, as the sound swelled and filled the hall with a resonance that for me seemed strange, yet strangely familiar. All my reading and intellectually acquired knowledge had not prepared me for anything like this. I knew what I was hearing and seeing bore a deeper significance than I could perceive; I knew this instinctively, and for a moment I felt as if I were about to break through the barrier of unknowing and understand it all.'

Back in the truck she and Doug listened to a cassette of a Tibetan opera on their headphones. Lulled half asleep by the music, it was almost as if the rhythmic syllables within the song contained sounds basic to any language, and to Elaine it seemed that the voices were speaking in French and other languages. Doug was amazed to find he could understand the words of the song which were coming across to him in English and wrote in his book, 'I had the certain feeling that something eternal and universal was locked away in the music.'

At Shegar, which stands at about 14,000 feet, their altitude acclimatisation really began. As the truck rumbled past the village of Tingri in the region where the Tibetan saint Milarepa had lived and meditated, Elaine felt she could begin to forge a link between the actual present and the legendary past. Born a poor peasant who became a black magician and murderer, Milarepa had atoned for his crimes through hardship and devotion. After years of meditating in caves and surviving on a diet of nettles, he had reached the ultimate spiritual goal of enlightenment. 'Even I felt this was taking the "simple life" too far. And yet there had been times, wandering alone in the barren wastes of the mountains with no ambitions or summits to worry about, when a kind of exhilaration and peace had pervaded my whole being, leaving no thoughts of the cold and discomfort I was experiencing. Was it then possible to train and control the mind to the point where far more severe conditions could be overcome for a whole lifetime? I had to admit I was curious. I wondered if insights into this kind of heightened perception still remained in New Tibet.' Elaine and Doug had originally wanted to camp in the village of Tingri but the others were keen to push ahead and reach the mountain as quickly as possible. Elaine felt oppressed by the limited single-mindedness of the climbers and her instinct was to set off then and there to explore Tibet. But in the end she was persuaded to continue with them and climb with Nick the easier peaks while the others tackled the face. Overpowered by the strength of Doug's personality and argument, she decided to postpone her decision until Base Camp.

They caught their first glimpse of Shishapangma as the truck ground its way across the Thong La Pass. The aptness of the description of Tibet as the roof of the world became apparent. 'It was as if we were looking down on the mighty Himalaya.' They were now entering a part of Tibet that had not been seen by a westerner since the Chinese take-over nearly thirty years before. In Nyalam, the end of the truck ride, there were further frustrations. The yaks which were to carry their equipment to Base Camp had not arrived, and when they eventually did they were in terrible physical condition and were accompanied by some extremely unenthusiastic yak-boys in denims. Tempers amongst the climbers were frayed; the frustrations and personality clashes which were to mark the whole expedition started to emerge. 'The arguments began to spread not unlike the clash of antlers in the contest for the leadership of the herd.' Elaine found herself to be the butt of the frequent chauvinistic taunts. When Nick became ill and made for his sleeping bag, coughing violently, someone shouted, 'Come on Elaine, why don't you jump in with him and rub his chest with something nice.' She was becoming tired of being referred to as if she was the expedition groupie. 'Long ago I had learned that men put women climbers into three types: wives are "hags", single girls are "tarts" and good climbers are "dykes". God, I thought, they're probably expecting me to be their cook and potwasher for three months.'

They pitched tents at Base Camp in a blizzard on a rocky ridge a week behind schedule. The tension between Elaine and the men was escalating and her complicated relationship with Doug was showing signs of strain as it had done on their previous trek to Makalu. Elaine wanted to leave them immediately and wander off on her own, but this presented difficulties because her visa stated she was a climber, not a tourist. By upsetting the authorities she might put the whole expedition in jeopardy. She decided to continue to the Advance Base Camp, but at 19,000 feet she was beginning to feel the ill-effects of altitude, severe dehydration due to the rapidity of their ascent. She had been higher before, but she had never gained altitude so quickly. Against her instincts she went with the others on their first exploratory climb. But before long Nick, too, was feeling the effects of the altitude, vomiting violently and trailing behind. A heated debate began amongst the men as to how to proceed. Elaine could stand the bickering no longer and continued alone up the moraine. 'What the hell was I doing here in the middle of all this? The mountains were silent – dazzlingly mockingly beautiful in the morning sunshine. The cold space around me was so vast, so empty, a place of purity and savage desolation. I was drawn back to the mountains because they never failed to remind me that there was also a clear space within, a space which so easily became crowded with the all-consuming business of everyday living. To leave the noise and bustle of the world behind was to be aware once more of that elusive inner peace .... What, then, was the point of slogging all the way up here, if only to drag the mental clutter and hassles along with them?' When Elaine recognised what kind of climb faced her, she was once more sharply aware of the dangers involved. 'Why was I afraid of this mountain, where before I had suffered no more fear than was necessary for survival ...? This time the lure was Tibet. There was something here I wanted to discover, something no more tangible than that desire to reach the top of the mountain, and I did not want to get myself killed before the quest had properly begun. Of course, Tibet, like climbing or anything else, could offer no insight to a closed mind. This experience too could degenerate into simply clinging to a self-image. For me the great delight of climbing had been the freedom from preoccupation with self that came from the intense concentration inspired by risk.' She suddenly realised that Alex was yelling behind her and heading off to the right. When she reached him he was standing beside a glacier.

As he uncoiled the rope at the edge of the glacier, a smooth undulating sweep of new snow flowing from the col above, deceptively hiding potentially lethal crevasses in the ice, he said: 'Better tie on for this one.' Two of the climbers had returned to camp, one with lung problems, and the other with severe altitude sickness. Elaine and the three remaining men spent the night bivouacking, cramped on a small ledge dug into the snow. During the night the wind rose to severe gusts which felt as if the flimsy bivouac tent would be ripped from its moorings. The next morning they set off on a rising traverse across steep blue ice with sheer rock below and crazily-angled *seracs*. Elaine looked at the shiny ice above and then down the dizzying drop to the boulders far below. 'I wondered what kind of controlled insanity was driving me to push myself to the limit. It wasn't difficult but I was feeling the altitude and a fall here would be my last.' She struggled to the top of the second ridge and realised it would be suicidal to continue. She let Doug accompany her back as far as the bivouac site, and they descended the ridge together. 'You gave it a good try – this speed of ascent is fast in anyone's books,' he said. 'Oh well, three down, three to go. Maybe one day I'll have a Himalayan trip that works out.' He looked very lonely as he plodded back up to the mountain.

She now had to traverse the glacier again alone, not roped to Alex as she had been the day before. Their footprints had been obliterated by the snow. She later said that this was probably the most frightening experience of her life as there was so much time to think about it. 'I had never crossed a glacier alone before. I had also known a few who had died doing just that. It seemed a pointless and lonely way to die. Slowly fear built up like a rock in my chest until I couldn't move. . . . I gradually became aware of a calm voice telling me to relax, that it was easy to get across. As my mind became calm it slowly emptied of everything except the endless whiteness of the snow, and I walked out into it.'

Back at camp Mr Wu was not optimistic that he would be able to get her visa status changed to tourist, but he gave her a letter in Chinese countersigned by Mr Pemba which said she had to return to Lhasa for health reasons. With this as her only authorisation for travelling round Tibet, she repacked – a set of warm clothes, emergency bivouac gear, sugar and *tsampa* and a pile of books on Milarepa, Tibetan history and Buddhist philosophy, together with canisters of film. 'I felt the tightening of the stomach which comes with excitement. In a kind of limbo between the mountain and the unknown came a rare moment of prescience and I knew I was on the edge of greater dangers and deeper insights than I had previously known.' She set off – alone at last.

Within a few hours she found herself in the most dangerous situation she had ever been in in her life. Crossing a river on a slippery log, she lost her balance and felt her heavy pack pulling her head-first into the river. 'Then there was nothing but icy water and confusion. Swimming-pool experience had taught me that when you fall into deep water you have only to wait and your head will break the surface . . . this did not happen . . . my lungs were screaming. Into the panic came the quiet voice telling me to stop struggling and think. . . . I became aware that I was lying face-down and that my pack had shunted forward and was holding my head under the water.' Eventually Elaine managed to roll over on her back and, with the pack beneath her, to breathe once more. She had been close to drowning in three feet of water. Sitting on the bank trying to sort out her soaking equipment with her wet hair turning to clumps of ice in the blizzard, her dazed mind told her that if she wanted to avoid dying of hypothermia, she should get moving.

In Nyalam she was informed that there would be a truck to Lhasa the following day. Four days later, with still no transport in sight, Elaine set off on foot. After twenty miles on starvation rations she was befriended in the village of Pankyeling by a Tibetan family, which consisted of an old lady, her two sons and their shared wife, and her eight-year-old son Tashi. The young men admired her climbing boots and offered to exchange them for a handsome new pair of black and red felt Tibetan boots, which they bound round her calves. The wife, Phurbu, had her hair in two long black glossy plaits. Braided into the hair was a string of turquoise and coral. She told Elaine that this signified that a girl was married. Laughing, she took Elaine's turquoise bracelet and braided it into her hair. 'Now you are *nama*!' After she had eaten a supper of rice, chilis and potatoes and some dried goat meat, the authorities caught up with her and, with the family and half the village waving at the roadside, she was bundled into a truck which was to take her back to Lhasa.

In fact she was embarking on the start of a voyage which was to make a turning point in her life. She became more and more deeply engrossed in the legend of the religious ascetic, Milarepa, of whom Lobsang P. Lhalungpa had written: 'Never, in the thirteen centuries of Buddhist history in Tibet, has there been such a man, who not only inspired an intellectual elite and spiritual luminaries, but also captured the imagination of the common people. . . . Throughout pre-Communist Tibet Milarepa was held in universal veneration. It was so in the past and is still so among the thousands of refugees in the settlements of northern India, Bhutan and Sikkim.'

At the village of Tingri, Elaine escaped from the truck and was soon surrounded by a crowd, one of whom invited her to be her guest. Tashi, a middle-aged woman, had a strong, handsome face set in a severe expression which broke into a broad smile when she saw Elaine's boots and the turquoise coiled into her hair. Elaine was nervous that her presence in her home could bring risk to the family, but after a generous amount of the intoxicating *chang* she was persuaded and gratefully slipped under a pile of bedcovers on a stone bench. She heard the family preparing for bed, whispering their evening *mantras*. 'My mind, released from the earthly bounds of waking, flitted away from the darkened house to the courtyard where the sleeping cattle shuffled in their straw, and beyond, over the dusty plain to where the mountains shone white and cold beneath the stars.' Living with this hospitable family she found herself begin to relax, to drop the guard she realised had been her defence ever since leaving Colorado. The days slipped by and she was content to become absorbed in the daily household routines. The atmosphere was one of cheerful calm; the family shared the limited space in the dimly lit room with a profound sensitivity towards one another. One day she showed them her book on Milarepa. They in turn proudly hunted behind pots and bottles and found an old faded copy hidden behind the clutter. 'It was hard to find words for such an unexpected surprise. Here I was, staying with a family which had kept the tradition alive through the turbulence of the past twenty years. How absurd it had been to think of searching for empty caves on the mountainside and how deeply ingrained was the western conception of tangible goals. Suddenly I realised that to come upon the forgotten landmark that had once been one of Milarepa's caves would be no more illuminating that standing on the summit of a mountain.' Living with this Tibetan family and seeing how bravely and cheerfully they coped with the hardships of life, in spite of having lost everything including their country, made Elaine realise how much she needed to escape from her confined past. She was beginning to admit to herself that whatever she had been seeking in the last ten years in the headlong pursuit of higher summits and harder rock pitches, she had not found, and only now could she begin to be free.

Her peaceful and contemplative life was suddenly interrupted when Mr Pemba discovered her whereabouts and the authorities sent her on her way once more, this time in a minibus with a group of highly organised Japanese mountaineers. Retracing her outward journey, she saw the great fort at Gyantze that Sir Francis Younghusband had found so impregnable in 1904, and she visited the monastery known as Kumbum, the Golden Temple of the Hundred Thousand Buddhas. A straggle of children became her guides, and as the evening light deepened to a rich red glow, she felt that 'Tibet had become a Dali landscape of colour and light – unreal and intangible'.

Hitch-hiking to Lhasa with a young American called Rob who had picked up a smattering of Chinese, Elaine found herself in trouble once more. At Nagartze they stopped for the night at a Chinese army barracks. 'A few soldiers wandered around and a handful of mangy mongrels were cleaning up the scraps from the floor. Suddenly I was struck violently on the back of the leg. I became aware that I was lying on the floor, and that the screams I could hear were my own.' One of the dogs had gone berserk and bitten her above the knee. A medical orderly arrived and began to swab the wounds with hydrogen peroxide, but it was decided that they should continue on to Lhasa to get to a proper hospital. There, the Chinese doctor was sympathetic and the treatment simple and functional, but she decided to wait until her return home before starting rabies shots.

When the rest of the expedition arrived back in England, Elaine heard that Doug, Alex MacIntyre and Roger Baxter-Jones had reached the summit, with Nick ferrying loads to the lower camp. The fifth climber, Paul Braithwaite, had retired with lung problems before the start of the climb. Their final celebrations with the Chinese Mountaineering Association had been amicable, ending with a sumptuous banquet and a pile of certificates confirming their achievement. Two months later Alex was killed when he was descending Annapurna – a solitary stone hurtling down sent him falling 800 feet to his death. His mother put up a stone at Annapurna Base Camp which reads: 'It is better to live one day as a tiger than a hundred as a sheep.' Later still Roger was killed while acting as a guide in the Alps. Elaine wrote in her book: 'So many deaths leave you numb; the sport has become a battlefield. All you can do is remember friends when they were still alive, doing what they wanted and doing it well, and wish only that the cost had not been so high.'

Although the modern Chinese treatment of Tibet had changed the country that she travelled through, nothing could diminish the experience, and her respect for the Tibetans whom Peter Fleming described as 'curiously compounded of mysticism and jollity, of shrewdness and superstition, of tolerance and strict convention'. Looking back on her journey, her thoughts reverted to Milarepa's teachings. 'Any search is a journey, a fulfilment in itself, a process of learning. To live with an awareness of impermanence is a gift indeed.' She felt she could find what she was looking for, alone.

Shishapangma was to be the last military-style and organised expedition Elaine would undertake. She wanted to use her expertise and her new-found values in a different way and undertake new challenges. To extend herself in yet another direction seemed the true meaning of adventure. Her walk alone in the Himalayan area the previous year had so fired her imagination that she now began to plot a major trans-Himalayan expedition over ancient commercial trails. It would start from Gangtok in Sikkim and continue across the length of Nepal to Srinagar at the other end of the Himalayan range in Kashmir. She and another British woman reckoned it would take them about seven months, which in fact was as long a trip as they could afford. They would need climbing skills to get through the mountain passes, but basically were far more concerned with learning about the area and its people than achieving competitive and technical climbs. Neither, or so it seemed, felt the need to prove they could get to the top of yet another mountain.

The two set off in the autumn of 1983 with two Sherpa porters. All went well for the first few weeks. But when they reached Tashi Lapcha, a 17,500-foot pass, they disagreed about the most suitable way to cross it. It had the reputation of being dangerous. Elaine and her porter decided to take the low road. Her companion and her porter rashly took the high pass, as a result of which they became so badly frostbitten that they had to drop out of the expedition and go to Kathmandu to recover. The plan was for them to rejoin Elaine in Jumla in western Nepal with food supplies, but in late March, when Elaine and her porter, Ang Tende, and his brother-in-law, who had joined them *en route*, reached Jumla, the injured woman had not arrived. They were not to meet again. For four weeks the trio walked through the cold passes and high valleys surviving on their meagre rations supplemented by green nettles. A severe drought had created a food shortage among the local people who were unable to come to their aid with their normal generosity. Elaine remembers, 'We became quite thin and it brought life down to basics – it was challenging and exciting.'

They reached the border of north-east India in April and hiked past Nanda Devi in the Himalayas where the temperature reached 100 degrees in the valleys and torrential rain soaked the snow on the high mountain passes. On the toughest day of their trip they struggled through waist-deep snow in their running shoes, fearing avalanches from the overburdened slopes above. When they got to the Nehru Institute of Mountaineering at Uttarkashi they had hoped to have a short rest, but news reached them that Ang Tende's father was ill in his distant village. After a detour by train, bus and plane to be by his side, they spent three weeks there until the father was well enough to leave with Ang's brother-in-law. Then they set off into the wild highlands of Ladakh. They were tired from their recent hardships. Crossing the 16,000-foot passes leading to the mountain region of Zanskar, they heard it aptly called 'the last place on earth'. But they found an occasional refuge in the homes of the local people who were of Tibetan origin, like the Sherpas.

Their last big challenge was at the village of Cha, where they had to cross a wisp of rotting twig bridge spanning a 150-foot mountain torrent. 'Even Ang, who had strolled casually over a number of terrifying aerial contraptions during the previous six months, was scared,' Elaine recalls. They forced themselves across, only to find that the bridge the other side of the town had collapsed and they had to retrace their steps.

Several weeks later, in mid-July, they came to the end of the trek in Srinagar. Elaine's 'Women's Trans-Himalayan Expedition' had turned from near-fiasco into yet another achievement.

In 1984 Elaine was thirty-five years old and was becoming more involved with the spiritual and less with the physical. 'I think the most valuable thing I learnt from climbing was that a training discipline and a single-pointed concentration bring not only physical skills but also a kind of mental awareness. I suppose this is how I first became interested in meditation.' But the mountains were not going to release her without a final struggle.

Three years previously she had met Julie Donnelly, a switchboard operator in her mid-thirties who had been totally blind since the age of eight. They had been on a short study course at Conishead Priory, Ulverston, living amongst the Buddhist community and had formed a close friendship. Elaine remembers how she would hand Julie leaves, flowers and rocks and watch her fingers explore the tracery of veins and ripples of fossilised shells. 'As she spoke of textures, sounds, smells, I began to enter a world of non-visual perception – a fluid and sometimes elusive world. . . . I was hooked. Here was a world as fascinating as my beloved Himalayas. Aligning my perceptions with Julie's had become as much of a challenge as understanding my extrovert and enigmatic Sherpa friends.'

Elaine described to Julie her years of trekking in the Himalayan foothills. Julie became fascinated and determined to join Elaine on one of her expeditions. They went rock-climbing in the Lake District and Derbyshire and found from the first climb that their *rapport* was so strong as to be almost instinctive. Elaine recalls, 'I can only explain it in Eastern terms – it was almost as if we'd known each other before.'

Soon they were planning a trek through the lower Sherpa villages of Nepal. 'How much further is it to the Everest Base Camp?' asked Julie. 'Oh come on, let's go for it – no point in doing things by halves.' Elaine called her book *The Windhorse*, known by Sherpas in Nepal as the jewelled horse on prayer flags which carries the wisdom of the world. She wrote it with Julie to describe their four-week trek which actually took them to Kala Patthar, at 18,200 foot, a summit 500 foot above Everest Base Camp.

The idea had grown in momentum and became a sponsored event to raise money for Guide Dogs for the Blind. Julie had been to a school for blind children, but she hadn't learnt to use a guide dog until she was twenty-seven. Until then being blind meant 'that person with the white stick'. When she acquired her dog, Bruno, he became a lifeline, escorting her through the complicated maze of the London Underground to the bank where she worked. She would be unable to take Bruno with her on the trip because of rabies restrictions and she would have to rely completely on Elaine. Both acknowledged that it was really the trust between them which was on trial. Elaine knew that the responsibility was hers, but also that she must trust Julie to keep cool on dangerous sections and to do exactly as directed. 'If she panicked or did not listen properly she would be endangering my life as well as her own.'

In the build-up to their departure, there were the usual last-minute hitches. The insurance company decided they were not a good risk and backed out of insuring them. Money was scarce, but Julie managed to elicit support from sponsors for all their equipment, while Elaine flew to Nepal to fulfil a commitment as a tour courier which also enabled her to make all the local arrangements for supplies, internal flights and Sherpa porters.

They flew to New Delhi and then on to Kathmandu, with Elaine trying to give Julie an impression of what the mighty Himalayas looked like from the air. On their arrival there was a message from

Tapkhay Lama, a Sherpa monk, who said he had hoped to be able to meet them, but he was establishing a monastery in his village near Paphlu and would be there when they flew in. When their tiny plane came to a jerky stop on the dirt runway at Paphlu, there Elaine saw her friend, the familiar red-robed figure of the lama. The desolate airstrip seemed a much friendlier place with Tapkhay's boisterous energy and humour, and they found they were laughing despite their tiredness. A young Sherpa stepped forward and introduced himself. 'I am Lhakpa – your Sirdar.' Elaine got the impression that he had worked with westerners for some time. His clothes were smart by Sola-Khumbu standards and he was soon calling them by their first names, unlike the usual custom which is to address people as *sati* (friend) or *diddi* (sister). In fact, as the nephew of Sherpa Tenzing, the first conqueror of Everest, he had been scaling the heights as an expedition guide since he was fourteen. Much later Lhakpa recalled his impression of that first meeting. 'When I heard I was to bear the responsibility of guiding two English women, one blind, to Everest Base Camp, my first thought was to back out. Then I met them and my doubts about Julie vanished. She found her way around better than most trekkers. It was Elaine who was the problem. There was a mistake over how many porters we were taking, and we got off on what she calls the wrong foot.' Elaine had, indeed, complained about the numbers of porters and the fact that the Sherpanis (female porters) didn't carry any loads.

In single file they followed the lama along the steep, rocky trail, with both Julie and Elaine concentrating hard on navigating the narrow ditches. They were walking through one of the most beautiful forested valleys in the Himalayas and breathing thin, clear air sweet with the smell of pine resin. They successfully crossed a river on a light bridge of wire mesh and started the climb up to Thumbuk where Tapkhay wanted to show them his new *Gompa* (monastery), but Julie was scared by the bridge and was getting short of breath from the height, so she needed to rest. They decided to stay the night nearby in the house of Tapkhay's uncle. On the way to the *Gompa* the following day they passed great stones built into the walls along the trail and carved with prayers. Julie would feel the script with her fingers. Before long her hands could decipher the mantra in all its different styles and sizes. As the Sherpas pitched the tents outside the *Gompa*, the two women sat on a sunny ridge listening to the breeze rippling the prayer flags and absorbing the atmosphere of solitude and peace. But presently Julie began to feel unwell. She had a bad cold, had lost her appetite and was acclimatising slowly to the height. Elaine found herself more worried by Julie's health than by her blindness. Had her expectations for Julie's enjoyment of the journey been too high? Before she had set off, people had asked her, 'Don't you feel it's a terrible responsibility taking a blind person on a trip like this?' If they had to beat an untimely retreat back to England, there would be plenty of people ready to say, 'We told you so!'

In fact there was never any question of retreat, but before they reached their goal there were times of despair, friction and chronic sickness. At moments they were both afraid of failure but neither would ask the other to back down.

As the trek progressed they made notes for the book, Elaine writing her notes with freezing fingers and Julie using a dictaphone, curled up in her sleeping bag. While climbing they used hand signals and tape recorders to communicate. Elaine later described how it worked. 'If Julie wanted to ask me a question, she'd give my hand a squeeze which meant, "I've switched on the tape-recorder, tell me what it looks like." '

In the dark evenings in their tent Julie found herself recounting the events of her life and her emotions which she had never shared with anyone before. The recording machine became the recipient of her most traumatic moments. Just before her eighth birthday the glaucoma she had suffered from birth became so bad that it was decided she would have to undergo operations to remove both eyes and replace them with glass ones. No one told her. 'Before when I had been admitted to hospital, I had always been told what the doctor was going to do while I was asleep.' After the final operation she went into post-operative shock and became very ill. 'Out of the blankness of unconsciousness I found myself above the hospital bed I was lying in, looking down at myself. I began to move away, very easily. I distinctly remember looking down and seeing a fine, silvery thread connecting "me" with my body. . . . Gradually I felt as if I was fading away, being drawn down a dark tunnel beyond which was a mass of light so brilliant it dazzled me . . . and although I felt afraid of it I wanted more than anything to get to the wonderful place I knew was beyond it. Then I heard a voice telling me I mustn't go there, not yet, I must come back to myself. It repeated this over and over again.' Her mother told her that the hospital sister, a devout Catholic, had sat by her bed the whole time she had been unconscious, telling her she mustn't leave them, that it wasn't the right time to die – willing her to come back.

Elaine, of course, knew about Julie's artificial eyes, but when she discovered the complications entailed in removing and cleaning them daily to avoid infection from the dust and dirt, she was mortified. If she had been pre-warned she would have made sure they always had some sterilised water. 'Why didn't you tell me?' she asked. 'To be honest,' answered Julie, 'I thought it might freak you out so much that you wouldn't do the trip.'

Before they even reached Everest Base Camp Julie started suffering from severe headaches, sickness and stomach cramps. These could either have been caused by the altitude, dehydration or by a germ picked up at one of the grubby wayside tea shops. As well as having to adjust her body to the continuous walking in the rarefied air and keeping her balance on the rocky trail, she knew that there was always a potentially dangerous cliff or drop nearby. Once she had to cross a single-plank bridge with no hand rails. The disorientating roar of the water, the wobbly plank underfoot and the apprehension Elaine transmitted through her hand produced in Julie a fear not easy to overcome. She was finding it difficult to keep down even small amounts of liquid, let alone the recommended four to six litres a day. She had become deeply depressed. Julie described her feelings in *The Windhorse*: 'I had never stopped to think what it would be like to be on unfamiliar ground for so long, to be so completely dependent on someone any time I wanted to go further than the loo tent – it's like being in a cage. The bars are the unknown empty space around me and the locked door is my fear.'

Lhakpa admitted to Elaine that he had doubts about her continuing the climb. But when they paused for a moment's rest on the edge of an icy precipice, Julie was grateful that, at least so far, she had not received any of the premonitions or early warnings of disaster which had become part of her life since childhood. Once she had dreamt that her brother had dashed into a rain-swept street and suddenly there had been a roar of brakes and he was flying through the air in a shower of glass. She had telephoned her mother the next morning to find that her brother was in hospital with severe head wounds after being hit by an ambulance.

Eventually her condition improved enough for them to continue, with Lhakpa occasionally carrying her. As they approached Thang-boche Monastery with the Gokyo mountains behind it they were greeted by smiling monks. For them the greatest tragedy was not to be blind or handicapped, but to be unable to hear or read Buddha's teachings – to be unable to understand how to transcend an endless cycle of lifetimes spent in trying to satisfy worldly desires. Later that evening Elaine returned to the monastery and watched the sinking sun flash on the gold spire of the *chorten*. She had been there many times before and had always found it both fascinating and disturb-ing. The previous year she had met the reincarnate Lama of Thangboche, and he had explained to her a little of the relationship between men and mountains and gods. She had asked the lama: 'Are these gods real, or are they just an imputation of men's minds?' He gave an enigmatic smile. 'All phenomena are imputations of the mind.' Elaine was being drawn closer and closer to Buddhism, but she still found some aspects beyond her reach.

The next day Julie was feeling more cheerful. They reached the confluence of two rivers and followed the left-hand valley to Pheriche. The climb was at last beginning to fulfil Julie's expecta-tions, and as it got steeper and harder, she seemed to adapt more easily and became her naturally extrovert self. At one moment on the crest of a bleak, windswept ridge she asked Elaine, 'Anywhere for a pee?' 'Oh boy, you really choose your moments – no self-respecting bush would be seen on this tundra. Hang on, there may be a boulder.' The temperature and velocity of the wind made the location unsuitable for the purpose and Julie was remarkably quick about her errand. 'This wind reaches places other winds cannot reach.' 'I got that on tape,' said Elaine. 'Good,' shouted Julie, 'I shall play it to my grandchildren as proof of my intrepidness.'

As they reached an altitude of 15,000 feet, it was hard for Elaine to believe that Julie had been so ill down at 11,500 feet in Khumjung. Julie was now determined to aim for Kala Patthar, the peak above Everest Base Camp. Elaine was dubious, still worried about the sudden attacks of exhaustion and sickness. She felt it might be better to keep to their schedule. But she was attracted by the idea. Kala Patthar was a rocky peak, 18,000 feet high with superb views, whereas Base Camp was a squalid tent city huddled in the shadow of the Khumbu ice-fall, polluted with the garbage of twenty years of Everest expeditions. Their decision was made.

Crossing frozen rivers proved to be one of their greater hazards. A series of widely spaced stones made it possible, but a slip would mean falling into the water under the ice. Lhakpa would carry Julie on his back, jumping from rock to slippery rock until he reached the far bank, leaping back to return for her rucksack. In a press interview after their return to England, Elaine later admitted that this was when she began to fall in love with him, as he muttered his catch-phrase, 'No problem'.

Earlier on in the trek at Khumjung she had left Julie in their tent for a few hours and had gone with him to his uncle's house. She had begun to feel almost an extension of the other woman, and she was guiltily relieved to escape briefly. Lhakpa's aunt had sat her by the fire and plied them with potato pancakes, chili sauce and melted rak (female yak) butter. The Sherpa's house was spartan but homely with the whole family living, working, eating and praying together in the one room. To Elaine it seemed 'very natural and human'. They listened to Lhakpa's cassettes of Sherpa songs and temple music, and he told her of his early years, studying in a monastery until he was ten and then leaving to work as a porter so that he could earn enough money to learn English at the Hillary School. He eventually started working for trekking groups and climbing expeditions until he became a qualified Sirdar. But he was not ambitious to climb high mountains. 'You make a lot of money,' he told her, 'but it's easy to get yourself killed and you can't spend it if you're dead.' They found they had a great deal in common, having reached the same conclusions by different paths.

Continuing their climb, they paused for breath at the top of a ridge, looking down at the Pheriche valley far below. Ahead to the north the symmetrical pyramid of a new mountain, Pumori, came into view against a flawless blue sky. Just below it was Kala Patthar – a peak of black rocks. Some yaks were grazing on the few patches

of spiky grass between the rocks and ice. At the small village of
Lobuche they prepared for their final ascent. Julie felt the exhilaration of being part of a team and the conviction that she had at last
disproved the notion that 'blind people only do things especially
designed for the blind and are therefore segregated from the rest of
society'. If their exploit could encourage other people to break
down some barriers, it would all have been worthwhile.

Her euphoric mood evaporated the following day. She started
feeling sick and totally exhausted on the long final climb, surrounded by boulders and ice. They were moving painfully slowly,
with rests every few minutes to sip liquid and take pills for the
nausea. Lhakpa suggested carrying her to the top, taking the
essential photographs, and carrying her down. But Julie was adamant that she could make it on her own. She kept herself going by
sheer force of will, but she later admitted, 'It was unmitigated hell.'
Elaine wrote in *The Windhorse*: 'I felt like a slave-driver, pushing
Julie on when it was obvious she'd had enough. The rules of this
strange game we had set ourselves were quite clear. None of us
could help her at all, except to encourage her to push herself
through more of the same self-inflicted pain.' Then, at last, there
was a long slender horizontal boulder with a cairn of stones
balanced on the cantilevered end that jutted out into space. Elaine
took Julie's hand and pulled her up the vertical rock-step. 'Here,
come and sit down. We're here.' Julie burst into tears. 'I don't
believe it . . . all those days and weeks and months. All that effort.'
But as Elaine gazed down at Everest Base Camp far below and
described the view, Julie felt she already knew what it was like and
could feel the resonance of the mountains all around her.

The descent was in some ways harder then the climb which had
left Julie both mentally and physically exhausted. She began to feel
homesick and more disorientated than she had ever been in her life.
Her aspirations that reaching the summit would somehow solve all
her inner emotional problems evaporated and left her with a sense
of total disillusion. 'Kala Patthar had become a symbol for my other
goals, but the fulfilment came as a nasty shock. I had succeeded, yet
I feel I failed to cope with it emotionally.' She had once suffered
from anorexia nervosa, a result of the breakdown of her first
marriage. This now returned. Much to Elaine's dismay, Julie began

to refuse food and they seemed to become more and more estranged. The strain had been greater than they realised. It took all their joint courage to break the deadlock between them. Eventually Julie emerged from her black hole of depression and gradually started to eat again, although she remained very weak for some time. It was during this difficult period that Elaine turned more and more to Lhakpa for support. His calm strength and sense of humour helped them to reach Lukla for their return flight to Kathmandu.

Back in England, the two women were involved in a whirlwind of publicity and television interviews with pictures in the papers of them at the summit, smiling prettily into Lhakpa's camera. The book had to be finished in three months and, for Julie, writing her account was a more painful experience than the actual climb. In the past she had always taken pride in presenting herself as a success at everything she undertook, being careful never to appear as an object of pity. Now she had to put on paper for the public gaze her moments of despair and traumatic early memories. But she discovered that admitting her weaknesses gave her a certain pride – she had achieved her aim and consequently put her handicap in its place. She wasn't advocating that all blind people should go mountaineering, but they could at least achieve the goals of their choice.

Elaine had found the journey more enriching than she had imagined possible. She had also discovered that her non-visual senses had become heightened. She tried to analyse what it was they had been trying to prove, she knew that whatever it was it would be foolish to try to cling to it. 'It was good to have done it. Now, let it go.'

There is a Sherpa tradition that it is the girl who starts a courtship, so when Elaine returned to trek in the Himalayas with a party of Americans guided by Lhakpa, she waited in vain for him to speak. When it was time for her to go back to England she asked him if he would like to join her. Although no one from his village had ever before visited England, Lhakpa didn't hesitate. His normally immobile face ignites with laughter as he remembers his first impression of getting lost on the London Underground for a whole day, and his amazement at the tiny hills beyond Coniston, which Elaine called mountains. They were married in a local registry office and later returned to Nepal for a three-hour wedding in his father's farmhouse, blessed by the lama. The whole village of fifty people turned out for the festivities: all the men danced and the women watched. The wedding procession should have proceeded from the bride's house, but as this was in Gloucestershire, it was considered a little too far, even for Sherpas.

Elaine and Lhakpa now live half the year in England. The other half is spent taking parties trekking in her beloved Himalayas. 'In their society,' she says, 'you create your own privacy within yourself. You may only have one room for a family, but everyone has their own space. We use concrete – they use meditation. In many ways theirs is a more sophisticated society.'

Their favourite trek is the Everest culture trek in the Solu Khambu region where Lhakpa's family have lived for generations. They visit the Chiwong Monastery which, although away from the tourist trails, is the focus for the most important event in the Sherpa year, the Mani Rimdu festival. The High Lama travels from his mountain retreat to preside over the ceremonies and the masked dances performed by the Lamas. Sherpas and Tibetans travel for days through the mountains to be at the festival. 'As they use the lunar calendar the trek has to be within the right phase of the moon. Every year it is different for us, but it's the same as far as the constellations are concerned and coming up one particular valley I can now stop and say to people, "when we get to the top the moon will be hanging very low on the horizon behind the summit" – it happens every time.' This year, they are leading an expedition to a mystical and virtually unknown region of the Himalayas, Dolpo, previously forbidden to outsiders and still extremely difficult to approach, where the rare snow leopard still roams. Their highest trek is to the 21,288-foot Mera Peak in Nepal, but to Elaine reaching the highest peak herself is no longer important. 'I think,' she says, 'the final mountains are in the mind.'

Bibliography

The author wishes to acknowledge and thank the following authors and publishers for their co-operation and help:

Dervla Murphy
John Murray (Publishers) Ltd., *Full Tilt* (1965), *The Waiting Land* (1967), *In Ethiopia with a Mule* (1968), *On a Shoestring to Coorg* (1976), *Where the Indus is Young* (1977), *A Place Apart* (1978), *Wheels Within Wheels* (1979), *Race to the Finish?* (1981), *Eight Feet in the Andes* (1983), *Muddling Through Madagascar* (1985), *Tales from Two Cities* (1987), *Cameroon with Egbert* (1989)

Monica Kristensen
Grøndahl & Søn Forlag, A. s., *Towards 90° South* (1987), translated by Neil McIntyre, *The Magic Land* (1989)

Christina Dodwell
W. H. Allen & Co., *Travels with Fortune* (1979)
The Oxford Illustrated Press, *In Papua New Guinea* (1983)
Hodder & Stoughton Ltd., *An Explorer's Handbook* (1984), *A Traveller in China* (1985), *A Traveller on Horseback* (1987), *Travels with Pegasus* (1989)

Clare Francis
Pelham Books Ltd., *Come Hell or High Water* (1977), *Come Wind or Weather* (1978)
BBC and Pelham Books Ltd., *The Commanding Sea* (Clare Francis and Warren Tate) (1981)

Elaine Brook
Jonathan Cape Ltd., *The Windhorse* (with Julie Donnelly) (1986), *Land of the Snow Lion* (1987)

About the Author

Sonia Melchett is the author of two previous books: a novel, *Tell Me Honestly*, and *Someone is Missing: A Memoir*, her autobiography. She is married with three children and lives in London.